CANADIAN HISTORY
IN DOCUMENTS, 1763-1966

CANADIAN HISTORY IN DOCUMENTS, 1763-1966

EDITED BY J.M.BLISS

RYERSON PRESS

MCGRAW-HILL COMPANY OF CANADA LIMITED

Toronto, Montreal, New York, London, Sydney, Johannesburg, Mexico, Panama, Düsseldorf, Singapore, Rio De Janeiro, Kuala Lumpur, New Delhi.

ISBN-0-7700-6011-0

ACKNOWLEDGMENTS

Grateful acknowledgment is made to the following for permission to quote the passages indicated:

The Right Honourable Lester B. Pearson; Documents XXVIII: 2 and 3

Roger Duhamel, Queen's Printer; Document XXXI:4—excerpts from the Preliminary Report of the *Royal Commission on Bilingualism and Biculturalism*

Le Devoir, Montreal; Document XXX:4—excerpts from an interview published in the issue of July 5, 1963

The Globe and Mail, Toronto; Document XXXII:2:c

Harvest House Limited Publishers, Montreal; Document XXX:2

Les Presses de l'Université Laval, Quebec; Document XXXI:3

McClelland and Stewart, Toronto; Documents XXXII:2:b and XXXII:3

A complete description of sources will be found on page 385. Every effort has been made to credit copyright holders. The publisher would appreciate information leading to the correction of any errors or omissions.

6 7 8 9 10 11 12 EP 8 7 6 5 4 3 2

PRINTED AND BOUND IN CANADA

PREFACE

The primary sources of history should be as widely read as the secondary accounts that are built up from them. Only in documents does the reader find history exactly as it was written and spoken. Here are the arguments, the claims and counter-claims, charges and counter-charges, the passions, and the personalities of the historical actors themselves. Here, also, are their dreams, illusions, irrationalities, and distortions. Nothing intrudes itself between the reader and the speeches and writings of these historical subjects. William Lyon Mackenzie, Francis Bond Head, John A. Macdonald, Louis Riel, Wilfrid Laurier, and John Diefenbaker, to name only a few of the figures represented in this volume, speak directly to the reader. If one has even the mildest interest in the past he will find these men informative, stimulating, and entertaining.

In choosing the material for *Canadian History in Documents, 1763-1966*, I have particularly avoided the type of document which conveys to the reader nothing but facts that are easily summarized in a standard text. Only four essential pieces of legislation are reprinted in this volume. Instead of reprinting the Military Service Bill of 1917, for example, it seemed much more important and more interesting to have Robert Borden and Henri Bourassa explain their respective positions on conscription.

My aim has been, wherever possible, to select documents that approach problems in Canadian history from two or more directions. Francis Bond Head's assessment of the struggle in Upper Canada is placed beside William Lyon Mackenzie's radically different view. The often forgotten opponents of Confederation are allowed to give their perceptive warnings. Stephen Leacock and Henri Bourassa present their diametrically opposed concepts of imperialism; King and Bennett clash on solutions for unemployment; Walter Gordon and *The Globe and Mail* suggest quite different analyses of the present Canadian-American dilemma. This juxtaposition of opinions on most topics (unfortunately limitations of material and space have made it impossible to treat every topic in this way) should help the reader to understand the issues in Canadian history as *issues*. He should begin to see our history as a continuum of events bred and nourished by controversy and conflict—a continuum that extends into 1966, 1967, and every future year.

The topics chosen for documentary study are, on the whole, those which are given special emphasis in most introductory courses in

Canadian history and in the general histories of Canada. In addition to political and constitutional themes, the volume includes studies of the Canadian economy in the early nineteenth century, western expansion in the Laurier years, and Canadian society at the beginning of the twentieth century. Several topics relate to the problems of racial harmony in the country. The last five sections of the volume illustrate some of the major problems of postwar Canada. The final section concentrates on the contemporary issue of Canada's relationship with the United States. Considerable care has been taken in preparing these sections to include documents that seem likely to retain their significance when the passage of time finally permits historians to set the postwar decades in clearer perspective.

Spatial requirements have necessitated severe condensation of most of the documents; but very early in the project it was decided to limit the total number of documents to be included rather than to condense so severely that the volume became a collection of snippets. The commentary introducing each selection includes background essential for the study of the document and suggests the document's significance in relation to its topic. The list of sources beginning on page 385 will direct the interested reader to what is usually the most accessible expanded form of each document. A few of the documents are published here for the first time. At least half of them are not contained in any other anthology currently in print. No attempt has been made to modernize spelling and punctuation, although inconsistencies and typographical errors in the sources have been corrected. The cross reference guide at the back of the volume will help the reader to trace themes and the role of individuals in Canadian history.

While the book should be read in conjunction with a text or a general history of Canada, it should be possible to study the documents with a minimal resort to secondary sources. It is hoped that readers will not treat the documents as mere background reading to a general text. If they are read for their own value, keeping in mind the suggestions made in the first paragraph of this Preface, they will yield more of the real tone of history to the reader than he has ever expected to find in "dull documents".

The editor hopes that *Canadian History in Documents* will be particularly useful for senior high school students and university students taking introductory courses in Canadian history. The organization of the volume into major topics and the problematic approach in selecting documents have made the volume adaptable as a source book for classroom assignments. Either before or after a topic has been considered in class, a basic documentary study can be made from this volume. For high school students the documentary studies can be the basis of reports and minor essays. University students should find their appetites whetted for further probing of primary sources.

Much assistance has been given me in the preparation of the volume, not least from librarians always willing to locate obscure materials. I am also indebted to Mr. Fred Gaviller, Miss Mary Honderich, and Mrs. Mary Austin for translating several documents heretofore available only in French. Professor John Moir of the University of Toronto has very kindly read the manuscript and made a number of corrections and suggestions. My own editor, W. G. Lovatt of The Ryerson Press, has guided me through many difficulties, great and small, in the conception and execution of the project. All errors of fact or weaknesses in emphasis are, of course, my responsibility. In helping to prepare the manuscript and in living with the project through every stage, my wife, Elizabeth, has contributed most to its completion.

J.M.B.

Toronto,
October, 1966

CONTENTS

I. Organizing A New Colony

I:1 THE ROYAL PROCLAMATION, 1763

Having acquired New France by the Treaty of Paris in 1763, Great Britain originally planned to transform the new territory into a typical, British North American colony. The Proclamation of 1763 outlines this intention. The proposals to introduce English laws and a representative assembly into the new colony were designed to attract English-speaking settlers from the New England colonies into Quebec. It was expected that gradually the French Canadians (or simply "Canadians" as they were then called) and their lands would be fully integrated into British North America.*

Whereas we have taken into Our Royal Consideration the extensive and valuable acquisitions in America, secured to our Crown by the late Definitive Treaty of Peace concluded at Paris, the 10th day of February last; and being desirous that all Our loving Subjects, as well of our Kingdom as of our Colonies in America, may avail themselves with all convenient Speed, of the great Benefits and Advantages which must accrue therefrom to their Commerce, Manufactures, and Navigation, We have thought fit, with the Advice of our Privy Council, to issue this our Royal Proclamation. . . .

*The sources from which the documents have been transcribed are listed beginning on page 385.

And whereas it will greatly contribute to the speedy settling our said new Governments, that our loving subjects should be informed of our Paternal care, for the security of the Liberties and Properties of those who are and shall become Inhabitants thereof, We have thought fit to publish and declare . . . that We have . . . given express Power and Direction to our Governors of Said Colonies respectively, that so soon as the state and circumstances of the said Colonies will admit thereof, they shall, with the Advice and Consent of the Members of our Council, summon and call General Assemblies within the said Governments respectively, in such Manner and Form as is used and directed in those Colonies and Provinces in America which are under our immediate Government; and We have also given Power to the said Governors, with the consent of our Said Councils, and the Representatives of the People, to be summoned as aforesaid, to make, constitute, and ordain Laws, Statutes, and Ordinances for the Public Peace, Welfare and good Government of our said Colonies, and of the People and Inhabitants thereof, as near as may be agreeable to the Laws of England, and under such Regulations and restrictions as are used in other Colonies; and in the mean time, and until such Assemblies can be called as aforesaid, all Persons Inhabiting in or resorting to our Said Colonies may confide in our Royal Protection for the Enjoyment of the Benefit of the Laws of our Realm of England; for which Purpose We have given Power under our Great Seal to the Governors of our said Colonies respectively to erect and constitute with the Advice of our said Councils respectively, Courts of Judicature and Public Justice within our said Colonies for hearing and determining all Causes, as well Criminal as Civil, according to Law and Equity, and as near as may be agreeable to the Laws of England. . . .

I:2 GOVERNORS MURRAY AND CARLETON ON CANADIAN PROBLEMS

The first two British Governors of Quebec, James Murray and Sir Guy Carleton, both sympathized with the French Canadians whose legal affairs had become chaotic because of the introduction of British justice and who were barred from holding any administrative positions by the Test Act. Selection (a), an excerpt of a letter from Governor Murray to the Lords of Trade, shows both his concern for the Canadians and the bitter personal dislike he had developed for the recently arrived British merchants. In selection (b) Carleton explains to the House of Commons (in the debate on the Quebec Act) the Canadian objections to English civil law and the still postponed Assembly.

a. Governor Murray

My Lords,

Little, very little, will content the New Subjects but nothing will satisfy the Licentious Fanaticks Trading here, but the expulsion of the Canadians who are perhaps the bravest and the best race upon the Globe, a Race, who cou'd they be indulged with a few priveledges which the Laws of England deny to Roman Catholicks at home, wou'd soon get the better of every National Antipathy to their Conquerors and become the most faithful and most useful set of Men in this American Empire.

I flatter myself there will be some Remedy found out even in the Laws for the Relief of this people, if so, I am positive the populer clamours in England will not prevent the Humane Heart of the King from following its own Dictates. . . . certain I am, unless the Canadians are admitted on Jurys, and are allowed Judges and Lawyers who understand their Language his Majesty will lose the greatest part of this Valuable people. . . .

b. Sir Guy Carleton

Lord North: Are the Canadian inhabitants desirous of having assemblies in the province?

Carleton: Certainly not.

Lord North: Have they not thought with horror of an assembly in the country, if it should be composed of the old British inhabitants now resident there?

Carleton: No doubt it would give them great offence.

North: Would they not greatly prefer a government by the governor and legislative council to such an assembly?

Carleton: No doubt they would. . . .

North: Is that the only idea of the assembly, that you ever knew suggested to the Canadians, and to which they returned their answer?

Carleton: I put the question to several of the Canadians. They told me assemblies had drawn upon the other colonies so much distress, had occasioned such riots and confusions, that they wished never to have one of any kind whatever. . . .

North: Have you never heard, that they imagined they should be obliged to pay the expence of government as soon as they had assemblies, but that until they had them they were not to pay the expence?

Carleton: No, that was not the idea of the Canadians; they dislike it as not being conformable to their ancient customs. . . .

North: Do you think, if all their customs of descent and heritage were preserved, that they would be dissatisfied with the introduction of trial by jury?

Carleton: With regard to any portion of their law, one custom separate from another, I believe they would be extremely hurt to have any part of their customs taken from them, except where the commercial interest of the country may require a reasonable preference, and such commercial laws as can be especially mentioned to them. I believe they would make no objection to any such commercial laws, if they may know what those laws are. But laws in the bulk, which nobody can explain to them, they think would be delivering them over a prey to every body that goes there as an attorney or lawyer. . . .

North: If their favourite laws and favourite customs were preserved to them, would they not, in every other case, take the law of England?

Carleton: They do not know what the law of England is; they call the law of England the mode of administering justice. They do not know the difference between Canadian law and English, in the mode of administering it. The essential laws of England, in deciding matters of property, they have not the least idea of. The intelligent part of the Canadians think and hope, that their laws and customs may be continued, because they know what they are. . . .

North: Did the supreme legislative council ever make any laws to secure property, according to the Canadian customs?

Carleton: There were some ordinances made; but I never could learn that anything was clear or certain in the law, nor did I understand clearly what was the law and custom; nor does it seem to be a clear question in the country. I have heard the same man argue for the English law in one cause, because it suited his cause, and I have heard him argue for the French law in another cause. . . .

North: Do you conceive it would be impracticable at this time, without giving general lessons of politics to all the people, to explain the advantages they would derive from the English government, without the abolition of all their usages?

Carleton: They have very often told me, that during the military government, the English frequently expressed to them the happiness, and great advantages they would receive, by the introduction of the law of the English government, and by the protection of the civil laws of the country; that they were to become a happy people by the change. Several years after, when they had experienced what it was, and found that they were debarred of what they looked upon as the civil rights of subjects, and that they understood that, as Roman Catholics, they could not enjoy places of profit, or trust, or honour, they thought it was adding mockery and insult to severity; and were astonished that people could hold such language to them. . . .

I:3 THE CASE OF THE BRITISH MERCHANTS

Shortly after the end of the French regime, British merchants began to settle in Quebec. Although they formed less than one percent of the total population, the new traders vigorously pressed their views on the British government. By 1774, as this petition shows, the merchant community had been driven to threatening drastic steps in its struggle against the imminent change of policy.

The Case of the British Merchants trading to Quebeck, and others of his Majesty's natural-born Subjects, who have been induced to venture their Property in the said Province on the Faith of his Majesty's Proclamation, and other Promises solemnly given.

[The merchants then reminded the government of its stated intention to summon an assembly and introduce the laws of England in the new colony. They continued as follows:]

. . . We humbly beg leave to represent, that many of us have, through a confidence in the said royal proclamation, and other instruments proceeding from, and allowed by, his majesty's royal authority, ventured to send considerable quantities of merchandize into the said province, and to give large credits to divers persons residing in the same, both of his majesty's new Canadian subjects, and of his antient [sic] British subjects, who have, through a like confidence in the said proclamation, resorted to, and settled themselves in, the said province. And that we have employed our property and credit in this manner, in a firm belief, that we should have the remedies allowed us by the laws of England for the security and recovery of it; and that if we had supposed the French laws, which prevailed in the said province under the French government, to be still in force there, or to be intended

to be revived in the same, we would not have had any commercial connections with the inhabitants of the said province,
either French or English. And therefore we beg leave to represent, that we think ourselves entitled, upon the mere grounds
of justice, (without desiring any favour to be shown us on
account of our being his majesty's antient [sic], and faithful,
and protestant subjects, that are attached to his royal person
and government by every tie of religion, interest, and habitual
duty and affection) to insist that, if it be resolved to persist
in this new measure of reviving all the former laws of Canada
concerning property and civil rights, and abolishing the laws
of England that have prevailed there in their stead since the
establishment of the civil government in one thousand seven
hundred and sixty-four, the execution thereof may at least
be postponed until we shall have had sufficient time to withdraw our effects from the said province, and by the remedies
and methods of trial allowed and appointed by the laws of
England in that behalf; through a reliance on which remedies
and methods of trial we were induced to venture our said
effects there, and permit those debts to be contracted. And
this time, we humbly represent, cannot well be less than three
years. . . .

I:4 THE QUEBEC ACT, 1774

> With an eye to the storm brewing in its older colonies
> the British government tried to ensure the loyalty of
> its new subjects by acknowledging the institutions
> unique to their community. The religious and legal
> provisions of the Quebec Act indicate an almost com-
> plete reversal of the policy of the Proclamation of
> 1763. They have formed the foundation of French
> Canada's survival in British North America.

An Act for making more effectual Provision for the Government of the Province of Quebec in North America.

V. And, for the more perfect Security and Ease of the Minds
of the Inhabitants of the said Province, it is hereby declared,

That his Majesty's Subjects, professing the religion of the Church of Rome, of and in the said Province of Quebec, may have, hold, and enjoy, the free Exercise of the Religion of the Church of Rome, subject to the King's Supremacy . . . and that the Clergy of the said Church may hold, receive, and enjoy, their accustomed Dues and Rights, with respect to such Persons only as shall profess the said Religion.

VI. Provided, nevertheless, That it shall be lawful for His Majesty, His Heirs or Successors, to make such Provision out of the rest of the said accustomed Dues and Rights, for the Encouragement of the Protestant Religion, and for the Maintenance and Support of a Protestant Clergy within the said Province, as he or they shall, from Time to Time, think necessary and expedient.

VII. [Catholic office-holders are excused from taking the oath acknowledging the King's headship of the Church and are required instead to subscribe to the following oath]: . . . "I, A.B., do sincerely promise and swear, That I will be faithful, and bear true Allegiance to His Majesty King George, and him will defend to the utmost of my Power, against all traiterous Conspiracies, and Attempts whatsoever, which shall be made against His Person, Crown and Dignity; and I will do my utmost Endeavour to disclose and make known to His Majesty, His Heirs and Successors, all Treasons, and traiterous Conspiracies, and Attempts, which I shall know to be against Him or any of Them; and all this I do swear without any Equivocation, mental Evasion, or secret Reservation, and renouncing all Pardons and Dispensations from any Power or Person whomsoever to the Contrary.

So Help Me GOD."

VIII. And be it further enacted by the Authority aforesaid, That all His Majesty's Canadian Subjects, within the Province of Quebec, the religious Orders and Communities only excepted, may also hold and enjoy their Property and Possessions, together with all Customs and Usages relative thereto, and all other their Civil Rights, in as large, ample, and beneficial Manner, as if the said Proclamation, Commissions, Ordinances, and others Acts and Instruments had not been made, . . . and that in all Matters of Controversy, relative to Property and Civil Rights, Resort shall be had to the Laws of Canada, as the Rule for the Decision of the same. . . .

XI. And whereas the Certainty and Lenity of the Criminal Law of England, and the Benefits and Advantages resulting from the use of it, have been sensibly felt by the Inhabitants, from an Experience of more than Nine Years, during which it has been uniformly administered; be it therefore enacted by the Authority aforesaid, That the same shall continue to be administered, and shall be observed as Law in the Province of Quebec. . . .

XII. . . . And whereas it is at present inexpedient to call an Assembly; be it therefore enacted by the Authority aforesaid, That it shall and may be lawful for His Majesty, His Heirs and Successors . . . and with the Advice of the Privy Council to constitute and appoint a Council for the Affairs of the Province of Quebec, to consist of such Persons resident there, not exceeding Twenty-three, nor less than Seventeen, as His Majesty, His Heirs and Successors, shall be pleased to appoint; . . . which Council, so appointed and nominated, or the major Part thereof, shall have Power and Authority to make Ordinances for the Peace, Welfare, and good Government of the said Province, with the Consent of His Majesty's Governor. . . .

II. Reorganizing The Colony

II:1 DEMANDS FOR A CHANGE

Although they bided their time until after the American Revolution, the British inhabitants of Quebec were far from satisfied with the Quebec Act. They were gradually joined by a number of the French Canadian leaders who recognized the potential advantages to their race of representative government. After 1783 their position was greatly strengthened by the wave of Loyalist settlers who naturally wanted to live under representative institutions. The following two selections represent the major demands: selection (a) is a petition for an Assembly by the British merchants and a few French Canadians; selection (b) is from a Loyalist petition requesting a division of the Province.

a. Petition for an Assembly, 1784

The humble Petition of Your Majesty's Ancient and New Subjects; Inhabitants of the Province of Quebec.

MAY IT PLEASE YOUR MAJESTY.

AFTER the Conquest of the Province of Canada by the Arms of Great Britain, Your Petitioners in compliance with Your Majesty's gracious and royal Proclamation, bearing date the 7th day of October, 1763, Settled and became established,

in the New acquired Colony of Quebec; in the full reliance
on the faith of the Crown of Great Britain, as expressed in
that Proclamation, for the enjoyment of those Laws, that
Freedom and Security in Canada, which the Principles of the
English Constitution afforded, in every part of the British
Dominions in America. YOUR PETITIONERS and the
Inhabitants of the Province, have chearfully on every occa-
sion, obeyed the Controuling power of the Parliament of
Great Britain, and with patience have suffered, during a
period of Anarchy and War, rather than wound Your
Majesty's feelings, or embarrass the Throne with Remon-
strances and Petitions, at a time when the safety of the
Nation, made sacred every moment of Public deliberation.
The Actions and Conduct of Your Petitioners when truly
represented, will best express to Your Majesty, the Sincerity
of their Loyalty and Attachment to the Crown and Government of Great Britain.

. . . YOUR PETITIONERS fully persuaded that the Welfare
and Happiness of Your Majesty's Subjects, are objects of Your
Majesty's serious and benign Consideration—beg leave to lay
their Petition at the foot of the Throne and ardently to request Your Majesty's Interposition for the Repeal of the
Quebec Bill; allowing such Priviledges as are already granted
to the Roman Catholick Religion; as being inadequate to the
Government of this extensive Province; the Cause of much
Confusion in our Laws, and fraught with trouble and uneasiness to Your Majesty's loyal Subjects here. And that Your
Majesty will be pleased to Concur in establishing your affec-
tionate Subjects of this Province, in the full Enjoyment, of
their civil Rights as British Subjects; and in granting them a
Free, Elective House of Assembly. . . .

b. A Loyalist Petition, 1785

To the King's Most Excellent Majesty.

The Petition of Sir John Johnston, Baronet, and others,
whose names are hereunto subscribed, on Behalf of the
Officers and Soldiers of the Provincial Troops and Indian

Department, who served under their Command during the late Rebellion; and of the other Loyalists, their Associates, who have taken Refuge in Canada.

Most humbly Sheweth, . . .

That the Tenure of Lands in Canada is such as to subject them to the rigorous Rules, Homages and Reservations, and Restrictions of the French Laws and Customs, which are so different from the mild Tenures to which they had ever been accustomed, and which continue to be enjoyed by the rest of Your Majesty's Subjects, has occasioned a general Discontent, and would have induced many to decline accepting their Locations, and to resolve on abandoning their Enterprize, but for the Influence of Your Petitioners, who had first led them into the Service, and on whose Endeavours they relied for obtaining, through Your Majesty's Favour, the Grant of such Terms and Tenures, and the Establishment of the same Laws as they formerly enjoyed under the auspices of Your Majesty's Government. In full Confidence of this happy Event they were prevailed upon to persevere in their Settlements, on which they have already, at some Expence, and much Labour, erected Habitations, and cleared Part of the Lands allotted to them.

For the Attainment of these Objects, so essential to the Happiness of Your Majesty's faithful Subjects, so conducive to the Increase of these new Settlements, and so salutary in their Consequences to the Public, we have, upon mature deliberation, formed a Plan, which with the reasons in support of it, we humbly presume to submit to Your Majesty's Royal Consideration.

1st It is proposed, that the County of Point Boudet, on the Lake St. François, in the River St. Lawrence, and from thence Westward, shall be comprehended within One District, distinct from the Province of Quebec, under the Government of a Lieutenant Governor and Council, to be appointed by Your Majesty, with the necessary Powers of internal Regulation, but subordinate to the Governor and Council of Quebec, in the same manner as the Island of Cape Breton now is, to the Government of Nova Scotia. This Territory will include all the Settlements made or intended to be made by the disbanded Corps, and the other Loyalists, while it leaves all French Canada and the French Seigneuries as they were before. . . .

The Inhabitants of this Territory, already amounting to several Thousands, conceive with all Humility that they have the strongest Grounds to hope for such an exempt Jurisdiction as they ask for; They were born British Subjects, and have ever been accustomed to the Government and Laws of England. It was to restore that Government, and to be restored to those Laws, for which from Husbandmen they became Soldiers, animated with the Hope, even in the most gloomy Aspect of Public Affairs, that should they fail in their Attempts to recover their former Habitations by a Restoration of Your Majesty's Government, they would still find a Resource in some Parts of the British Dominions, where they might enjoy the Blessings of British Laws and of the British Government; and they still possess the greatest Confidence, that by Your Majesty's Gracious Interposition they will be exempted from the Burthens of French Tenures, which, however congenial they may be to Men born and bred under them, would be in the highest Degree exceptionable to Englishmen.

The Petitioners have the more Confidence in the Success of their Application, from reflecting that they do not ask for more than has already been granted to their Fellow Sufferers in Nova Scotia, for less indeed than is enjoyed by those who are settled in the Province of New Brunswick, and only to be in the same situation with the Settlers in the Island of Cape Breton. . . .

II:2 THE CONSTITUTIONAL ACT, 1791

The demands of the Loyalists, who had fought to live under British customs and laws, could not be ignored. The Constitutional Act (or Canada Act) was an amendment of the Quebec Act designed to apply the British constitution as nearly as possible to colonial conditions without affecting the guaranteed rights of French Canadians. Note should be taken of the failure to define the role of the Executive Council and the ambiguity of the provisions for the Clergy Reserves. (What was meant by a "Protestant" clergy?) These flaws in the Act paved the way for much of the controversy that was to engulf the Canadas.

II. And whereas his Majesty has been pleased to signify, by his message to both Houses of Parliament, his Royal intention to divide his Province of Quebec into two separate Provinces, to be called the Province of Upper Canada and the Province of Lower Canada: Be it enacted by the authority aforesaid, that there shall be within each of the said Provinces respectively a Legislative Council and an Assembly, to be severally composed and constituted in the manner hereinafter described; and that in each of the said Provinces respectively, His Majesty, His Heirs, or Successors, shall have power during the continuance of this Act, by and with the advice and consent of the Legislative Council and Assembly of such Provinces respectively, to make laws for the peace, welfare and good Government thereof, . . .

III. And be it further enacted by the authority aforesaid, that for the purpose of constituting such Legislative Council, as aforesaid, in each of the said Provinces respectively, it shall and may be lawful for his Majesty, his heirs, or successors, by an instrument under his or their sign manual, to authorize and direct the Governor or Lieutenant-Governor, or person administering the Government, in each of the said Provinces respectively, . . . to summon to the said Legislative Council, to be established in each of the said Provinces respectively, a sufficient number of discreet and proper persons, being not fewer than seven, to the Legislative Council for the Province of Upper Canada, and no fewer than fifteen to the Legislative Council for the Province of Lower Canada; . . .

V. And be it further enacted by the authority aforesaid, that every member of each of the said Legislative Councils shall hold his seat therein for the term of his life, . . .

XIII. And be it further enacted by the authority aforesaid, that for the purpose of constituting such Assembly as aforesaid in each of the said Provinces respectively, it shall and may be lawful for his Majesty, his heirs or successors, by an instrument under his or their sign manual, to authorize and direct the Governor or Lieutenant-Governor, or person administering the Government in each of the said Provinces respectively, . . . to summon and call together an Assembly in and for such Province.

XXVI. And be it further enacted by the authority aforesaid, that it shall and may be lawful for his Majesty, his heirs, or successors, to authorize the Governor or Lieutenant-Governor of each of the said Provinces respectively, or the person administering the Government therein, to fix the places and times of holding the first and every other session of the Legislative Council and Assembly of such Province, giving due and sufficient notice thereof, and to prorogue the same from time to time, and to dissolve the same by proclamation or otherwise, whenever he shall judge it necessary or expedient.

XXX. And be it further enacted by the authority aforesaid, that whenever any bill, which has been passed by the Legislative Council and by the House of Assembly in either of the said Provinces respectively, shall be presented for his Majesty's assent to the Governor or Lieutenant-Governor of such Province, or to the person administering his Majesty's Government therein, such Governor or Lieutenant-Governor, or person administering the Government shall, and he is hereby authorized and required to declare, according to his discretion, but subject nevertheless to the provisions contained in this Act, and to such instructions as may from time to time be given in that behalf by his Majesty, his heirs or successors, that he assents to such bill in his Majesty's name, or that he withholds his Majesty's assent from such bill, or that he reserves such bill for the signification of his Majesty's pleasure thereon.

XXXI. Provided always, and be it further enacted by the authority aforesaid, that whenever any bill which shall have been so presented for his Majesty's assent . . . shall . . . have been assented to in his Majesty's name, such Governor, Lieutenant-Governor, or person as aforesaid shall, and he is hereby required, by the first convenient opportunity to transmit to one of his Majesty's principal Secretaries of State, an authentic copy of such bill so assented to; and that it shall and may be lawful, at any time within two years after such bill shall have been so received by such Secretary of State for his Majesty, his heirs or successors, by his or their Order-in-Council to declare his or their disallowance of such bill, . . .

XXXV. And whereas by the above mentioned [Quebec] Act passed in the fourteenth year of the reign of his present Majesty it was declared that the clergy of the Church of Rome in the Province of Quebec might hold, receive, and enjoy their accustomed dues and rights, with respect to such persons only as should profess the said religion; provided nevertheless that it should be lawful for his Majesty, his heirs or successors, to make such provision out of the rest of the said accustomed dues and rights for the encouragement of the Protestant religion and for the maintenance and support of a Protestant clergy within the said Province as he or they should from time to time think necessary and expedient: . . . be it enacted by the authority aforesaid that the said declaration and provision contained in the said above mentioned Act, and also the said provision so made by his Majesty in consequence thereof by his instructions above recited, shall remain and continue to be of full force and effect in each of the said two Provinces of Upper Canada and Lower Canada respectively, except in so far as the said declaration or provisions respectively, or any part thereof, shall be expressly varied or repealed by any Act or Acts which may be passed by the Legislative Council and Assembly of the said Provinces respectively, and assented to by his Majesty, his heirs or successors, under the restriction hereinafter provided.

XXXVI. And whereas his Majesty has been graciously pleased, by message to both Houses of Parliament, to express his Royal desire to be enabled to make a permanent appropriation of land in the said Provinces for the support and maintenance of a Protestant clergy within the same, . . . therefore, for the purpose of more effectually fulfilling his Majesty's gracious intentions as aforesaid, and of providing for the due execution of the same in all time to come, be it enacted by the authority aforesaid that it shall and may be lawful for his Majesty, his heirs or successors, to authorize the Governor, or Lieutenant-Governor of each of the said Provinces respectively, or the person administering the Government therein, to make from and out of the lands of the Crown within such Provinces such allotment and appropriation of lands for the support and maintenance of a Protestant clergy within the same as may bear a due proportion to the amount of such lands within the same as have at any time been granted by or under the authority of his Majesty: And that, whenever any grant of lands within either of the said Provinces shall hereafter be made by or under the authority of his Majesty, his heirs or successors, there shall at the same time be made, in respect of the same, a proportionable allotment and appropriation of lands for the above mentioned purpose, within the township or parish to which such lands so to be granted shall appertain or be annexed, or as nearly adjacent thereto as circumstances will admit; and that no such grant shall be valid or effectual unless the same shall contain a specification of the lands so allotted and appropriated, in respect of the lands to be thereby granted; and that such lands so allotted and appropriated shall be, as nearly as the circumstances and nature of the case will admit, of the like quality as the lands in respect of which the same are so allotted and appropriated, and shall be, as nearly as the same can be estimated at the time of making such grant, equal in value to the seventh part of the lands so granted.

XXXVII. And be it further enacted by the authority aforesaid that all and every the rents, profits, or emoluments, which may at any time arise from such lands so allotted and appropriated as aforesaid, shall be applicable solely to the maintenance and support of a Protestant clergy within the Province in which the same shall be situated, and to no other purpose whatever.

XXXVIII. And be it further enacted by the authority aforesaid that it shall and may be lawful for his Majesty, his heirs and successors, to authorize the Governor or Lieutenant-Governor of each of the said Provinces respectively, . . . to constitute and erect within every township or parish which is now or hereafter may be formed, constituted or erected within such Province, one or more parsonage or rectory, or parsonages or rectories, according to the establishment of the Church of England; and from time to time by instrument under the great seal of such Province to endow every such parsonage or rectory with so much or such a part of the lands so allotted and appropriated as aforesaid, . . .

XLIII. And be it further enacted by the authority aforesaid, that all lands which shall be hereafter granted within the said Province of Upper Canada shall be granted in free and common soccage, . . .

III. The Road To Rebellion: Lower Canada

III:1 EARLY FRENCH CANADIAN GRIEVANCES

This *Mémoire,* presented to the Colonial office in 1814, is an exceptionally clear and accurate analysis of the developing controversy in Lower Canada. It is also remarkable in containing the clearest early expression of what would later become the doctrine of responsible government. Its probable author is Pierre Bédard, one of the first leaders of the popular party in Lower Canada. The moderation of the *Mémoire* should be contrasted with the tone of the Ninety-Two Resolutions.

We consider our present constitution to be the one most capable of making us happy, and our greatest hope would be to be able to enjoy it in accordance with the wishes of His Majesty and His Parliament. Unfortunately, however, the manner in which it has been hitherto administered creates an affect quite contrary to its purpose.

This unhappy result is the consequence of the way in which parties in this province have taken shape.

When our constitution was granted, the English-speaking subjects controlled the offices of the government. The only Canadians admitted to the government were chosen, on

English recommendation, from a group of Canadian "followers" of the English.

Since the granting of the constitution the same situation has prevailed. The English subjects continue to occupy government offices and have become the official party of the administration. The channel of recommendation for office remains as before and only a few Canadians whose adherence to the English party was well known have been given positions.

Because the mass of the population is Canadian the majority of the House of Assembly has been composed of Canadians, and the English with a few Canadian "followers" have formed the minority. Because the Canadians of the majority, freely elected by the people, have not been found to pander to the English, they have not been able to hold official positions. The members who have been made Executive Councillors have been chosen from the minority. The governing party has been linked with the minority in the House of Assembly; and the majority, that is to say the House of Assembly itself, which is supported by the mass of the people, has been regarded as a foreign body, scarcely recognized by the government and the other branches of the Legislature, and left in opposition as if destined to be guided by authority.

In effect the members of the English party, who had failed in their efforts to have the constitution denied to the Canadians, have found themselves, as the governing party, in possession of a means of preventing the Canadians from enjoying the constitution except on terms set out by the English.

Each time that the Canadians have wished to propose something which does not conform to the ideas of this party, they have found themselves in opposition to the government and have been treated as irresponsible subjects and as a group struggling against their government. . . . The government programme is prepared by Councillors representing the minority. . . . It is then taken to the House to be passed by the majority, and the majority has no alternative but to pass it or to find itself opposed to the minority, which is to say the government, and to be treated as though they were disloyal to the government.

The divisions of the House of Assembly are becoming national. The English, on the one hand, form the minority with whom the government is connected, and the Canadians, on the other hand, form the majority supported by the mass of the people. The passions created by these national divisions are transferred from the House of Assembly to the people; the whole country is divided into two parties, the English party of the government on the one side and the mass of the people on the other. This appearance of opposition by the French Canadian Catholics to their government continually increases the prejudice of the common part of the English party against them, and the Canadians are treated in a manner most insulting to a people conscious of its loyalty. And thus the more the Canadians want to enjoy their constitution, the more they strengthen the sole pretext by which the English party exists as a party, that is the supposed disloyalty of the Canadians. . . .

Because the Canadians form the major part of the population, the part on which the Government may rely in time of need, it is only just that they be able to communicate with the Governor for themselves, rather than be represented by the party opposed to them in whatever way it may please, however respectable that party may be. The only way the Governor has of knowing the Canadians is through the Councillors and people in power who are members of the English party.

The House of Assembly offers a way of obtaining this communication by regular means, bypassing the recommendations of the English party. If the Governor had the power to appoint to his Council the chief members of the majority of the House of Assembly, he would have a means of hearing both parties and not be obliged to know one party only through information received from the other; and would no longer be deprived of ideas and advice that he could obtain from the old inhabitants of the country, nor be compelled to listen only to those of the opposing party, which is not the one having the greatest knowledge of the country nor the most interests corresponding to those of the country.

After having heard both parties, he would be able to decide which measures to take and would be able to send exact information to England.

He would not be obligated to follow advice which he considered to be improper; he would only have the advantage of profiting from just advice.

He would not be at the disadvantage of finding himself so often in opposition to the House of Assembly. . . .

If it were possible that a number of positions of Councillors or other places of honour and profit, were given to those who have the most influence on the majority in the House of Assembly, and if these positions rested entirely on their ability to maintain this influence, and if it were certain and well known that there would no longer be another method of obtaining them, there would be every reason to believe that the two parties would quickly reunite in the Assembly and that this national division, so contrary to the aim of the Government, would disappear just as quickly outside the Assembly, and that this shameful semblance of opposition between the Canadians and their government, which disgraces the people of the country and makes it appear in the light, so little merited, of a people of rebels, would cease to mar one of the most beautiful dependencies of the Empire in America. . . .

The Canadians, unable to protect themselves, have nowhere to turn for protection but to the mother country. This country having been lost once, they have no homeland to turn to. An Englishman still has his native land.

If the Canadas come under the domination of the United States their population will be submerged by that of the United States, and they will become nothing, without any influence in their government, unable to protect their religion. . . .

The English party is opposed to their interests, having much more of an affinity with the Americans through their customs, their religion, and their language. They encourage the American population as a means of ridding themselves of the Canadians whom they always regard as a foreign population, as a French Catholic population. . . . Thus the English party is opposed to the Canadian party precisely in that area which affects its life and existence as a nation. . . .

III: 2 GOVERNOR CRAIG: AN ENGLISH VIEW

> Very few of the English-speaking inhabitants of Lower Canada sympathized with, or were even tolerant of, the French Canadian point of view. This despatch to the Colonial Office from the most outspoken of the early Governors, Sir James Craig (1807-11) illustrates an extreme but fairly typical attitude towards the French Canadians. Craig's governorship was labelled the "Reign of Terror" by French Canadians who became increasingly alienated from the English in these years.

It may not be useless in order to bring the whole under one view, that I should now present a summary of the various objects which it has been my intention to submit to the consideration of His Majesty's Ministers, . . .

They are—1st. That this is already a powerful Province in so far as depends upon numbers of Inhabitants, and that in the short period of 20 or 25 years these will probably exceed half a million.

2d. That the great Mass of this population, indeed that proportion that admits of no balance from the other part, so far from being united to us by any bond of affection, views us with mistrust, jealousy and hatred.

3d. That they are, and consider themselves as French, attached to that nation from identity of Religion, laws, language, and manners. This is general, and runs thro' all Ranks and descriptions, the exceptions as I believe being very few.

4th. That this people immersed in a degree of ignorance that is scarcely to be exceeded, and credulous in the extreme are particularly open to the arts and delusions that may be practiced on them by factious, and designing Men.

5th. That they are at this moment compleatly in the hands of a party of such factious and designing Men.

6th. That the whole Proceedings of this Party are calculated to alienate the people from any attachment they might be supposed to entertain for a Government under which they cannot but confess they have enjoyed the most perfect security, liberty and prosperity, and to pave the way for their return to their ancient connection with that which they esteem their Mother Country.

7th. That there is reason to fear that they have been successful in their attempts, and that the People do look forward to a change in their Government.

8th. That the Clergy under the general influence of attachment to France are further from religious motives decidedly our Enemies.

9th. That the Party who have the lead in the Country have also the compleat command of the House of Assembly, and are therefore placed in a situation particularly favourable to their views, and of consequence in the same proportion dangerous to His Majesty's Interests.

10th. That from the composition of the House of Assembly, it is likely that it will ever be in the hands of any party who may have a view in taking the direction of it; and that Government possesses no influence by which such view, whatever it may be, can be counteracted.

11th. That from prejudice, jealousy and ignorance, it is little to be expected that the House as at present constituted will accede to measures that may advance the real prosperity of the Colony.

12th. That the Government is equally destitute of all influence over the Clergy with whom it has scarcely a connection, and that this influence is entirely in the hands of an individual who holds his power under the confirmation at least of a foreign authority, which authority is now under the compleat direction of our inveterate Enemy.

*　　*　　*

The first and most obvious remedy that presents itself, is to deprive them of the constitution, as they term it, that is of that representative part of the Government which was unquestionably prematurely given them—neither from habits, information or assimilation, with the Government of England, were they prepared for it, nor was this circumstance of their unprepared state unforeseen by many of the best informed of the Canadians themselves, who opposed its being granted to them. It was in fact brought about by the English part of the Inhabitants, who in their Enthusiasm for the Constitution which they so justly Esteemed as it exists in their own Country, could not conceive that any inconvenience, or any thing but happiness, and prosperity, could result from its establishment elsewhere. . . .

Short of the decisive step of taking away the House altogether, one or other of these two measures either of reuniting the Provinces, or of forming a new division of the Counties seems to offer the only option, from which a hope can be entertained of rendering that House less capable of doing mischief; when I say this, I mean as offering the only expectation of ever effecting a Balance, to the Canadian Party, but under any shape in which it may be thought proper to continue the House, the enactment of a qualification with respect to the Representatives seems to be indispensably necessary. It really My Lord appears to me an absurdity, that the Interests of certainly not an unimportant Colony, involving in them those also of no inconsiderable portion of the Commercial concerns of the British Empire, should be in the hands of six petty shopkeepers, a Blacksmith, a Miller, and 15 ignorant peasants who form part of our present House, a Doctor or Apothecary, twelve Canadian Avocats, and Notaries, and four, so far respectable people that at least they do not keep shops, together with ten English members compleat the List; there is not one person coming under the description of a Canadian Gentleman among them. . . .

III: 3 THE NINETY-TWO RESOLUTIONS, 1834

> As the deadlock between the Lower Canadian Assembly on the one side and the Governor and his Council on the other became more pronounced, moderate men were gradually replaced by extremists. The classic statement of extreme grievances is the Ninety-Two Resolutions passed by the Lower Canada Assembly in 1834. This long, rambling, repetitive document, of uncertain authorship, contains both the complaints of the Assembly and a bare outline of the future programme of the radicals. For a full understanding of the situation in the Canadas the Resolutions should be read in conjunction with the *Mémoire*, Mackenzie's *Seventh Report on Grievances*, and Durham's *Report*.

1. Resolved, That His Majesty's loyal subjects, the people of this province of Lower Canada, have shown the strongest attachment to the British Empire, of which they are a portion; that they have repeatedly defended it with courage in time of war; that at the period which preceded the Independence of the late British Colonies on this continent, they resisted the appeal made to them by those colonies to join their confederation.

9. Resolved, That the most serious defect in the Constitutional Act, its radical fault, the most active principle of evil and discontent in the province; the most powerful and most frequent cause of abuses of power; of the infraction of the laws; of the waste of the public revenue and property, accompanied by impunity to the governing party, and the oppression and consequent resentment of the governed, is that

injudicious enactment, . . . which invests the Crown with that exorbitant power (incompatible with any government duly balanced, and founded on law and justice, and not on force and coercion) of selecting and composing without any rule or limitation, or any predetermined qualification, an entire branch of the legislature, supposed from the nature of its attributes to be independent, but inevitably the servile tool of the authority which creates, composes and decomposes it, and can on any day modify it to suit the interests or the passions of the moment.

17. Resolved, That . . . the principal Agent of His Majesty's Government in this Province . . . has destroyed the hope which His Majesty's faithful subjects had conceived of seeing the Legislative Council reformed and ameliorated, and has confirmed them in the opinion that the only possible mode of giving to that body the weight and respectability which it ought to possess, is to introduce into it the principle of election.

41. Resolved, . . . that the neighbouring States have a form of government very fit to prevent abuses of power, and very effective in repressing them; that the reverse of this order of things has always prevailed in Canada under the present form of government; that there exists in the neighbouring States a stronger and more general attachment to the national institutions than in any other country, and that there exists also in those States a guarantee for the progressive advance of their political institutions towards perfection, in the revision of the same at short and determinate intervals, by conventions of the people, in order that they may without any shock or violence be adapted to the actual state of things.

44. Resolved, That the unanimous consent with which all the American States have adopted and extended the elective system, shows that it is adapted to the wishes, manners and social state of the inhabitants of this continent; . . . and that we do not hesitate to ask from a Prince of the House of Brunswick, and a reformed Parliament, all the freedom and

political powers which the Princes of the House of Stuart and their Parliaments granted to the most favoured of the plantations formed at a period when such grants must have been less favourably regarded than they would now be.

49. Resolved, That this House and the people whom it represents do not wish or intend to convey any threat; but that, relying as they do upon the principles of law and justice, they are and ought to be politically strong enough not to be exposed to receive insult from any man whomsoever, or bound to suffer it in silence; that the style of the said extracts from the despatches of the Colonial Secretary, as communicated to this House, is insulting and inconsiderate to such a degree that no legally constituted body, although its functions were infinitely subordinate to those of legislation, could or ought to tolerate them; . . .

52. Resolved, . . . that the majority of the inhabitants of this country are in nowise disposed to repudiate any one of the advantages they derive from their origin and from their descent from the French nation, which, with regard to the progress of which it has been the cause in civilization, in the sciences, in letters, and the arts, has never been behind the British nation, and is now the worthy rival of the latter in the advancement of the cause of liberty and of the science of Government; from which this country derives the greater portion of its civil and ecclesiastical law, and of its scholastic and charitable institutions, and of the religion, language, habits, manners and customs of the great majority of its inhabitants.

64. Resolved, That the claims which have for many years been set up by the Executive Government to that control over and power of appropriating a great portion of the revenues levied in this province, which belong of right to this House, are contrary to the rights and to the constitution of the country; and that with regard to the said claims, this House persists in the declarations it has heretofore made.

73. Resolved, That it was anciently the practice of the House of Commons to withhold supplies until grievances were redressed; and that in following this course in the present conjuncture, we are warranted in our proceeding, as well by the most approved precedents, as by the spirit of the constitution itself.

75. Resolved, That the number of the inhabitants of the country being about 600,000, those of French origin are about 525,000, and those of British or other origin 75,000; and that the establishment of the civil government of Lower Canada for the year 1832, according to the yearly returns made by the Provincial Administration, for the information of the British Parliament, contained the names of 157 officers and others receiving salaries, who are apparently of British or foreign origin, and the names of 47 who are apparently natives of the country, of French origin: that this statement does not exhibit the whole disproportion which exists in the distribution of the public money and power, the latter class being for the most part appointed to the inferior and less lucrative offices, and most frequently only obtaining even these by becoming the dependents of those who hold the higher and more lucrative offices; . . .

79. Resolved, That this House, as representing the people of this province, possesses of right, and has exercised within this province when occasion has required it, all the powers, privileges and immunities claimed and possessed by the Commons House of Parliament in the kingdom of Great Britain and Ireland. . . .

84. Resolved, That besides the grievances and abuses before mentioned, there exist in this province a great number of others (a part of which existed before the commencement of the present administration, which has maintained them, and is the author of a portion of them), with regard to which this House reserves to itself the right of complaining and demanding reparation, and the number of which is too great to allow

of their being enumerated here: that this House points out, as among that number,

1stly. The vicious composition and the irresponsibility of the Executive Council, . . . and the secrecy with which not only the functions, but even the names of the members of that body have been kept from the knowledge of this House, . . .

2dly. The exorbitant fees illegally exacted in certain of the public offices, and in others connected with the judicial department, under regulations made by the Executive Council, by the judges, and by other functionaries usurping the powers of the legislature.

4thly. The cumulation of public places and offices in the same persons, and the efforts made by a number of families connected with the administration, to perpetuate this state of things for their own advantage, . . .

5thly. The intermeddling of members of the Legislative Councils in the election of the representatives of the people, for the purpose of influencing and controlling them by force, and the selection frequently made of returning officers for the purpose of securing the same partial and corrupt ends; the interference of the present Governor-in-chief himself in the said elections; his approval of the intermeddling of the said legislative councillors in the said elections; . . .

6thly. The interference of the armed military force at such elections, through which three peaceable citizens, whose exertions were necessary to the support of their families, and who were strangers to the agitation of the election, were shot dead in the streets, . . .

7thly. The various faulty and partial systems which have been followed ever since the passing of the Constitutional Act, with regard to the management of the waste lands in this province, and have rendered it impossible for the great majority of the people of the country to settle on the said lands; the fraudulent and illegal manner in which, contrary to His Majesty's instructions, Governors, Legislative and Executive Councillors, Judges and subordinate officers have appropriated to themselves large tracts of the said lands; . . .

85. Resolved, . . . that this House expects from the honour, patriotism and justice of the reformed Parliament of the United Kingdom, that the Commons of the said Parliament will bring impeachments, and will support such impeachments before the House of Lords against the said Matthew Lord Aylmer, for his illegal, unjust and unconstitutional administration of the government of this province; and against such of the wicked and perverse advisers who have misled him, as this House may hereafter accuse, . . .

86. Resolved, That this House hopes and believes, that the independent members of both Houses of the Parliament of the United Kingdom will be disposed, both from inclination and from a sense of duty, to support the accusations brought by this House, to watch over the preservation of its rights and privileges which have been so frequently and violently attacked, more especially by the present administration; and so to act, that the people of this province may not be forced by oppression to regret their dependence on the British Empire, and to seek elsewhere a remedy for their afflictions. . . .

III:4 THE BREAKING POINT

> Rebellion was touched off by the British government's final statement of policy in the Ten Resolutions, introduced by Lord John Russell in the House of Commons in March 1837, and flatly rejected by the Lower Canadian Assembly. The most important of the Resolutions are given below (a), followed by a sample of radical newspaper reaction to them. The editorial (b) is by Dr. E. B. O'Callaghan in *The Vindicator*.

a. Lord John Russell's Ten Resolutions, 1837

4. That in the existing state of Lower Canada, it is unadvisable to make the Legislative Council of that province an elective body; but that it is expedient that measures be adopted for securing to that branch of the Legislature a greater degree of public confidence.

5. That while it is expedient to improve the composition of the Executive Council in Lower Canada, it is unadvisable to subject it to the responsibility demanded by the House of Assembly of that province.

8. That for defraying the arrears due on account of the established and customary charges of the administration of justice, and of the civil government of the said province, it is expedient, that . . . the Governor of the said province be empowered to issue from and out of any other part of his Majesty's revenues, in the hands of the Receiver-General of the said province, such further sums as shall be necessary to effect the payment of the before - mentioned sum of £142,160. 14s. 6d. . . .

b. A Lower Canadian Reply To Russell

It gives us great pleasure to announce, that the feeling created throughout this wealthy and populous District, by Lord John Russell's infamous resolutions, is one of unmixed INDIGNATION. They are met everywhere with "curses not loud but deep," and a fixed, stubborn determination, to resist any and every attempt to enslave the country.

The Reformers are already on the alert. . . . and before the summer will have gone over their heads, the people of Lower Canada will tell, both their representatives and their rulers, that they are not the stuff from which slaves are made.

It could not be otherwise. Those who have combatted, and successfully combatted, the attempts of Dalhousie to pay away their money without the authority of law; those who have, year after year, protested against the unconstitutional interference of the British Parliament in our internal affairs, will not allow it to go abroad to the world, that their principles and protests are nothing better than waste paper. They will not permit it to be said that, at the back of even a House of Commons, they now sanction what they have up to this day so doggedly, so repeatedly, so consistently, and so honorably resisted.

A combined and dishonorable junction of Whigs and Tories, in a House of Commons 'reformed' but in name, may pass Resolutions to annihilate the last remnant of Liberty left in the Colonial Legislatures. A House of Lords, the fundamental principle of whose Constitution is inimical to human freedom, may endorse the determination of the combined enemies of freedom in the Lower House, but neither the Resolutions, the authors, nor their supporters, can change the nature of things. *Robbery will be robbery still.*

Russell may, therefore, order *his Deputy, Gosford, to plunder our public chest.* A second Falstaff, he may say to his worthy chum—'Rob me the Exchequer, Hal!'—and his Deputy and chum may rob it accordingly: but even this will not legalize the plunder. Our rights must not be violated with impunity. A HOWL of indignation must be raised from one extremity of the Province to the other, against the ROBBERS, and against all those WHO PARTAKE OF THE PLUNDER.

"HENCEFORTH, THERE MUST BE NO PEACE IN THE PROVINCE— *no quarter for the plunderers.* Agitate! *Agitate!!* AGITATE!!! Destroy the Revenue; denounce the oppressors. Everything is lawful when the fundamental liberties are in danger. 'The guards die—they never surrender.'

IV. The Road To Rebellion: Upper Canada

IV: 1 GOVERNOR SIMCOE'S PLANS FOR UPPER CANADA

Upper Canada's first Lieutenant-Governor, John Graves Simcoe, was a conservative soldier determined to create a carbon copy of English society in the North American wilderness. The following excerpts from his correspondence outline his principle aims and the motive behind them. Selection (a) is from a letter Simcoe wrote to the Duke of Portland; (b) is from a letter to the Archbishop of Canterbury.

a. The Constitution

It appears proper that I should state to your Grace, that, uncontrovertibly, on my receiving the administration of the Government of this Province, under the Canada Act, I did conceive, and stated to His Majesty's Ministers, that I considered the Act as the Magna Carta of the Colony, and that it was my duty to render the Province as nearly as may be "a perfect Image and Transcript of the British Government and Constitution"—The *forms* of the British Constitution, from the very seed plot in the Province to their Maturity in the Parent State, being in my Judgement, essentially necessary for the preservation of the Public Tranquillity, and the best Security for Colonial Allegiance— . . .

It may not be unnecessary for me to observe to Your Grace, that when I speak of assimilating the modes of Government to those of the Parent State, I principally allude, in matters of less consequence, to checking the Elective P.inciple from operating so universally as it does in the United States; but which, as may be seen in some of the Acts, though I have been enabled to restrain, I by no means had the Power to abolish. . . .

b. **An Established Church**

I must beg leave to premise, that I am decisively of opinion, that a regular Episcopal establishment, subordinate to the primacy of Great Britain, is absolutely necessary in any extensive colony which this country means to preserve, and in particular, if the advantages which she aims at, are expected to be derived and increased proportionably to its degree of population. But in regard to a colony in Upper Canada, which is to be blessed with the laws and upright administration of them, which distinguishes and ennobles the country, and which colony is peculiarly situated amongst a variety of republics, every establishment of Church and State that upholds the distinction of ranks, and lessens the undue weight of the democratic influence, ought to be introduced, and will no doubt, in the hands of Great Britain, hold out a purer model of government in a practical form, than has been expatiated upon in all the theoretic reveries of self-named philosophers.

The neglect of the principle of overturning republicanism in former periods, by giving support and assistance to those causes which are perpetually offering themselves, to effect so necessary an object, is much to be lamented; but it is my duty to be as solicitous as possible, that they may now have their due influence, if I wish the government to be a permanent one; and I am happy to feel the utmost conviction, that the best mode of population, and the best line of connexion, with the United States, is combined in giving *due* support to that church establishment, which I consider so necessary to promote the national religion, of which I am a sincere and humble believer, and to maintain the true and venerable constitution of my country.

IV:2 THE RELIGIOUS PROBLEM

The most serious issue in Upper Canada before the rebellion was the question of religious privilege. The problem of the Clergy Reserves was only the most obvious instance of the attempts by the Church of England to exercise power as an established Church. The following two selections present the opinions of the Upper Canadian Assembly on (a) the Clergy Reserves, and (b) the question of an established church.

a. The Clergy Reserves

We further most humbly represent, most gracious Sovereign, that the lands set apart in this Province, for the maintenance and support of a Protestant Clergy, ought not to be enjoyed by any one denomination of Protestants, to the exclusion of their Christian brethren of other denominations, equally conscientious in their respective modes of worshipping God, and equally entitled, as dutiful and loyal Subjects, to the protection of your Majesty's benign and liberal government. We therefore humbly hope, it will, in your Majesty's wisdom, be deemed expedient and just, that, not only the present reserves, but that any funds arising from the sales thereof, should be devoted to the advancement of the Christian Religion generally, and the happiness of all your Majesty's Subjects of whatsoever denomination; or if such application, or distribution should be deemed inexpedient, that the profits arising from such appropriation, should be applied to the purposes of education, and the general improvement of this province.

b. **An Established Church**

. . . A country in where there is an established church from which a vast majority of the subjects are dissenters, must be in a lamentable state: the Committee hope that this Province will never present such a spectacle. It is well known that there is in the minds of the people generally a strong and settled aversion to any thing like an established Church, and altho from the conviction so happily and justly entertained, that His Majesty's Government will never adopt a measure so deeply affecting the interests and feelings of the inhabitants of this Province, without the most indulgent consideration of their wishes on the subject, there is less anxiety than would otherwise exist, yet the apprehension that it was the intention of His Majesty's Government to incorporate the Church of England or any other church with the Government as an appendage of the state—and to invest it with peculiar rights or privileges civil or pecuniary, from which other sects were excluded, would excite alarm through the Country, and the actual execution of such a measure would produce the most general and lasting discontent. There is besides no necessity for such an establishment. It cannot be necessary for the security of the Government; the loyalty of the people is deep and enthusiastic, and it may be doubted how far it would be improved or increased by any state establishment of clergymen. Religious instruction, it is true, will promote and strengthen loyalty and all other virtues; but no more when communicated by clergymen of the Church of England than by those of other sects, and probably less if they are or appear to be political teachers and servants of the state, rather than ministers of the Gospel. It cannot be necessary for the ends of religion; other denominations of course will not be benefited by it; and the church itself will derive probably but little if any real advantage. The piety and religious prosperity of a church can gain but little from men who are induced by secular motives to assume the sacred functions of the clerical office. . . .

IV: 3 WILLIAM LYON MACKENZIE'S
SEVENTH REPORT ON GRIEVANCES,
1835

Upper Canada's problems went far beyond religion—
they were also economic, political, and social. Most of
the reformers' grievances were summed up in William
Lyon Mackenzie's *Seventh Report on Grievances*
which was presented to the Assembly in 1835. The
excerpts given here also indicate the differences
among the reformers in their suggestions for constitutional change.

The almost unlimited extent of the patronage of the Crown,
or rather of the Colonial Minister for the time being and his
advisers here, together with the abuse of that patronage, are
the chief sources of Colonial discontent. Such is the patronage
of the Colonial Office that the granting or withholding of
supplies is of no political importance unless as an indication
of the opinion of the country concerning the character of the
government, which is conducted upon a system that admits
its officers to take and apply the funds of the Colonists without any legislative vote whatever. . . .

The patronage of the Crown, as now exercised in this
Province, includes the payments of gifts, salaries, pensions,
and retired allowances to the Clergy of the Methodist, Presbyterian, Protestant Episcopal & Roman Catholic orders, and
to nearly the whole of the civil officers of the government, . . .
The Royal patronage also embraces the judicial establishment, many pensions, the nomination of one branch of the
Legislature, by the name of the Legislative Council, and the
appointment of its speaker and other officers,—the selection of
the officers of the House of Assembly—the control of the
Indian Department, of King's College, and of Upper Canada
College, the appointment of the twelve District Boards of
Education, and the direction of the expenditure of public
monies in aid of Emigration—the selection of the Executive
Council—the uncontrolled management of millions of Acres

of public Lands—the appointment of 1500 commissioned Militia Officers—the sole control of the Military and Naval Forces—and (subject to the votes of the House of Commons in this case) the regulation of the whole Military and Naval expenditure. . . .

The Canada Company, the several incorporated establishments for Banking, Canalling and other purposes, and the Harbour, Dock & Wharf Companies, in nearly all cases, unite their patronage with that of the local government, and steadily strive to increase the influence of the Crown. . . .

The present system is altogether inefficient for ensuring the application of the revenue to the purposes for which it is intended to be applied. The House of Assembly, acting by one or more of its committees in a session, cannot examine the accounts and vouchers of the several public accountants, owing to the very complex, obscure and unsatisfactory manner in which they are furnished; and as for the Executive Council, the law recognizes them not as auditors of the revenue, nor do they merit the public confidence as a board of audit. . . .

Many items of information required by the House and its Committees from the Government with respect to the public accounts, the receipt and expenditure of public monies, college and other funds, monies placed in the hands of individuals for the payment of clergymen or the building of churches and chapels, &c. have as yet been withheld, and the receipts and expenditure of the post-office department have been very unnecessarily delayed. . . . The remedy for neglecting to supply returns in most cases, would be by a statute providing the time and manner of making them, and naming the officers who should render them to the Legislature; but it is well known that such an enactment would fail in the Council, which has an interest in preventing the enforcement of practical accountability to the people. . . .

This body [the Legislative Council] forms a part of the patronage of the British Government; they are the nominees of the Minister of the colonies, who can add to their numbers at his discretion. In continually rejecting the many valuable measures earnestly prayed for by the people, they may be fairly presumed to act in obedience to the power from whence their appointments were derived. Your committee examined some of the members of the council holding offices of emolument under the government, and from their answers it will readily be seen whether they are or are not under the influence of the Lieutenant Governors for the time being.

Capital may be brought into any country, but under an arbitrary, imprudent, and irresponsible government it will be impossible to retain a large share of it. Notwithstanding the encouragement given to emigration, as stated in Mr. Robinson's accounts; it appears . . . that the population of the colony has not increased much beyond the natural rate in an agricultural settlement of great extent, fertile soil, and spare population. The emigration at Quebec in these four years, as also at New York, has been very extensive. The more wealthy class of emigrants pass through Canada to the United States. . . . .

The Governors of colonies, like other men, are individually liable to all the infirmities of human nature, and in their political capacity, when left to act without restraint, they, no doubt, sacrifice occasionally the interests and happiness of the people, to the gratification of their own passions and caprices. One great excellence of the English constitution consists in the limits it imposes on the will of a King, by requiring responsible men to give effect to it. In Upper Canada no such responsibility can exist. The Lieutenant Governor and the British Ministry hold in their hands the whole patronage of the Province; they hold the sole dominion of the country, and leave the representative branch of the Legislature powerless and dependent. . . .

In Upper Canada the efforts of the Legislature have been directed towards improving the Executive Council. Yet it appears on enquiry that that body affects to have done neither good nor harm— . . .

In the appointment to offices, and concerning the accepting or rejecting Legislative Bills, it does not appear that they have ever been consulted. . . . It appears to Your Committee that the Executive Council is a nondescript with which it is folly further to contend.

There have been three classes of persons examined before Your Committee—the first, of whom the Venerable Dr. Strachan is one, are of opinion that the Government is well enough as it is, and that as to responsibility it is as responsible as other Governments.

The second class desire a responsible Ministry, some heads of departments well paid, to direct the government, to prepare bills and most of the business of the session, and to hold office or lose it according as they may happen to be in the minority or majority in the House of Assembly. This system was never attempted in any of the old colonies, but Your Committee have asked many questions with a view of ascertaining what is the public opinion concerning its practicability here; and it appears that Mr. Mackenzie, in his letters to Lord Goderich, expressed a belief that with some modifications it might be productive of a greater share of good government and public prosperity than is at present enjoyed by the people.

A third class contend for elective institutions, and affirm that while Governors come from without, and Judges are commissioned from without, favoritism towards their connexions will prevail to an extent that would destroy the influence of any set of "Ministers," constituted upon the principle desired by the second class; that the influence of Downing Street will continue to prevail as hitherto; and that the favourites of the Secretary of State will, as at present, be placed in important offices to the exclusion of better qualified men. . . .

The class of persons who are in favor of elective institutions contend, that they were found to work well in the old North American colonies while in a colonial state, that the people of Upper Canada are entitled to the enjoyment of institutions equally free with those enjoyed by the old colonists during the time they were colonial, and under British protection—

that few politicians are now found contending that these continental colonies, capable of containing large population, will for a long series of years be required to submit to the inconveniences resulting from perpetual interference by the Home Government in their internal concerns. . . . that elective institutions are the only safeguards to prevent the Canadas from forming disadvantageous comparisons between the condition of the colonists and the adjoining country . . . and that hence there is no disloyalty in freely and calmly discussing which of these modes of government that have been granted to British subjects and countries will best suit Canada.

. . . A painful experience has proved how impracticable it is for such a succession of strangers beneficially to direct and control the affairs of the people 4000 miles off; and being an impracticable system, felt to be intolerable by those for whose good it was professedly intended, it ought to be abolished, and the domestic institutions of the province so improved and administered by the local authorities as to render the people happy and contented. . . .

The growing condition of this part of the Empire, in population, wealth and commerce, requires there should be an entire confidence between the Executive and the Commons House of Assembly; and this confidence cannot exist while those who have long and deservedly lost the esteem of the country are continued in the public offices and councils. Under such a state of things, distrust is unavoidable, however much it is to be deplored as incompatible with the satisfactory discharge of the public business.

. . . the whole system has so long continued virtually in the same hands, that it is little better than a family compact. Abuses have grown up so as to be interwoven with every thing; and these abuses are concealed, or palliated, excused and sustained by those who are interested to uphold them as the means of retaining office for their private, and not for the public, good.

. . . This country is now principally inhabited by loyalists and their descendants, and by an accession of population from the mother country, where is now enjoyed the principles of a free and responsible government; and we feel the practical enjoyment of the same system in this part of the empire to be equally our right; without which it is in vain to assume that we do or can possess in reality or in effect "the very image and transcript of the British Constitution."

IV:4 FRANCIS BOND HEAD IN DEFENCE OF THE FAMILY COMPACT

The often maligned "Family Compact" of Upper Canada should not be hastily condemned. In his 1839 account of the Upper Canadian situation, former Lieutenant-Governor Francis Bond Head attempted to show how such a "compact" was a necessary part of any civilized society. This view of the "Family Compact" should be compared with the analysis made by Lord Durham (Section V).

. . . this "FAMILY COMPACT," is nothing more nor less than that "social fabric" which characterizes every civilized community in the world. It is that social fabric, or rather fortress, within which the British yeoman, farmer, and manufacturer is enabled to repel the extortionate demands of his labourers; and to preserve from pillage and robbery the harvest of his industry after he has reaped it!

"The bench," "the magistrates," "the clergy," "the law," "the landed proprietors," "the bankers," "the native-born inhabitants," and "the supporters of the Established Church," form just as much "a family compact" in England as they do in Upper Canada, and just as much in Germany as they do in England. . . .

The "family compact" of Upper Canada is composed of those members of its society who, either by their abilities and character have been honoured by the confidence of the executive government, or who, by their industry and intelligence, have amassed wealth. The party, I own, is comparatively a small one; but to put the multitude at the top and the few at the bottom is a radical reversion of the pyramid of society which every reflecting man must foresee can end only by its downfall. . . .

IV:5 BOND HEAD EXPLAINS HIS POLICY

> Francis Bond Head, who arrived in Upper Canada as Lieutenant-Governor in 1836, personified the conservative or "Family Compact" point of view. He quickly provoked open conflict. This excerpt from an 1837 despatch to the Colonial Office outlines his position. Head's bitter denunciation of the United States is typical of this point of view (see also Simcoe's plans, Document IV:1, on page 34) and shows how much the Canadian struggle was shaped by attitudes about the American experience.

. . . The two parties here are constitutionalists on the one side, and democrats on the other. The dispute on this continent is not, as it is in England, which of two parties shall attain the honour of conducting the government of their Sovereign; but here the great mass of society is striving to secure to their children the blessings of the British constitution, which a small party, from self-interested motives, is endeavouring to pull down. The idle, the profligate, and the unprincipled, see that democracy in the United States is rapidly hurrying to anarchy, and they well know, or rather they reckon, that anarchy, or, in other words, *plunder,* is the shortest method of obtaining wealth. . . .

No one can read an account of the early stages of the American Revolution, without being struck with the resemblance of much that we now witness to that unfortunate period of our history.

It was then a capital error in the Government of the mother-country, that they seemed to believe the Americans to be sincerely contending for the single object of freedom from taxation by the British Parliament, and they imagined that by renouncing that power, and by disabling themselves (by 18

Geo. III.) from raising money in the Colonies, even for the necessary support of the Government, they would overcome all difficulties. But it was soon evident that the outcry raised about taxation was but the means to another end. Separation from the mother-country was, from the first, the self-interested object of the few ruling demagogues who gave the impulse; and they persevered just as resolutely *after* the ostensible ground of difference had been renounced as before. The Government soon learnt that their measure of conciliation availed them nothing.

So here, in our time, the Government has gone back step by step for years, giving ground before the pretensions of Mr. Papineau and the Assembly, however insolently advanced; weakening by each concession the confidence of the King's loyal and attached subjects, and encouraging as well as strengthening an unprincipled faction avowedly hostile to British rule. No approach to an amicable adjustment has followed any or all of these concessions. On the contrary, they have been so many unprofitable sacrifices of principles and usages necessary to the maintenance of good government, and at the last an end is arrived at, when the King's Ministers are reduced to choose between an unequivocal and direct violation of the Colonial Constitution, or an abandonment of the power of governing. A firm determination early evinced to yield nothing to clamour, to surrender nothing for the mere sake of conciliation, would have secured to the Government the respect of all classes, and would have averted the necessity of resorting to measures which admit in principle of no defence.

Whatever may have been the brilliant theory of subverting the British Constitution in America, we who are living on this continent clearly see before our eyes its effects; namely, that in the United States the will of the people has become stronger than the power of the law. Public credit, life, and property hang therefore upon the conduct of a dense mass of men, in no one of whose hands can it be wise that such vast interests should be committed. The only remedy is in a revolution, of which it is easier to foresee the beginning than the end.

To save the people of Upper Canada from following in the footsteps of the United States, has been the object of every act of my administration.

IV:6 MACKENZIE'S CALL TO REVOLUTION, 1837

In his *Seventh Report on Grievances* Mackenzie was at his best as a slashing critic of the government. His other side—Mackenzie the revolutionary—is shown in these excerpts from a broadside circulated at the beginning of the rebellion. Especially noticeable is his attempt to give religious justification for the act of rebellion.

There have been Nineteen Strikes for Independence from European Tyranny, on the Continent of America. They were all successful! The Tories, therefore, by helping us will help themselves.

The nations are fallen, and thou still art young,
The sun is but rising when others have set;
And tho' Slavery's cloud o'er thy morning hath hung,
The full tide of Freedom shall beam round thee yet.

BRAVE CANADIANS! God has put into the bold and honest hearts of our brethren in Lower Canada to revolt—not against "lawful" but against "unlawful authority." The law says we shall not be taxed without our consent by the voices of the men of our choice, but a wicked and tyrannical government has trampled upon that law—robbed the exchequer—divided the plunder—and declared that, regardless of justice they will continue to roll their splendid carriages, and riot in their palaces, at our expense—that we are poor spiritless ignorant peasants, who were born to toil for our betters. But the peasants are beginning to open their eyes and to feel their strength—too long have they been hoodwinked by Baal's priests—by hired and tampered with preachers, wolves in sheep's clothing, who take the wages of sin, and do the work of iniquity, "each one looking to his gain in his quarter."

CANADIANS! Do you love freedom? I know you do. Do you hate oppression? Who dare deny it? Do you wish perpetual peace, and a government founded upon the eternal heaven-born principle of the Lord Jesus Christ—a government bound to enforce the law to do to each other as you would be done by? Then buckle on your armour, and put down the villains who oppress and enslave our country. . . .

That power that protected ourselves and our forefathers in the deserts of Canada . . . will be in the midst of us in the day of our struggle for our liberties, and for Governors of our free choice, who would not dare to trample on the laws they had sworn to maintain. In the present struggle, we may be sure, that if we do not rise and put down Head and his lawless myrmidons, they will gather all the rogues and villains in the Country together—arm them—and then deliver our farms, our families, and our country to their brutality—to that it has come, we must put them down, or they will utterly destroy this country. If we move now, as one man, to crush the tyrant's power, to establish free institutions founded on God's law, we will prosper, for He who commands the winds and waves will be with us—but if we are cowardly and mean-spirited, a woeful and a dark day is surely before us. . . .

CANADIANS! It is the design of the Friends of Liberty to give several hundred acres to every Volunteer—to root up the unlawful Canada Company, and give *free deeds* to all settlers who live on their lands—to give free gifts of the Clergy Reserve lots, to good citizens who have settled on them—and the like to settlers on Church of England Glebe Lots, so that the yeomanry may feel independent, and be able to improve the country, instead of sending the fruit of their labour to foreign lands. The fifty-seven Rectories will be at once given to the people, and all public lands used for Education, Internal Improvements, and the public good. £100,000 drawn from us in payment of the salaries of bad men in office, will be reduced to one quarter, or much less, and the remainder will go to improve bad roads and to "make crooked paths straight;" law will be ten times more cheap and easy—the bickerings of priests will cease with the funds that keep them up—and men of wealth and property from other lands will soon raise our farms to four times their present value. We have given Head and his employers a trial of forty-five years—five years longer than the Israelites were detained in the wilderness. The promised land is now before us—up then and take it. . . .

. . . the prize is a splendid one. A country larger than France or England; natural resources equal to our most boundless wishes—a government of equal laws—religion pure and undefiled—perpetual peace—education to all—millions of acres of lands for revenue—freedom from British tribute—free trade with all the world—but stop—I never could enumerate all the blessings attendant on independence!

Up then, brave Canadians! Get ready your rifles, and make short work of it; a connection with England would involve us in all her wars, undertaken for her own advantage, never for ours; with governors from England, we will have bribery at elections, corruption, villainy and perpetual discord in every township, but Independence would give us the means of enjoying many blessings. Our enemies in Toronto are in terror and dismay—they know their wickedness and dread our vengeance. . . . now's the day and the hour! Woe be to those who oppose us, for "In God is our trust."

V. The British Response

V:1 LORD DURHAM'S *REPORT*, 1839

Lord Durham spent only five months in the Canadas and less than two weeks in Upper Canada. His *Report* contained many inaccuracies about Upper Canada and was bitterly resented in Lower Canada for its unsympathetic view of French Canadians. Its major recommendation, responsible government, originated with the Baldwins and other moderate reformers rather than with Lord Durham himself. Nevertheless, the *Report* is perhaps the most significant document in Canadian history, as well as a milestone in the history of the British Empire. Once the doctrine of responsible government had been accepted and promoted by an official of the British government, ultimate implementation was virtually assured. Here was both a relatively simple solution to the twenty-year deadlock in the Canadas and a giant first step toward eventual independence from Great Britain.

The excerpts given below cover Durham's analysis of the problems and his major recommendations, but the entire *Report* should be studied for a full appreciation of its value.

TO THE QUEEN'S
MOST EXCELLENT MAJESTY

. . . the evils I had it in charge to remedy, are evils which no civilized community can long continue to bear. There is no class or section of Your Majesty's subjects in either of the Canadas, that does not suffer from both the existing disorder and the doubt which hangs over the future form and policy of the Government. While the present state of things is allowed to last, the actual inhabitants of these Provinces have no security for person or property, no enjoyment of what they possess, no stimulus to industry. The development of the vast resources of these extensive territories is arrested; and the population, which should be attracted to fill and fertilize them, is directed into foreign states. Every day during which a final and stable settlement is delayed, the condition of the Colonies becomes worse, the minds of men more exasperated, and the success of any scheme of adjustment more precarious.

LOWER CANADA

. . . I expected to find a contest between a government and a people: I found two nations warring in the bosom of a single state: I found a struggle, not of principles, but of races; and I perceived that it would be idle to attempt any amelioration of laws or institutions until we could first succeed in terminating the deadly animosity that now separates the inhabitants of Lower Canada into the hostile divisions of French and English.

. . . The national feud forces itself on the very senses, irresistibly and palpably, as the origin or the essence of every dispute which divides the community; we discover that dissensions, which appear to have another origin, are but forms of this constant and all-pervading quarrel; and that every contest is one of French and English in the outset, or becomes so ere it has run its course.

. . . The French majority asserted the most democratic doctrines of the rights of a numerical majority. The English minority availed itself of the protection of the prerogative, and allied itself with all those of the colonial institutions which enabled the few to resist the will of the many. But when we look to the objects of each party, the analogy to our own politics seems to be lost, if not actually reversed; the French appear to have used their democratic arms for conservative purposes, rather than those of liberal and enlightened movement; and the sympathies of the friends of reform are naturally enlisted on the side of sound amelioration which the English minority in vain attempted to introduce into the antiquated laws of the Province.

. . . The ascendancy which an unjust favouritism had contributed to give to the English race in the government and the legal profession, their own superior energy, skill and capital secured to them in every branch of industry. They have developed the resources of the country; they have constructed or improved its means of communication; they have created its internal and foreign commerce. The entire wholesale, and a large portion of the retail trade of the Province, with the most profitable and flourishing farms, are now in the hands of this numerical minority of the population.

. . . It is not any where a virtue of the English race to look with complacency on any manners, customs or laws which appear strange to them; accustomed to form a high estimate of their own superiority, they take no pains to conceal from others their contempt and intolerance of their usages. They found the French Canadians filled with an equal amount of national pride; a sensitive, but inactive pride, which disposes that people not to resent insult, but rather to keep aloof from those who would keep them under. The French could not but feel the superiority of English enterprise; they could not shut their eyes to their success in every undertaking in which they came into contact, and to the constant superiority which they were acquiring. They looked upon their rivals with alarm, with jealousy, and finally with hatred. The English repaid them with a scorn, which soon also assumed the same form of hatred. The French complained of the arrogance and injustice of the English; the English accused the French of the vices of a weak and conquered people, and charged them with meanness and perfidy. . . .

The English population, an immigrant and enterprising population; looked on the American Provinces as a vast field for settlement and speculation, and in the common spirit of the Anglo-Saxon inhabitants of that continent, regarded it as the chief business of the Government, to promote, by all possible use of its legislative and administrative powers, the increase of population and the accumulation of property; . . .

Without going so far as to accuse the Assembly of a deliberate design to check the settlement and improvement of Lower Canada, it cannot be denied that they looked with considerable jealousy and dislike on the increase and prosperity of what they regarded as a foreign and hostile race; they looked on the Province as the patrimony of their own race; they viewed it not as a country to be settled, but as one already settled; and instead of legislating in the American spirit, and first providing for the future population of the Province, their primary care was, in the spirit of legislation which prevails in the old world, to guard the interests and feelings of the present race of inhabitants, to whom they considered the new-comers as subordinate; . . .

. . . A jealousy between two races, so long habituated to regard each other with hereditary enmity, and so differing in habits, in language and in laws, would have been inevitable under any form of government. That liberal institutions and a prudent policy might have changed the character of the struggle I have no doubt; but they could not have prevented it; they could only have softened its character, and brought it more speedily a more decisive and peaceful conclusion. Unhappily, however, the system of government pursued in Lower Canada has been based on the policy of perpetuating that very separation of the races, and encouraging these very notions of conflicting nationalities which it ought to have been the first and chief care of Government to check and extinguish. From the period of the conquest to the present time, the conduct of the Government has aggravated the evil, and the origin of the present extreme disorder may be found in the institutions by which the character of the colony was determined.

. . . It may fairly be said, that the natural state of government in all these Colonies is that of collision between the Executive and the representative body. In all of them the administration of public affairs is habitually confided to those who do not co-operate harmoniously with the popular branch of the legislature; and the Government is constantly proposing measures which the majority of the Assembly reject, and refusing its assent to bills which that body has passed. . . .

The powers for which the Assembly contended, appear in both instances to be such as it was perfectly justified in demanding. It is difficult to conceive what could have been their theory of government who imagined that in any colony of England a body invested with the name and character of a representative Assembly, could be deprived of any of those powers which, in the opinion of Englishmen, are inherent in a popular legislature. . . .

From the commencement, therefore, to the end of the disputes which mark the whole Parliamentary history of Lower Canada, I look on the conduct of the Assembly as a constant warfare with the executive, for the purpose of obtaining the powers inherent in a representative body by the very nature of representative government. It was to accomplish this purpose, that it used every means in its power; but it must be censured for having, in pursuit of this object, perverted its powers of legislation, and disturbed the whole working of the constitution. It made the business of legislation, and the practical improvement of the country, subordinate to its struggle for power; and, being denied its legitimate privileges, it endeavoured to extend its authority in modes totally incompatible with the principles of constitutional liberty. . . .

UPPER CANADA

. . . In the preceding account of the working of the constitutional system in Lower Canada, I have described the effect which the irresponsibility of the real advisers of the Governor had in lodging permanent authority in the hands of a powerful party, linked together not only by common party interests, but by personal ties. But in none of the North American Provinces has this exhibited itself for so long a period or to such an extent, as in Upper Canada, which has long been entirely governed by a party commonly designated throughout the Province as the 'family compact', a name not much more appropriate than party designations usually are, inasmuch as there is, in truth, very little of family connexion among the persons thus united. For a long time this body of men, receiving at times accessions to its numbers, possessed almost all the highest public offices, by means of which, and of its influence in the Executive Council, it wielded all the powers of government; it maintained influence in the legislature by means of its predominance in the Legislative Council; and it disposed of the large number of petty posts which are in the patronage of the Government all over the Province. Successive Governors, as they came in their turn, are said to have either submitted quietly to its influence, or, after a short and unavailing struggle, to have yielded to this well-organized party the real conduct of affairs. The bench, the magistracy, the high offices of the Episcopal Church, and a great part of the legal profession, are filled by the adherents of this party: by grant or purchase, they have acquired nearly the whole of the waste lands of the Province; they are all-powerful in the chartered banks, and, till lately, shared among themselves almost exclusively all offices of trust and profit. The bulk of this party consists, for the most part, of native-born inhabitants of the Colony, or of emigrants who settled in it before the last war with the United States; the principal members of it belong to the Church of England, and the maintenance of the claims of that church has always been one of its distinguishing characteristics.

A monopoly of power so extensive and so lasting could not fail, in process of time, to excite envy, create dissatisfaction, and ultimately provoke attack; and an opposition consequently grew up in the Assembly which assailed the ruling party, by appealing to popular principles of government, by denouncing the alleged jobbing and profusion of the official body, and by instituting inquiries into abuses, for the purpose of promoting reform, and especially economy. . . .

It was upon this question of the responsibility of the Executive Council that the great struggle has for a long time been carried on between the official party and the reformers; for the official party, like all parties long in power, was naturally unwilling to submit itself to any such responsibility as would abridge its tenure, or cramp its exercise of authority. Reluctant to acknowledge any responsibility to the people of the Colony, this party appears to have paid a somewhat refractory and nominal submission to the Imperial Government, relying in fact on securing a virtual independence by this nominal submission to the distant authority of the Colonial Department, or to the powers of a Governor, over whose policy they were certain, by their facilities of access, to obtain a paramount influence. . . .

During all this time, however, though much irritation had been caused by the exclusive claims of the Church of England, and the favour shown by the Government to one, and that a small religious community, the clergy of that church, though an endowed, were not a dominant, priesthood. They had a far larger share of the public money than the clergy of any other denomination; but they had no exclusive privileges, and no authority, save such as might spring from their efficient discharge of their sacred duties, or from the energy, ability or influence of members of their body. But the last public act of Sir John Colborne, before quitting the Government of the Province in 1835, which was the establishment of the fifty-seven rectories, has completely changed the aspect of the question. . . . This is regarded by all other teachers of religion in the country as having at once degraded them to a position of legal inferiority to the clergy of the Church of England; and it has been resented most warmly. In the opinion of many persons, this was the chief pre-disposing cause of the recent insurrection, and it is an abiding and unabated cause of discontent. . . .

. . . The apparent right which time and custom give to the maintenance of an ancient and respected institution cannot exist in a recently settled country, in which every thing is new; and the establishment of a dominant church there is a creation of exclusive privileges in favour of one out of many religious denominations, and that composing a small minority, at the expense not merely of the majority, but of many as large minorities. . . .

It is most important that this question should be settled, and so settled as to give satisfaction to the majority of the people of the two Canadas, whom it equally concerns. And I know of no mode of doing this but by repealing all provisions in Imperial Acts that relate to the application of the clergy reserves, and the funds arising from them, leaving the disposal of the funds to the local legislature, and acquiescing in whatever decision it may adopt. . . .

In addition . . . there are permanent causes of discontent, resulting from the existence of deep-seated impediments in the way of its industrial progress. The Province is without any of those means by which the resources of a country are developed, and the civilization of a people is advanced or upheld. . . .

. . . A very considerable portion of the Province has neither roads, post offices, mills, schools, nor churches. The people may raise enough for their own subsistence, and may even have a rude and comfortless plenty, but they can seldom acquire wealth; nor can even wealthy land-owners prevent their children from growing up ignorant and boorish, and from occupying a far lower mental, moral and social position that they themselves fill. Their means of communication with each other, or the chief towns of the Province, are limited and uncertain. . . .

The principal evils to which settlers in a new township are subject result from the scantiness of population. A township contains 80,000 acres of land; one-seventh is reserved for the clergy and one-seventh for the Crown; consequently five-sevenths remain for the disposal of Government, a large proportion of which is taken up by grants to U.E. loyalists, militiamen, officers and others: the far greater part of these grants remain in an unimproved state. These blocks of wild land place the actual settler in an almost hopeless condition; he can hardly expect, during his lifetime, to see his neighbourhood contain a population sufficiently dense to support mills, schools, post-offices, places of worship, markets or shops; and without these, civilization retrogrades. . . .

GENERAL REVIEW AND RECOMMENDATIONS

. . . It is not in the terrors of the law, or in the might of our armies, that the secure and honourable bond of connexion is to be found. It exists in the beneficial operation of those British institutions which link the utmost development of freedom and civilization with the stable authority of an hereditary monarchy, and which, if rightly organized and fairly administered in the Colonies, as in Great Britain, would render a change of institutions only an additional evil to the loss of the protection and commerce of the British Empire.

. . . I rely on the efficacy of reform in the constitutional system by which these Colonies are governed, for the removal of every abuse in their administration which defective institutions have engendered. If a system can be devised which shall lay in these countries the foundation of an efficient and popular government, ensure harmony, in place of collision, between the various powers of the State, and bring the influence of a vigorous public opinion to bear on every detail of public affairs, we may rely on sufficient remedies being found for the present vices of the administrative system.

. . . It is not by weakening, but strengthening the influence of the people on its Government; by confining within much narrower bounds than those hitherto allotted to it, and not by extending the interference of the imperial authorities in the details of colonial affairs, that I believe that harmony is to be restored, where dissension has so long prevailed; and a regularity and vigour hitherto unknown, introduced into the administration of these Provinces. It needs no change in the principles of government, no invention of a new constitutional theory, to supply the remedy which would, in my opinion, completely remove the existing political disorders. It needs but to follow out consistently the principles of the British Constitution, and introduce into the Government of these great Colonies those wise provisions, by which alone the working of the representative system can in any country be rendered harmonious and efficient. . . .

. . . Every purpose of popular control might be combined with every advantage of vesting the immediate choice of advisers in the Crown, were the Colonial Governor to be instructed to secure the co-operation of the Assembly in his policy, by entrusting its administration to such men as could command a majority; and if he were given to understand that he need count on no aid from home in any difference with the Assembly, that should not directly involve the relations between the mother country and the Colony. This change might be effected by a single dispatch containing such instructions; or if any legal enactment were requisite, it would only be one that would render it necessary that the official acts of the Governor should be countersigned by some public functionary. This would induce responsibility for every act of the Government, and, as a natural consequence, it would necessitate the substitution of a system of administration, by means of competent heads of departments, for the present rude machinery of an Executive Council. The Governor, if he wished to retain advisers not possessing the confidence of the existing Assembly, might rely on the effect of an appeal to the people, and, if unsuccessful, he might be coerced by a refusal of supplies, or his advisers might be terrified by the prospect of impeachment. But there can be no reason for apprehending that either party would enter on a contest, when each would find its interest in the maintenance of harmony; and the abuse of the powers which each would constitutionally possess, would cease when the struggle for larger powers became unnecessary. . . .

. . . I admit that the system which I propose would, in fact, place the internal government of the Colony in the hands of the colonists themselves; and that we should thus leave to them the execution of the laws, of which we have long entrusted the making solely to them. Perfectly aware of the value of our colonial possessions, and strongly impressed with the necessity of maintaining our connexion with them, I know not in what respect it can be desirable that we should interfere with their internal legislation in matters which do not affect their relations with the mother country. The matters, which so concern us, are very few. The constitution of the form of government,—the regulation of foreign relations, and of trade with the mother country, the other British Colonies, and foreign nations,—and the disposal of the public lands, are the only points of which the mother country requires a control. . . . The colonists may not always know what laws are best for them, or which of their countrymen are the fittest for conducting their affairs; but, at least, they have a greater interest in coming to a right judgment on these points, and will take greater pains to do so than those whose welfare is very remotely and slightly affected by the good or bad legislation of these portions of the Empire. If the colonists make bad laws, and select improper persons to conduct their affairs, they will generally be the only, always the greatest, sufferers; and, like the people of other countries, they must bear the ills which they bring on themselves, until they choose to apply the remedy. . . .

. . . Instead of confiding the whole collection and distribution of all the revenues raised in any country for all general and local purposes to a single representative body, the power of local assessment, and the application of the funds arising from it, should be entrusted to local management. . . .

. . . A plan by which it is proposed to ensure the tranquil government of Lower Canada, must include in itself the means of putting an end to the agitation of national disputes in the legislature, by settling, and once and for ever, the national character of the Province. I entertain no doubts as to the national character which must be given to Lower Canada; it must be that of the British Empire; that of the majority of the population of British America; that of the great race which must, in the lapse of no long period of time, be predominant over the whole North American Continent. Without effecting the change so rapidly or so roughly as to shock the feelings and trample on the welfare of the existing generation, it must henceforth be the first and steady purpose of the British Government to establish an English population, with English laws and language, in this Province, and to trust its government to none but a decidedly English legislature.

. . . The English have already in their hands the majority of the larger masses of property in the country; they have the decided superiority of intelligence on their side; they have the certainty that colonization must swell their numbers to a majority; and they belong to the race which wields the Imperial Government, and predominates on the American Continent. If we now leave them in a minority, they will never abandon the assurance of being a majority hereafter, and never cease to continue the present contest with all the fierceness with which it now rages. . . .

On these grounds, I believe that no permanent or efficient remedy can be devised for the disorders of Lower Canada, except a fusion of the Government in that of one or more of the surrounding Provinces; and as I am of opinion that the full establishment of responsible government can only be permanently secured by giving these Colonies an increased importance in the politics of the Empire, I find in union the only means of remedying at once and completely the two prominent causes of their present unsatisfactory condition. . . .

If the population of Upper Canada is rightly estimated at 400,000, the English inhabitants of Lower Canada at 150,000, and the French at 450,000, the union of the two Provinces would not only give a clear English majority, but one which would be increased every year by the influence of English emigration; and I have litle doubt that the French, when once placed, by the legitimate course of events and the working of natural causes, in a minority, would abandon their vain hopes of nationality. . . .

But while I convince myself that such desirable ends would be secured by the legislative union of the two Provinces, I am inclined to go further, and inquire whether all these objects would not more surely be attained, by extending this legislative union over all the British Provinces in North America; and whether the advantages which I anticipate for two of them, might not, and should not in justice be extended over all. Such a union would at once decisively settle the question of races; it would enable all the Provinces to co-operate for all common purposes; and, above all, it would form a great and powerful people, possessing the means of securing good and responsible government for itself, and which, under the protection of the British Empire, might in some measure counterbalance the preponderant and increasing influence of the United States on the American Continent. I do not anticipate that a colonial legislature thus strong and thus self-governing, would desire to abandon the connexion with Great Britain. On the contrary, I believe that the practical relief from undue interference, which would be the result of such a change, would strengthen the present bond of feelings and interests; and that the connexion would only become more durable and advantageous, by having more of equality, of freedom, and of local independence. . . .

. . . I am averse to every plan that has been proposed for giving an equal number of members to the two Provinces, in order to attain the temporary end of out-numbering the French, because I think the same object will be obtained without any violation of the principle of representation, . . . and because, when emigration shall have increased the English population in the Upper Province, the adoption of such a principle would operate to defeat the very purpose it is intended to serve. It appears to me that any such electoral arrangement, founded on the present provincial divisions, would tend to defeat the purposes of union, and perpetuate the idea of disunion.

. . . I pray Your Majesty's earnest attention to this Report. It is the last act arising out of the loyal and conscientious discharge of the high duties imposed upon me by the Commission with which Your Majesty was graciously pleased to entrust me. I humbly hope that Your Majesty will receive it favourably, and believe that it has been dictated by the most devoted feeling of loyalty and attachment to Your Majesty's Person and Throne, by the strongest sense of public duty, and by the earnest desire to perpetuate and strengthen the connexion between this Empire and the North American Colonies, which would then form one of the brightest ornaments in Your Majesty's Imperial Crown.

All which is humbly submitted to Your Majesty.

DURHAM.

VI. The Struggle For Responsible Government

VI: 1 LORD JOHN RUSSELL'S OBJECTIONS TO RESPONSIBLE GOVERNMENT

Durham's *Report* was not well received in Britain. Although the Whig Government implemented Durham's recommendation that Upper and Lower Canada be united, it would not accept the second major recommendation, responsible government. In a speech before Parliament in 1839, Lord John Russell outlined British objections to responsible government.

. . . It does not appear to me that you can subject the Executive Council of Canada to the responsibility which is fairly demanded of the ministers of the executive power in this country. In the first place, there is an obvious difference in matter of form with regard to the instructions under which the Governor of a colony acts. The Sovereign in this country receives the advice of the ministers and acts by the advice of those ministers, and indeed, there is no important act of the Crown for which there is not some individual minister responsible. There responsibility begins and there it ends. But the Governor of Canada is acting, not in that high and unassailable position in which the Sovereign of this country is placed. He is a Governor receiving instructions from the Crown on the responsibility of a Secretary of State.

Here, then, at once, is an obvious and complete difference between the Executive of this country and the Executive of a colony. The Governor might ask the Executive Council to propose a certain measure. They might say that they could not propose it unless the members of the House of Assembly would adopt it, but the Governor might reply that he had received instructions from home commanding him to propose that measure. How, in that case, is he to proceed? Either one power or the other must be set aside,—either the Governor or the House of Assembly; or else the Governor must become a mere cipher in the hands of the Assembly and not attempt to carry into effect the measure which he is commanded by the home Government to do.

But if we endeavour to carry out this analogy, there is one case that all the world allows is a case in which it could be applied—I mean the case of foreign affairs. . . . Again neither could this analogy be maintained with regard to trade between Canada and the mother country or Canada and any other foreign country; how then can you adopt a principle from which such large exceptions are to be made? If you were to do so you would be continually on the borders of dispute and conflict; . . .

It is quite impossible to allow it to be laid down as a general principle that any part of the government of this country, conducted by ministers having the sanction of this House shall be overruled by a colony, and that such colony shall not be subject to the general superintending authority of the Crown of these realms. I can conceive, sir, and I think that it would be the part of wisdom and justice to say, that there are matters affecting the internal affairs of these Provinces,—that there are matters in which neither the Imperial Parliament nor the general Government need interfere and on which they should be anxious to consult the feelings of the people of the colonies. . . . I know no reason why the Legislative Assembly, whether of each separately, or of both Provinces united, should not be listened to with deference; but I am not prepared to lay down as a principle—a new principle

—for the future government of the colonies, that we ought to subject the Executive there to the same restrictions as prevail in this country. . . .

VI: 2 JOSEPH HOWE'S LETTERS

Russell's speech rejecting responsible government prompted Joseph Howe of Nova Scotia to write the most eloquent defense of responsible government ever to come out of British North America. In four brilliant and witty open letters to Russell, Howe reiterated again and again his main theme that the colonists were asking no more than the rights of ordinary Englishmen. The excerpts below are collected from all of the letters.

My Lord,—I beg your Lordship to believe that no desire to seek for notoriety beyond the limited sphere in which Providence has placed me, tempts me to address these letters to you. Born in a small and distant Province of the empire, and contented with the range of occupation that it affords, and with the moderate degree of influence which the confidence of some portion of its population confers, I should never have thought of intruding upon your Lordship, had not the occupations of my past life, and the devotion to them of many days of toil and nights of anxious inquiry led me to entertain strong opinion upon a subject which your Lordship has undertaken recently to discuss; and which, while it deeply concerns the honour and the interests of the empire, appears to be, by Her Majesty's present ministers, but little understood. Whether or not the Anglo-Saxon population, upholding the British flag on this side of the Atlantic, shall possess the right to influence, through their representatives, the Government under which they live, in all matters touching their internal affairs (of which their fellow-subjects living elsewhere know nothing and with which they have no right to interfere) is a question, my Lord, that involves their happiness and freedom. . . .

. . . If the Frenchmen in one Province do not understand, or cannot be entrusted with this valuable privilege, why should we, who are all British or of British descent, be deprived of what we do understand and feel that we can never be prosperous and happy without? . . .

You ask me for the remedy. Lord Durham has stated it distinctly: the Colonial Governors must be commanded to govern by the aid of those who possess the confidence of the people, and are supported by a majority of the representative branch. Where is the danger? Of what consequence is it to the people of England, whether half-a-dozen persons, in whom that majority have confidence, but of whom they know nothing and care less, manage our local affairs; or the same number, selected from the minority, and whose policy the bulk of the population distrust? Suppose there was at this moment a majority in our Executive Council who think with the Assembly, what effect would it have upon the funds? Would the stocks fall? Would England be weaker, less prosperous or less respected. because the people of Nova Scotia were satisfied and happy?

But, it is said, a colony being part of a great empire must be governed by different principles from the metropolitan state. That, unless it be handed over to the minority it cannot be governed at all; that the majority, when they have things their own way, will be discontented and disloyal; that the very fact of their having nothing to complain of will make them desire to break the political compact, and disturb the peace of the empire. Let us fancy that this reasoning were applied to Glasgow, or Aberdeen, or to any other town in Britain, which you allow to govern itself. . . . You allow a million of people to govern themselves in the very capital of the kingdom; and yet Her Majesty lives in the midst of them without any apprehension of danger, and feels the more secure, the more satisfaction and tranquillity they exhibit. Of course, if the Lord Mayor were to declare war upon France, or the Board of Aldermen were to resolve that the duties on brandy should no longer be collected by the general revenue officers of the kingdom, everybody would laugh, but no one would apprehend any great danger. Should we, if Lord Durham's principles be adopted, do anything equally outré, check us, for you have the power; but until we do, for your own sakes—for you are as much interested as we are—for the honour of the British name, too often tarnished by these squabbles, let us manage our own affairs, pay our own officers, and distribute a patronage, altogether beneath your notice, among those who command our esteem.

. . . Suppose the present Cabinet were to advise Her Majesty to cut off Sir Robert's ears, or to bombard the city of London, would she obey, or would she not say, "Gentlemen you are exceeding your powers, and unless you conduct yourselves with more discretion, you must resign"? It is plain, therefore, that there are bounds beyond which even in the mother country, neither the advisers nor the monarch can pass; and none who seek colonial responsibility are so mad as to require that corresponding restrictions shall not be binding here; that there shall not be a limit beyond which no Executive Councillor can pass, and over which no representative of Her Majesty will consent to be driven? . . .

. . . It will be seen, too, that by this system, whatever sections or small parties might think or say, the Governor could never, by any possibility, become, what British Governors have of late been everywhere, embroiled with the great body of the inhabitants over whom he was sent to preside. The Governor's responsibility would also be narrowed to the care of the Queen's prerogative, the conservation of treaties, the military defence, and the execution of the Imperial Acts; the local administration being left in the hands of those who understand it, and who were responsible. His position would then be analogous to that of the Sovereign—he could do no wrong in any matter of which the Colonial Legislature had the right to judge; but would be accountable to the Crown, if he betrayed the Imperial interests committed to his care. . . .

You well know, my Lord, that rebels have become exceedingly scarce at home, since the system of letting the majority govern has become firmly established; and yet they were as plentiful as blackberries in the good old times, when the sovereigns contended, as Sir Francis Head did lately, that they only were responsible. Turn back and you will find that they began to disappear altogether in England about 1688, and that every political change that makes the Executive more completely responsible to the Legislature and the Legislature to the country at large, renders the prospects of a new growth, "small by degrees and beautifully less." And yet, my Lord, who can assure us, that if the sovereigns had continued, as of old, alone responsible; if hundreds of able men all running the same course of honourable ambition, had not been encouraged to watch and control each other; and if the system of governing by the minority and not by the majority, and of excluding from power all who did not admire the mode, and quarrelled with the court, had existed down to the present day;—who, I ask, will assure us, that Chatham and Fox, instead of being able ministers and loyal men, might not have been sturdy rebels? Who can say that even your Lordship, possessed of the strong attachment to liberty which distinguishes your family, might not,—despairing of all good government under such a system,—instead of using your influence to extend by peaceful improvements the happiness of the people,—be at this moment in the field at their head and struggling, sword in hand, to abate the power of the Crown? . . .

. . . Can an Englishman, an Irishman or a Scotchman, be made to believe, by passing a month upon the sea, that the most stirring periods of his history are but a cheat and a delusion; that the scenes which he has been accustomed to treat with deep emotions are but mementoes of the folly, and not, as he once fondly believed, of the wisdom and courage of his ancestors; that the principles of civil liberty, which from childhood he has been taught to cherish and to protect by forms of stringent responsibility, must, with the new light breaking in upon him on this side of the Atlantic, be cast aside as useless incumbrance? No, my Lord, it is madness to suppose that these men, so remarkable for carrying their national characteristics into every part of the world where they penetrate, shall lose the most honourable of them all, merely by passing from one part of the empire to another. Nor is it to be supposed that the Nova Scotians, New Brunswickers and Canadians—a race sprung from the generous admixture of the blood of the three foremost nations of the world—proud of their parentage and not unworthy of it, to whom every stirring period of British and Irish history, every great principle which they teach, every phrase of freedom to be gleaned from them, are as familiar as household words, can be in haste to forget what they learnt upon their parents' knees; what those they loved and honoured clung to with so much pride, and regarded as beyond all price. . . .

. . . Am I not then justified, my Lord, in claiming for my countrymen that Constitution, which can be withheld from them by no plea but one unworthy of a British statesman— the tyrant's plea of power? I know that I am; and I feel also, that this is not the race that can be hoodwinked with sophistry, or made to submit to injustice without complaint. All suspicion of disloyalty we cast aside, as the product of ignorance or cupidity; we seek for nothing more than British subjects are entitled to; but we will be contented with nothing less. . . .

VI: 3 RESPONSIBLE GOVERNMENT ACHIEVED

After Durham's *Report* it was only a matter of time before Britain granted responsible government. For a short time Lord Sydenham tried to avoid the issue by acting as his own Prime Minister. In 1842, however, Sir Charles Bagot, his successor, gave *de facto* recognition to the principles of responsible government by inviting Baldwin and Lafontaine into his Council because they had the support of the majority of the Assembly. In selection (a) below Bagot explains why he felt he had no choice. Selection (b) is Lord

Elgin's analysis (written in 1847) of the new relationship between the Governor and Assembly under responsible government. In that year the British government finally acquiesced in the introduction of responsible government in Nova Scotia and the Province of Canada.

a. Sir Charles Bagot on the Inevitability of Responsible Government, 1842

. . . There was but one way to avoid it—by appointing a new Executive Council prepared to act without the sympathy and against an overwhelming majority of the House of Assembly: by denying *in toto* the principle of Responsible Government, and refusing to act upon it, at a crisis which would immediately have brought the question to an issue unfavourable to the Government. But having before me the Act of Union, Lord John Russell's despatch of the 14th October 1839, Lord Sydenham's avowed policy, the Resolutions of the House of Assembly last Session, and the present feeling and temper of its members, I was not prepared, to adopt such a policy. The consequences would have been most disastrous. The Assembly would have stopped the supplies about to be voted—the questions which led to the former troubles of Canada would have been revived—all attempts to resist the power of the Assembly and the tide of public opinion would have failed, and Canada would have again become the Theatre of a wide spread rebellion, and perhaps the ungrateful separatist or the rejected outcast from British Dominion. . . .

b. Lord Elgin's View of the New System, 1847

. . . It must also be remembered that it is only of late that the popular assemblies in this part of the world have acquired the right of determining who shall govern them—of insisting, as we phrase it, that the administration of affairs shall be conducted by persons enjoying their confidence. It is not wonderful that a privilege of this kind should be exercised at first with some degree of recklessness, and that, while no great

principles of policy are at stake, methods of a more question-
able character for winning and retaining the confidence of
these arbiters of destiny should be resorted to. My course in
these circumstances, is, I think, clear and plain. It may be
somewhat difficult to follow occasionally, but I feel no doubt
as to the direction in which it lies. I give to my ministers all
constitutional support, frankly and without reserve, and the
benefit of the best advice that I can afford them in their difficulties. In return for this, I expect that they will, in so far as
it is possible for them to do so, carry out my views for the
maintenance of the connexion with Great Britain and the
advancement of the interests of the province. On this tacit
understanding we have acted together harmoniously up to
this time, although I have never concealed from them that I
intended to do nothing which may prevent me from working
cordially with their opponents, if they are forced upon me.
That ministries and oppositions should occasionally change
places, is of the very essence of our constitutional system, and
it is probably the most conservative element which it contains. By subjecting all sections of politicians in their turn
to official responsibilities, it obliges heated partisans to place
some restraint on passion, and to confine within the bounds
of decency the patriotic zeal with which, when out of place,
they are wont to be animated. In order, however, to secure
these advantages, it is indispensable that the head of the
Government should show that he has confidence in the loyalty
of all the influential parties with which he has to deal, and
that he should have no personal antipathies to prevent him
from acting with leading men.

I feel very strongly that a Governor-General, by acting upon
these views with tact and firmness, may hope to establish a
moral influence in the province which will go far to compensate for the loss of power consequent on the surrender of
patronage to an executive responsible to the local Parliament.
Until, however, the functions of his office, under our amended
colonial constitution, are more clearly defined—until that
middle term which shall reconcile the faithful discharge of

his responsibility to the Imperial Government and the province with the maintenance of the quasi-monarchical relation in which he now stands towards the community over which he presides, be discovered and agreed upon, he must be content to tread along a path which is somewhat narrow and slippery, and to find that incessant watchfulness and some dexterity are requisite to prevent him from falling, on the one side into the *néant* of mock sovereignty, or on the other into the dirt and confusion of local factions.

VII. The Developing Economy

VII: 1 ALEXANDER MACKENZIE ON THE FUR TRADE

> Trading in furs, the great staple of the economy of New France, remained the chief commercial enterprise of British North America until the Montreal-based North West Company was absorbed by the Hudson's Bay Company in 1821. The following account of some aspects of the trade about 1800 is by Alexander Mackenzie, whose earlier trips to the Arctic and the Pacific were a product of his involvement in the fur trade. In these passages he is describing the XY Company, a rival of the North West Company that was soon to be absorbed by its larger competitor.

The agents are obliged to order the necessary goods from England in the month of October, eighteen months before they can leave Montreal; that is, they are not shipped from London until the spring following, when they arrive in Canada in the summer. In the course of the following winter they are made up into such articles as are required for the savages; they are then packed into parcels of ninety pounds weight each, but cannot be sent from Montreal until the May following; so that they do not get to market until the ensuing winter, when they are exchanged for furs, which come to Montreal the next fall, and from thence are shipped, chiefly to London, where they are not sold or paid for before the succeeding spring, or even as late as June; which is forty-two months after the goods were ordered in Canada; thirty-six after they had been shipped from England, and twenty-four after they had been forwarded from Montreal; so that the merchant, allowing that he has twelve months' credit, does not receive a return to pay for those goods, and the necessary expenses attending them, which is about equal to the value of the goods themselves, till two years after they are considered as cash, which makes this a very heavy business. . . .

The articles necessary for this trade, are coarse woollen cloths of different kinds; milled blankets of different sizes; arms and ammunition; twist and carrot tobacco; Manchester goods; linens, and coarse sheetings; thread, lines, and twine; common hardware; cutlery and ironmongery of several descriptions; kettles of brass and copper, and sheet-iron; silk and cotton handkerchiefs, hats, shoes, and hose; calicoes and printed cottons, &c., &c., &c. Spirituous liquors and provisions are purchased in Canada. These, and the expense of transport to and from the Indian country, including wages to clerks, interpreters, guides and canoe-men, with the expense of making up the goods for the market, form about half the annual amount against the adventure. . . .

. . . We shall now proceed to consider the number of men employed in the concern: viz. fifty clerks, seventy-one interpreters and clerks, one thousand one hundred and twenty canoe-men, and thirty-five guides. Of these, five clerks, eighteen guides, and three hundred and fifty canoe-men, were employed for the summer season in going from Montreal to the Grand Portage, in canoes, part of whom proceeded from thence to Rainy Lake, as will be hereafter explained, and are called Pork-eaters, or Goers and Comers. These were hired in Canada or Montreal, and were absent from the 1st of May till the latter end of September. For this trip the guides had from eight hundred to a thousand livres,* and a suitable equip-

*One livre was approximately equal to one English shilling. A pint of brandy cost about twelve livres, a shirt thirty livres and a canoe cost from two hundred to three hundred livres.

ment; the foreman and steersman from four to six hundred livres; the middlemen from two hundred and fifty to three hundred and fifty livres, with an equipment of one blanket, one shirt, and one pair of trowsers; and were maintained during that period at the expense of their employers. Independent of their wages, they were allowed to traffic, and many of them earned to the amount of their wages. About one-third of these went to winter, and had more than double the above wages and equipment. All the winterers were hired by the year, and sometimes for three years; and of the clerks many were apprentices, who were generally engaged for five or seven years, for which they had only one hundred pounds, provisions and clothing. Such of them who could not be provided for as partners, at the expiration of this time, were allowed from one hundred pounds to three hundred pounds per annum, with all necessaries, till provision was made for them. Those who acted in the two-fold capacity of clerk and interpreter, or were so denominated, had no other expectation than the payment of wages to the amount of from one thousand to four thousand livres per annum, with clothing and provisions. The guides, who are a very useful set of men, acted also in the additional capacity of interpreters, and had a stated quantity of goods, considered as sufficient for their wants, their wages being from one to three thousand livres. The canoe-men are of two descriptions, foremen and steersmen, and middlemen. The two first were allowed annually one thousand two hundred, and the latter eight hundred livres each. The first class had what is called an equipment, consisting of two blankets, two shirts, two pair of trowsers, two handkerchiefs, fourteen pounds of carrot tobacco, and some trifling articles. The latter had ten pounds of tobacco, and all the other articles: those are called North Men, or Winterers; and to the last class of people were attached upwards of seven hundred Indian women and children, victualled at the expense of the company.

The first class of people are hired in Montreal five months

before they set out, and receive their equipments, and one-third of their wages in advance; . . .

The necessary number of canoes being purchased, at about three hundred livres each, the goods formed into packages, and the lakes and rivers free of ice, which they usually are in the beginning of May, they are then despatched from La Chine, eight miles above Montreal, with eight or ten men in each canoe, and their baggage; and sixty-five packages of goods, six hundred weight of biscuit, two hundred weight of pork, three bushels of pease, for the men's provision; two oil-cloths to cover the goods, a sail, &c., an axe, a towing-line, a kettle, and a sponge to bail out the water, with a quantity of gum, bark, and watape, to repair the vessel. An European on seeing one of these slender vessels thus laden, heaped up, and sunk with her gunwale within six inches of the water, would think his fate inevitable in such a boat, when he reflected on the nature of her voyage; but the Canadians are so expert, that few accidents happen. . . .

The voyagers are frequently obliged to unload their canoes, and carry the goods upon their backs, or rather suspended in slings from their heads. Each man's ordinary load is two packages, though some carry three. Here the canoe is towed by a strong line. There are some places where the ground will not admit of their carrying the whole; they then make two trips, that is, leave half their lading, and go and land it at the distance required; and then return for that which was left. . . .

I shall now . . . give some further account of the people from Montreal. When they are arrived at the Grand Portage, which is near nine miles over, each of them has to carry eight packages of such goods and provisions as are necessary for the interior country. This is a labour which cattle cannot conveniently perform in summer, as both horses and oxen were tried by the company without success. They are only useful for light, bulky articles; or for transporting upon sledges, during the winter, whatever goods may remain there, especially provision, of which it is usual to have a year's stock on hand.

Having finished this toilsome part of their duty, if more goods are necessary to be transported, they are allowed a Spanish dollar for each package: and so inured are they to this kind of labour, that I have known some of them set off with two packages of ninety pounds each, and return with two others of the same weight, in the course of six hours, being a distance of eighteen miles over hills and mountains. This necessary part of the business being over, if the season be early they have some respite, but this depends upon the time the North men begin to arrive from their winter quarters, which they commonly do early in July. At this period, it is necessary to select from the Pork-eaters, a number of men, among whom are the recruits, or winterers, sufficient to man the North canoes necessary to carry, to the river of the rainy lake, the goods and provision requisite for the Athabasca country; as the people of that country (owing to the shortness of the season and length of the road, can come no further) are equipped there, and exchange ladings with the people of whom we are speaking, and both return from whence they came. This voyage is performed in the course of a month, and they are allowed proportionable wages for their services.

The North men being arrived at the Grand Portage, are regaled with bread, pork, butter, liquor and tobacco, and such as have not entered into agreements during the winter, which is customary, are contracted with, to return and perform the voyage for one, two, or three years: their accounts are also settled, and such as choose to send any of their earnings to Canada, receive drafts to transmit to their relations or friends: and as soon as they can be got ready, which requires no more than a fortnight, they are again despatched to their respective departments. . . .

The people being despatched to their respective winter quarters, the agents from Montreal, assisted by their clerks, prepare to return there, by getting the furs across the portage, and re-making them into packages of one hundred pounds weight each, to send them to Montreal; where they commonly arrive in the month of September. . . .

VII: 2 THE TIMBER TRADE

> British demand for Canadian timber products more
> than compensated for the decline of the Montreal
> fur trade. It arose when the Napoleonic Wars tem-
> porarily closed Britain's sources of supply along the
> Baltic Sea, and was then nurtured by tariff preference
> for colonial timber in the British market. Selection
> (a) is a brief summary of the qualities of Canadian
> white pine that made it so highly prized. In selection
> (b) a British traveller in Canada describes lumbermen
> and the timber rafts of the Ottawa Valley.

a. The Qualities of Canadian White Pine

. . . Yellow Pine [known to Canadians as white pine], the
description of Canada Timber which has been most abused,
is the most useful timber in the world; it gives us a mast
thirty feet long and ninety-six inches in diameter, cheaper by
one half and as good as can be produced in any other quarter.
This is the most magnificent form in which Yellow Pine
comes to hand; as illustrative of its utility, I may just here
mention (going to an opposite extreme) that it is the material
exclusively used for lucifer matches, and this paltry article
consumes deals by the thousand; and such are its properties
that it can be split into boards of 30 to the inch. Between
these extremes, the mast and the match, there extends a large
space, in which this timber proves itself useful. It is used by
engineers for patterns, it is exclusively used for sign boards,
for mouldings, for picture and looking-glass frames, for inside
work in house-building, for steamers' decks, for Venetian
blinds, and for various other purposes where lightness, clean-
ness, and mild quality are required. . . . This timber for
mast-yards, topmasts, and booms, is unequalled. The Baltic
produces nothing like it; it is tough, clean, durable, clear of
sap, obtainable in any length required, and is more free from
defects than any other timber with which I am acquainted. . . .

b. Lumbermen and Timber Rafts

Lumbermen and *Shantymen* are nearly synonymous; with this difference, that the former are generally the masters, or, what the Canadians call, the *Bourgeois* of the latter. The *Shantymen* live in hordes of from thirty to forty together; throughout the day they cut down the pine trees, and square them in the *pineries*, or the oaks in the groves, and afterwards draw the logs to what is termed the *bank*, with oxen. When spring draws on, they form the lumber into small rafts, called *cribs*, and drop away down the rapids to market. When they come to any extensive sheets of still-water, the cribs are brought into one grand flotilla; masts, white flags, and sails are sported; while, with long rude oars, they contrive to glide slowly along. Thus they will come from Lake Alumet, on the Ottawa, to Wolfe's Cove, Quebec, a distance of nearly 800 miles, in about six weeks. On these rafts they have a fire for cooking, burning on a sandy hearth; and places to sleep in, formed of broad strips of bark, resembling the half of a cylinder, the arch about four feet high, and in length about eight. To these *beds*, or *lairs*, *trams* or handles are attached, so that they can be moved about from *crib* to *crib*, or from *crib* to the shore, as circumstances render it necessary. When they are passing a *breaking-up rapid*, they live ashore in these lairs, until the raft is *new withed*, and fixed on the stillwater below.

As these people live in huts in the woods, as stated, which huts are houses only for a season, they are called *shanties*, and hence, *shantymen*; but there is something more attached to the name *shanty* than mere *hut*, in the lumberman's dictionary. Thus, so many men, oxen, so much pork, flour, &c., compose a *shanty*. . . . In these *shanties* they pass the time pretty well, considering them to be made up of Highlandmen, Irishmen, and Yankees. Great quantities of spurious whisky are swallowed, many battles fought, and so forth; yet these things being perfectly natural to the shantyman, he could hardly endure life without them. In the conceited towns he is held in abhorrence by the *clerk* and *counter-jumper*, who know no more of the laws of Nature, or the elements of human life, than a parcel of magpies. They fancy that the wood-cutter from the wilderness should be made up of nods and smiles, starch and ruffles, like their dear affected selves, never thinking that he is a creature by himself, like the sailor, bred amid dangers and difficulties, and made somewhat roguish by the sharking rogues of the cities. . . .

The truth is, that the lumberman can do very well without the *storekeeper*, but the latter not without the former; so the man of intrusion decoys the man of real business. The lumberman, with all his roughness of manner, is the person who does good to the country. He brings an article to market with much risk—the only staple commodity, in fact, that is; and, consequently, he is the means of bringing the greater portion of cash to Canada. What is the *storekeeper* but a person living on his exertions,—a person that might be dispensed with? He is the *rogue*, not the lumberman. His intent is to have *three values* for goods, which, were they not forced on the poor woodsman, he would not take. . . .

At Quebec, there are people called *Cullers*, who are appointed to select lots of timber according to quality. The refuse wood is called *culls*, and brings an inferior price. There is a good deal of corruption and bribery going on in this business, and many *rafts* of timber get a worse character than they deserve. The honest English captains of ships are the best *cullers*, in my opinion; and our merchants at home would be acting wisely, if they allowed them to select their own cargoes, instead of their agents there.

Nearly two-thirds of all the timber that comes to market is the *white pine*, which generally brings five-pence currency per cubic foot at Quebec, red pine eight-pence, and oak ten-pence. . . .

VII: 3 PROSPECTS FOR IMMIGRANTS TO UPPER CANADA, 1829

To make the westward Atlantic crossing profitable the timber ships specialized in bringing immigrants to

British North America at low fares—thus stimulating an already growing interest in settlement in the colonies. The opportunities for the settler in Upper Canada are comprehensively described in this excerpt from an 1829 pamphlet for prospective emigrants.

The Emigrant who directs his course to Upper Canada, a country which has for some years afforded an asylum for some thousands of poor settlers, need not apprehend the want of fertile land, nor, after two or three years, the necessities and many of the conveniences of life. Yet, notwithstanding the vast tracts of unoccupied land, he will, in order to secure a desirable farm, have to proceed a great distance into the back country, apart from society, and without the conveniences to be found only in a populous neighbourhood. He must not, however, be discouraged if he suffers much more, from the time he lands at Quebec or Montreal, until he plants himself and family in the woods, than he experienced in removing to America from the land of his forefathers. Every succeeding year will open more cheering prospects to him; the Emigrants who arrive after him will settle beyond him in the wilderness, and he will soon observe houses, villages, and cornfields occupying the place of gloomy and boundless forests. . . .

As to the classes to which British America offers inducements to emigrate, much will depend upon individual character; but it may, however, be observed, that in consequence of the high price of labour, gentlemen farmers do not succeed, and the condition of new countries do not admit of extensive establishments. The settlers who thrive soonest, are men of steady habits, accustomed to labour.

Practical farmers possessing from £200 to £600, may purchase, in any of the Colonies, farms with from twenty to thirty acres cleared, which may be cultivated agreeably to the system of husbandry practised in the United Kingdom. The embarrassed circumstances of many of the old settlers, brought on by improvidence, or by having engaged in the timber business, will compel them to sell their farms, and commence again on woodlands.

Joiners, stonemasons, saddlers, shoemakers, tailors, black-smiths, cart, mill, and wheelwrights, and (in the seaports), coopers may always find employment. Brewers may succeed, but in a few years there will be more encouragement for them. Butchers generally do well. For spinners, weavers, or those engaged in manufactures, there is not the smallest encouragement.

Active labouring men and women may always secure employment, kind treatment, and good wages.

To gentlemen educated for the professions of law, divinity, or physic, British America offers no flattering prospects. . . .

Young men of education, clerks in mercantile houses, or shopmen, need not expect the least encouragement, unless previously engaged by the merchants or shopkeepers in America. Many young men, however, of persevering minds, and industrious habits, have baffled every obstacle, and finally succeeded in establishing themselves in trade. Many of the richest merchants in the Colonies were of this description. . . .

Men of broken fortunes, or unprincipled adventurers, were generally the persons who have been engaged in the traffic long known by the emphatic cognomen of the "white slave trade," of transporting Emigrants to America. They travelled over the country among the labouring classes, allured them by flattering, and commonly false, accounts of the New World, to decide on emigrating, and to pay half of the passage-money in advance. A ship of the worst class, ill-found with materials, and most uncomfortably accommodated, was chartered to a certain port, where the passengers embarked: crowded closely in the hold, the provisions and water indifferent, and often unwholesome and scanty; inhaling the foul air generated by filth and dirt,—typhus fever was almost inevitably produced, and, as is too well known, many of the passengers usually became its victims. . . .

There are various ways in which men may always employ themselves, after they land in America. The heads of families cannot do better than by devoting all the time they possibly can to the clearing and preparing their new farms, for cultivation. It is often, however, necessary for them to work for provisions, or other assistance, among the old settlers; but prudent men never do so after the first year, except compelled by necessity.

Women, and children above ten years of age, can find employment, particularly during spring and autumn. Young unmarried labouring men ought to save, at least, half their wages. Food, except in the towns and at public works, is usually provided for labourers by their employers.

Children, whose parents are unable to support them, may be provided for by binding them until they become of age, as apprentices to farmers, with whom they are generally brought up as one of the family; and a cow, a sheep, and some seed, is usually given to them when they leave, to begin with on a farm. In this manner, orphans are generally taken care of. It rarely happens, that a man who has a family finds it necessary to bind any of his children to others; and he who has the most numerous offspring, is considered to have the best opportunity of prospering, in a country where land is abundant, and in which the price of labour is high.

A common plan with those who own cleared farms that they do not occupy, is to let these farms on the halves; that is, to stock the farm with horses, horned cattle, sheep, and hogs, provide half the necessary seed, and then give possession to a practical farmer, who will cultivate it, and find the labour. After harvest, the produce, even to that of the dairy, is equally divided between the proprietor and the farmer. Many farmers, who dislike commencing at once in the woods, have, by industry and frugality, supported their families very comfortably in this manner, for two or three years, besides accumulating sufficient stock and seed to commence on a new farm. . . .

In remarking generally on the condition of the inhabitants of our American Colonies, as respects their means, no class, except those engaged immediately or indirectly in commerce, has accumulated fortunes. The majority of the whole population possess considerable property in land and cattle; among the remainder, many are poor; but beggars are scarcely ever seen, unless it be in the towns, where some accidental calamity or natural infirmity brings occasionally a destitute individual to solicit charity. The Irish Emigrants are, but only for a short time after landing, frequently observed begging. . . .

There are scarcely any taxes, and very few public burdens,— duties on articles of luxury are trifling, and on necessary articles there are rarely any, consequently all that is required for supporting a family may be purchased at low rates, fine clothing excepted.

I have particularly to advise new settlers against running in debt to the shopkeepers; doing so, has prevented many hard labouring men from prospering. The low price of spirituous liquors is also a great bane to the success of Emigrants, and the facility with which rum can be procured, is the most prolific source of domestic misery and personal depravity that exists in America.

Wherever a settlement is formed, and some progress is made in the clearing and cultivation of the soil, it begins gradually to develop the usual features of an American village. First, a saw mill, a grist mill, and a blacksmith's shop appear, then a school-house and a place of worship; and in a little time the village doctor, and pedlar with his wares, introduce themselves.

Few habitations can be more rude than those of the first settlers, which are built of logs, and covered with bark or boards, but many in the United Kingdom are far less comfortable. The most that an Emigrant can do the first year is to erect his habitation, and cut down the trees on as much ground as will be sufficient to plant ten to twelve bushels of potatoes, and to sow three or four bushels of grain. . . .

In the course of five years an industrious man may expect, and should have, twelve acres under cultivation, one horse, two or three cows, a few sheep and pigs, and sufficient food for himself and family. In ten years the same man, with perseverance and frugality, ought to have from twenty-five to thirty under improvement, to possess a pair of horses, a waggon or cart, a sledge and cabriole, five or six cows, a yoke of oxen, sheep, hogs, poultry, &c. a comfortable house, a good barn, and plenty of food for himself and family. This is no extravagant calculation—I could name hundreds who began in a state of abject poverty, who, in the same period, accumulated, by steady industry, fully as much as I have stated.

VII:4 THE STATE OF MANUFACTURING, 1846

As Britain gradually adopted free trade in the 1840's British North Americans began to realize that a measure of self-sufficiency would now be necessary to compensate for the loss of their preferred trading position with the Mother Country. What were the chances of developing manufacturing industries in the colonies? In September, 1846, the *Canadian Economist* printed this summary of the progress to date.

This is an important inquiry, and more particularly so, since the change which has taken place in the commercial policy of Great Britain. Canada is now thrown upon her own resources, and if she wishes to prosper, those resources must be developed. . . . We now propose to give some additional particulars by which it will be seen that Canada is not destitute of the means of entering extensively into manufactures, and thereby greatly enlarging the means of her prosperity. And the first point we would notice is, the great water power which Canada possesses. This is an important element in the great resources at her command; and is an abundant compensation for the loss she experiences in the absence of all coal beds within her boundaries. . . . we cannot now say what untold wealth lies buried under the surface of our earth; but we do know and have experienced the great value of the surface itself, in the magnificent crops which it is yielding, and therefore we can afford to wait awhile for the more full development of our mineral wealth. We have, however, but to turn our attention to Lake Superior, where copper ore is found in great abundance, and where the first steps are now being taken to open up the beds which there have been discovered. But to return to the manufactories—

The cotton manufactory . . . in operation at Sherbrooke has been established about one year, and turns out about 1000 yards per day.

The one at Chambly was put into operation the past year, and turns out about 800 yards per day. The fabrics from both of these manufactories, although not equal in finish to those imported, are, nevertheless, superior in point of firmness and durability, and are sold at about the same price.

There is a woollen manufactory at Sherbrooke which has been in operation a number of years; . . .

In Cobourg, Canada West, a woollen manufactory has been put into operation this season, which, when in full employ, is calculated to work off near 5000 yards of cloth a week. About 100,000 lbs. of wool is grown in the Newcastle District annually, and this amount, doubtless, might and will be quadrupled in a few years. Indeed, there are but few parts of Canada West where wool could not be produced to a large extent; and in the Eastern Townships, of Canada East, the fine grazing lands there ought to produce, at least, 1,500,000 lbs. annually. The neighbouring state of Vermont produces about 4,000,000 lbs. annually. We have three cordage manufactories in Montreal where about 300 tons of hemp are manufactured, and the amount could be doubled in case of need.—To one of these manufactories is attached machinery for grinding and calcining Plaster of Paris for agricultural purposes, and for stucco work, where about 1000 tons per annum are disposed of.

Hemp surely can be grown in Canada West, and we hope soon to hear that the experiment which has already been made at Niagara, most successfully, in growing hemp, will be followed up in other favourable sections of the Province.

There are three paper manufactories in Canada East. The most important one is at Portneuf, about forty-five miles above

Quebec. It is owned by the Messrs. Miller of this City, who have expended but recently about £10,000 in enlarging the premises. They manufacture printing, writing, and wrapping paper—principally the former. They estimate that they can turn out about 600 tons of paper annually.

There is a paper manufactory at Chambly, in full operation, and another at Stanstead, both of which together turn out about the same quantity of paper as the Portneuf mills.

There are five or six paper mills in Canada West, . . . We think, that with these data there is sufficient assurance that, in a few years, Canada will be enabled to supply her own demand, with the exception of the more costly qualities of paper.

The most extensive manufactory, however, in Canada East, are the St. Maurice iron works, in the rear of Three Rivers. The iron ore found there is not only abundant, but is of the best description. The hammered iron manufactured from it, is quite equal to the best English iron; and the stoves cast from it are considered superior to the best Scotch castings. Although we have no statistics at hand to guide us in our estimates of the amount of iron manufactured there, yet we know that many thousands of tons are annually turned out even under the very great disadvantages with which the forges and blasts are worked. . . . Some idea may be formed of the magnitude of these works, when we state that from 1200 to 1500 mouths are dependent upon them.

The glass manufactory, noticed as established at St. Johns, has been in operation something more than one year. It has two furnaces, and can turn out 100 half boxes of glass a day. Sand, used in the manufacture of glass, is said to be found in abundance at Beauharnois and at Vaudreuil.

Leather, an article of great importance, is manufactured extensively throughout the Province. There are two or three tanneries in the vicinity of Montreal, which employ, severally, a capital of from £12,000 to £15,000.

Stoves are being cast in almost all sections of the Province, and we hope to see the time when we shall supply our own demand.

Nail factories already exist to such an extent that we do not require to import a single cut nail.

Axes are manufactured largely; if not to the full requirement of the Province, we have no doubt they might be.

Agricultural implements, thus far, have but imperfectly engaged the attention of the manufacturer, although we see no reason why we should not make them as well as our neighbours.

VII:5 CANADIAN RAILWAYS BY 1860

The 1850's were the first great age of railway construction in British North America. These passages from a traveller's study of Canada in 1860 discuss the pressing economic motives behind the railway boom, describe the Province's two main railways, and suggest some of the benefits resulting from the completion of the Grand Trunk. In fact, though, Canadian railroads never succeeded in tapping the traffic from the American mid-west. The Grand Trunk was always in financial difficulty.

The grand system of water communication afforded by the St. Lawrence, and the lakes connected with it, though of incalculable value to Canada in the earlier stages of its settlement, when the population was too scanty to admit of more expensive modes of transit, is liable to the disadvantage of being closed for more than half the year by frost. Even in the season favourable to navigation, it has, from the natural obstacles in its course, to be supplemented by canals, in which the navigation is unavoidably tedious. The Welland Canal, for instance, by which the Falls of Niagara are avoided, has no less than 30 locks. So great is the traffic nevertheless, that in one year (1853) there passed through it 2743 British, and 2705 American and other vessels; but all this busy traffic is stopped by the ice that locks river and canals from November to May. For six months, Quebec and the other ports and harbours of the river are unavailable, and all trade is in a great measure suspended. In addition to the need thus created of some means of communication that might be independent of the change of seasons, the introduction of railways into the United States made their adoption in Canada an indispensable measure of self-preservation; as it was found that the rapidity and certainty of transport on the American railways was carrying away from the St. Lawrence even the trade of Western Canada itself. "Unless," it was said, "Canada could combine with her unrivalled inland navigation, a railroad system connected therewith, and mutually sustaining each other; the whole of her large outlay of five millions on canals must remain for ever unproductive."

Railways have, accordingly, been constructed with an energy and rapidity commensurate with the general progress of the country. In 1856, before the completion of the Grand Trunk, Canada possessed 2000 miles of fully equipped railway, obtained at a cost of £18,000,000; . . .

The two great railways of Canada, to which all the others are tributary, are the Great Western and the Grand Trunk lines, and an arrangement has been entered into between them for the division of the traffic on certain sections, by which injurious competition has been avoided.

The former, the Great Western, runs from Windsor on the Canadian side of the Detroit river, opposite the city of Detroit, to the river Niagara, which it crosses two miles below the Falls by the fine suspension bridge before mentioned, and thence communicates with the railways of New York and Boston. . . .

The Grand Trunk line has a two-fold commencement; one at the harbour of Portland in the State of Maine, on the Atlantic coast; the other at Quebec, on the St. Lawrence. The Portland section of the Grand Trunk was previously in existence, and known as the "Atlantic and St. Lawrence Railway of Maine;" but it has now been leased in perpetuity by the Grand Trunk Company, at the rate of six per cent. These two branches unite at Richmond, on the Canadian frontier, and the line then runs thence to Montreal, where it meets lines from Boston and New York, and then, crossing the St. Lawrence by the gigantic Victoria Bridge, enters a country where it has no competitors, but meets many shorter lines, which run at right angles to it through new countries, and serve it as feeders, till it reaches Toronto, where it is connected with the Great Western by a short line called the "Hamilton and Toronto Railway," and with the "Ontario, Simcoe, and Huron" line, which runs due north from Toronto to Lake Simcoe, skirting part of the southern shore of the lake and of Georgian Bay, to Collingwood Harbour.

From Toronto the Grand Trunk passes, still keeping the same south-westerly direction to Sarnia at the southern extremity of Lake Huron, where it is brought into communication with the States of Michigan, Illinois, Iowa, Minnesota, and Wisconsin. In this course of 1112 miles, it connects all the principal towns of Canada, and receives as tributaries lines that have struck out through the forest to new and remoter regions, which they are rapidly awakening to life. . . .

Now that the Grand Trunk Line is complete, the long and dangerous passage by the Gulf of St. Lawrence may be avoided, and Portland become the harbour of debarkation for emigrants. From thence the facilities of transport to the lakes and Upper Canada are much superior to those offered by the American lines. The whole distance, too, may be travelled in one vehicle, and the importance to emigrants of being forwarded at once to their places of destination can hardly be overrated. In some instances, large tracts of country, before unpeopled and almost unknown, have been called into social life by this enterprise. . . .

By this Grand Trunk route, but one trans-shipment has to be made, even for the countries on the Mississippi; and in a report published in the present year, we find that important commercial firms in Chicago, St. Louis, Cincinnati, and other great Western entrepôts were beginning to avail themselves of it. The Company had also entered into a contract with the Hudson's Bay Company to deliver the whole of their stores destined for the Red River settlement in *twenty-eight days*, from Liverpool to St. Paul's, Minnesota, and the time was found amply sufficient. Among other circumstances that contribute to the attractions of Canada, both for travellers and settlers, it should not be forgotten that the lines of the electric telegraph now extend over nearly the whole of it, and communicate with other lines ramifying over the entire North American continent.

VIII. Political Deadlock in Canada

VIII:1 GEORGE BROWN ON FRENCH DOMINATION

By the early 1850's it was becoming evident that the union of Upper and Lower Canada merely aggravated the tension between the province's two racial groups. Equality of representation in the Assembly, so important to Canada West when it was a minority, now meant that the rapidly growing English Protestant section of the province could not pass legislation to suit its ends without French Catholic support from Canada East. That support was often denied as the two communities failed to develop common goals in an era of rapid and confusing economic change. George Brown, editor of the Toronto *Globe*, became the leader of Canada West's outcry against the "tyranny" of the system. This 1852 letter of Brown's to a group of his supporters illustrates the bitter sectionalism which soon destroyed the Reform coalition and led to the formation of Brown's "Clear Grits," whose favourite cure-all for sectional dispute was representation by population.

. . . On almost every issue the Ministerialists were obliged to take up the defensive; they acknowledged that it would be well if such views could be carried out—but they voted as if they thought the contrary, and palliate their inconsistency on the unworthy plea of expediency. It would have been desirable, they admit, to have had a vote of the Assembly in favour of secularizing the Reserves—but the French Canadians were opposed to it, and it was dangerous to insist on it. It would have been well to apply the 550,000 acres at once to educational purposes—but the French Canadians thought it best to await the settlement of the whole Reserve question. It would have been well to prevent new incumbents being placed on the pension-list—but the French Canadians were in the way. The Rectories were better settled by Act of Parliament—but the French Canadians are immoveable on this question, and absurd as the Law-suit is, it has been commenced and had better go on. The accumulation of real estate in the hands of Clerical corporators is evil in the extreme—but the French Priests are indignant on this point, and we dare not meddle with it. The Jesuit College Bill was indefensible, and we voted against it on the second reading—but you saw the storm our votes drew down on us from the French papers, and we had all to *reverse them* on the third reading. The Three Rivers Tax Bill was highly improper, but what could we do?—the French Canadians demanded it. The sectarian clause of the Upper Canada School Bill is a great evil—but the Roman Catholics demand Separate Schools; the French Hierarchy of Lower Canada have taken up their cause—and what can we do? The division of the University funds among the petty sectarian Colleges is wrong, truly; but there has been extravagance in the management of the Institution. The sectarian money grants annually voted, are vicious in principle, but how can we cut them off, when they have existed so long? Population is the only true basis for Parliamentary Representation; but it would swamp the French Canadians, and they will never consent to it. . . .

Such is the attitude of the Ministerialists on the proceedings of the late session. What limit can be set to this strain of argument? Disguise it as they will, the sum and substance of it is simply this: "If the Reformers of Upper Canada insist on their views being carried out, it will cause a disruption between us and the French Canadians—we must in that case go out of office, and the Tories will come in; we are not so foolish as to do this, and therefore Upper Canada principles of Reform and Progress must stand in abeyance." . . .

And in what a contemptible attitude does all this place the Reformers of Upper Canada! Does it not confess them the abject vassals of the French Canadian priesthood? Mark the long list of important reforms from which we are debarred by the *fiat* of Popery. And mark, too, the humiliating draughts we have been compelled to swallow under compulsion of the same power. What has French Canadianism been denied? Nothing. It bars all it dislikes—it extorts all it demands—and it grows insolent over its victories. And is this a state of things to delight the Reformers of Upper Canada? All this humiliation, all this sacrifice of principle, all this iniquitous legislation under the sanction of Western liberalism—for the noble consideration that *"the party"* is in office! Shame, shame on such degradation! I do not wonder that the well-tried Reformers of your neighbourhood seek some means of giving vent to the indignation that such things excite within them. I do not wonder that they long to see their leaders stand upright before the world, as they once did, bold in the confidence of truth, and scorning to barter principle for the miserable pageant of office without power.

But the Tories would come in, if we acted honestly—and they might remain in for ten years! And what if they did? It is our duty to act uprightly and leave consequences in higher hands. Shall we do evil that good may come? And such a good!—a base vassalage to French Canadian Priestcraft. . . .

VIII:2 GEORGE ETIENNE CARTIER AND FRENCH CANADA'S POSITION

"They will never consent to it" Brown said in 1852, accurately assessing French Canada's attitude towards "rep by pop." In this 1858 speech in a debate in the Assembly, George Etienne Cartier, by now the chief

French Canadian spokesman, presents Canada East's arguments—and fears. Comparison of Brown's and Cartier's positions will show how little room there was for political agreement.

Mister Speaker, the honourable member for Toronto (Mr. George Brown) can hardly be serious in what he says. This member has spoken as if it were a question concerning only Upper Canada, whereas it concerns Lower Canada just as much as Upper Canada.

Representation based on population is unknown in the world. If one were going to decree it, it would be necessary to guarantee an absolute majority of the votes of the electorate. Is this practical? In the United States it often happens that the minority governs. . . .

There is not a State of the Union which is bound to elect its representatives by an absolute majority. A relative majority is enough. Representation based on population does not exist in Great Britain. There is even a great inequality in the number of representatives, with regard to population, [between] England, Scotland, and Ireland.

Did Upper Canada conquer Lower Canada? If not by virtue of what right can it ask for representation based on population in the aim of governing us? Everyone knows that the union of the two provinces was imposed on Lower Canada which did not want it at any price. But Lower Canada has discharged the offices of the Union loyally and sincerely with the determination of upholding it on the present basis.

Mr. H. Foley (Waterloo-North)—Yes, you make it work in your way; Lower Canada governs Upper Canada with the help of ministers who represent a minority of the section of the province to which they belong.

Several voices—Hear! Hear!

Mr. Cartier—Say rather that the people from Upper Canada demand representation based on population in the aim of dominating Lower Canada.

Mr. Foley—That is exactly what you do to Upper Canada.

Mr. Cartier—I have indeed ascertained the ends of the honourable member from Toronto in proposing representation based on population. He demands it with great clamor because he hopes thereby to produce for himself enough supporters to control Lower Canada. . . .

. . . I have no unjust design towards Upper Canada in fighting against this measure. I fight it rather because I wish to fulfill loyally the Act of Union, which has been a great source of benefit for the two sections of the province. What would Upper Canada be without the Union? An exceedingly backward country which would not be able to collect its customs duties. It has drawn many advantages from the Union. Lower Canada had saved its money and when this system was imposed on it, it saved Upper Canada from bankruptcy. . . .

The government does not fear this question. It is happy to have the occasion to discuss it. I may say, in the name of all the members from Lower Canada, except one, that Lower Canada will adopt other political institutions before accepting the yoke of a man like the honourable member from Toronto (Mr. Brown).

VIII:3 JOHN A. MACDONALD ON THE RACIAL BALANCE

> The political crisis naturally heightened Canada's always latent racial animosity. John A. Macdonald analyzed the situation in this 1856 letter to a Lower Canadian journalist. The fact that Macdonald followed these principles throughout his career does much to explain his amazing success.

. . . But the truth is you British L. [Lower] Canadians never can forget that you were once supreme—that Jean Baptiste was your hewer of wood and drawer of water—You struggle like the Protestant Irish in Ireland—like the Norman Invaders in England not for equality, but ascendency—the difference between you and those interesting and amiable people being that you have not the honesty to admit it—You can't & [sic] won't admit the principle that the majority must govern—The Gallicans may fairly be reckoned as two thirds agt [*sic*] one third of all the new races who are lumped together as Anglo-Saxons—Heaven save the mark! . . . The only remedies are immigration and copulation and these will work wonders—The laws are as equally administered to the British as the French. At least, if we may judge by the names of your judges it ought to be so. Lumping your judges of Q.B. [Queen's Bench] Supreme and Circuit courts—you have full one half British—More than one half of the Revenue officers & indeed of all offices of emolument, are held by men not of French origin.—It would surprise you to go over the names of officials in a L.C. [Lower Canada] Almanac & reckon the *ascendency* you yet hold of official positions. Take care that the French don't find it out and make a counter-cry. . . . No man in his senses can suppose that this country can for a century to come be governed by a totally unfrenchified govt.— if a Lower Canadian Britisher desires to conquer he must "stoop to conquer"—He must make friends with the French —without sacrificing the status of his race or lineage he must respect their nationality—Treat them as a nation and they will act as a free people generally do—generously. Call them a faction, and they became factious—Supposing the numerical preponderance of British in Canada becomes much greater than it is. I think the French could give more trouble than they are said now to do—At present, they divide, as we do, they are split up into several sections—& are governed more [or] less by defined principles of action—As they become smaller & feebler, so they will be more united—from a sense of self preservation—they will act as one man & hold the balance of power. . . . So long as the French have 20 votes they will be a power, & must be conciliated—I doubt much however if the French will lose their numerical majority in L.C. in a hurry— What with the cessation of immigration from Europe—their own spread in the Townships, the opening up of the Ottawa & St. Maurice and the certainty that they will ere long be the laborers in our factories that are fast coming I am inclined to think they will hold their own for many a day yet. . . .

VIII:4 MACDONALD SUPPORTS THE *STATUS QUO*

By 1858 Canadian politics was in virtual deadlock. The Macdonald-Cartier, Liberal-Conservative party was being whittled away in Canada West, while Brown's Grits had formed a working relationship with the "Rouges" minority in Canada East. Evenly balanced parties and extreme sectional tensions were strangling governmental action. One suggested solution was Sandfield Macdonald's theory of the "double majority"—that a ministry would not legislate on matters of provincial concern without the support of a majority of the members from each section of the province. In this report from the Toronto *Leader* of an 1858 Assembly debate, John A. Macdonald rejects the double majority and struggles to postpone the inevitable revision of the constitution. As the last paragraph shows, however, the disaffected were not impressed.

Mr. Macdonald: . . . With reference to the Double Majority, he had to say he held the principles of Responsible Government; and he believed these principles were the only ones that could be successfully carried out. (Hear) He believed the Double Majority was opposed in every respect to the principles of Responsible Government and as such he would always vote against it. . . . His opinions were that they should govern the country by a government having the confidence of the majority of the representatives of the people in Parliament. (Hear) An Administration was principally occupied in the discussion of a legislation of a provincial importance, equally applying to both sections of the country. The whole or nearly the whole of the measures of any great importance equally affected the east and the west. And the only way in which this country could be governed on constitutional principles was by a government who agreed on these great questions and had the confidence of the people to carry out their legislation. If it were conceded that an Administration should be divided into sections, each having local interests, one for the east and one for the west, constitutional government was at once destroyed. . . . There were at the present time few questions comparatively important because all the great questions of purely local importance that had roused the people with an over-ruling interest had been settled already. Was the Government thereby, having a majority of the whole House and carrying on legislation according to the majority of the House, to be set aside for such a principle as the Double Majority . . . ? . . .

He had no hesitation in saying they suffered severely at the election from prejudice which had been partially excited, but of the whole number of votes polled in Upper Canada, there were more polled for gentlemen known to be friendly to the Ministry than those hostile to them. (Hear) Speaking of a dividing line, he had to say that either in religion or race the Government had a majority in the House. . . .

Mr. Mowat said the system which the Government was pursuing was one of tyranny towards Upper Canada. They were ruled by a minority of Upper Canadians. What was tyranny but government by a minority? They were not a free people so long as a system was sanctioned by which a mere fraction of the people could rule over them—by which they could not get a law passed, a single officer appointed, or a single resolution passed—unless a minority of their own people chose to grant it. Injustice never answered a good purpose to those who committed it. For a time they might think it advantageous, but so sure as they were assembled in that House they would find that injustice would turn against themselves some day. The only safe course in legislation was to act fairly and justly.

IX. The Drive For Confederation

IX:1 THE FIRST MISSION, 1858

After the famous "double shuffle" of 1858, the Cartier-Macdonald administration adopted the proposals for federation first put forward by Alexander Tilloch Galt as the only solution to the political deadlock. This memorial was presented to the British Colonial Secretary in September 1858 by a delegation representing the Canadian government. The mission was rebuffed on the ground that the proposal lacked a wide basis of support in British North America. Nevertheless, the memorial does present a very clear picture of the factors influencing the Canadians as early as 1858.

. . . It is our duty to state that very grave difficulties now present themselves in conducting the Government of Canada in such a manner as to show due regard to the wishes of its numerous population. The Union of Lower with Upper Canada was based upon perfect equality being preserved between these provinces, a condition the more necessary from the differences in their respective language, law and religion, and although there is now a large English population in Lower Canada, still these differences exist to an extent which prevents any perfect and complete assimilation of the views of the two sections.

100

At the time of the Union Act Lower Canada possessed a much larger population than Upper Canada, but this produced no difficulty in the Government of the United Provinces under that Act. Since that period, however, the progress of population has been more rapid in the western section, and claims are now made on behalf of its inhabitants for giving them representation in the Legislature in proportion to their numbers, which claims, involving, it is believed, a most serious interference with the principles upon which the Union was based, have been and are strenuously resisted by Lower Canada. The result is shown by an agitation fraught with great danger to the peaceful and harmonious working of our constitutional system, and consequently detrimental to the progress of the province.

The necessity of providing a remedy for a state of things that is yearly becoming worse, and of allaying feelings that are daily being aggravated by the contention of political parties, has impressed the advisers of Her Majesty's representatives in Canada with the importance of seeking for such a mode of dealing with these difficulties as may forever remove them. In this view it has appeared to them advisable to consider how far the Union of Lower with Upper Canada could be rendered essentially federative—in combination with the provinces of New Brunswick, Nova Scotia, Newfoundland and Prince Edward Island, together with such other territories as it may be hereafter desirable to incorporate with such confederation from the possessions of the Crown in British North America.

. . . But independent of reasons affecting Canada alone it is respectfully represented that the interests of the several Colonies and of the Empire will be greatly promoted by a more intimate and united Government of the entire British North American Possessions. The population, trade and resources of all these Colonies have so rapidly increased of late years and the removal of Trade restrictions has made them, in so great a degree, self-sustaining, that it appears to the Government of Canada exceedingly important to bind still more closely the ties of their common allegiance to the British Crown, and to obtain for general purposes such an identity in legislation as may serve to consolidate their growing power, thus raising, under the protection of the Empire, an important confederation on the North American Continent.

At present each Colony is totally distinct in its Government, in its customs and trade, and in its general legislation. To each other, no greater facilities are extended than to any Foreign State and the only common tie is that which binds all to the British Crown. This state of things is considered to be neither promotive of the physical prosperity of all, nor of that moral union which ought to be preserved in the presence of the powerful confederation of the United States.

With a population of three and a half millions, with a foreign commerce exceeding Twenty-five million Sterling, and a Commercial Marine inferior in extent only to those of Great Britain and the United States, it is in the power of the Imperial Government, by sanctioning a confederation of these Provinces, to constitute a Dependency of the Empire, valuable in time of peace, and powerful in the event of war—forever removing the fear that these Colonies may ultimately serve to swell the power of another Nation. . . .

The Government of Canada do not desire to represent the feelings of the other provinces. Their application is confined to the request that the Imperial Government will be pleased to authorise a meeting of Delegates on behalf of each Colony and of Upper and Lower Canada respectively, for the purpose of considering the subject of a Federative Union, and reporting on the principles on which the same could properly be based. . . .

IX:2 GEORGE BROWN EXPLAINS THE CANADIAN COALITION, 1864

The formation of the coalition between Brown, Macdonald and Cartier in 1864, for the express purpose of furthering a federation of British North America, was the initial giant step towards making Confederation a reality. In his speech to the Assembly on June 22, 1864, Brown explained why he had agreed to join his former enemies.

Hon. George Brown then arose, evidently labouring under the deepest emotion, which for a time almost choked his utterance. He said: "Did I conceal from the House that I feel in all its force the painful position I now occupy, I should be deceiving hon. members. For ten years I have stood opposed to the hon. gentlemen opposite in the most hostile manner it is possible to conceive of public men arrayed against each other in the political arena. . . . I am free to confess that, had the circumstances in which we are now placed been one whit less important, less serious, less threatening than they are, I could not have approached hon. gentlemen opposite, even with a view to these negotiations. But I think the House will admit that, if a crisis has ever arisen in the political affairs of any country which would justify such a coalition as has taken place, such a crisis has arrived in the history of Canada. . . .

When we look at the long record of able public men who have been sacrificed by the system under which we have been governed; when we look back on the discords and agitations of the last ten years, I do say, that if by any means we can find a solution of the difficulties, every man who has the slightest stake in the country will have cause to be grateful to those who accomplish it. (Cheers.) . . . I do not hesitate to say that, as our only justification for entering the Cabinet is that we may thereby attain the settlement of the sectional question, my duty will have ended when I see that that settlement can no longer be advanced by my remaining in the Government. (Hear, hear.) . . .

. . . I do frankly confess, Mr. Speaker, that if I never have any other parliamentary success than that which I have achieved this day in having brought about the formation of a Government more powerful than any Canadian Government that ever existed before, pledged to settle, and to settle forever, the alarming sectional difficulties of my country, I would have desired no greater honour for my children to keep years hence in their remembrance than that I had a hand, however humble, in the accomplishment of that great work. (The hon. gentleman resumed his seat amidst loud and prolonged cheers from all parts of the House, and many members crowded around him to offer their congratulations.)

IX:3 GEORGE BROWN DESCRIBES CHARLOTTETOWN, 1864

Because reporters were barred from the Charlottetown Conference, few accounts of its proceedings exist. One of the best is this letter from George Brown to his wife. Prominent in his account is the lively social life of the Conference—which added much to the amiability of the delegates.

. . . Having dressed ourselves in correct style, our two boats were lowered man-of-war fashion—and being each duly manned with four oarsmen and a boatswain, dressed in blue uniform, hats, belts etc. in regular style, we pulled away for shore and landed like Mr. Christopher Columbus who had the precedence of us in taking possession of portions of the American Continent. Our brother delegates were there before us. Five from Nova Scotia, five from New Brunswick and five from Prince Edward. Newfoundland goes heartily with the movement, but was not notified in time to take part in the proceedings.

At two o'clock the Conference was organized by the appointment of Col. Gray, Prime Minister of Prince Edward as President of the Convention. You are aware that the Conference was originally summoned merely to consider the question of a union of the Maritime Provinces and that Canada was no party to that Arrangement and had no interest in it. We came their [sic], not as recognized members of the Conference, but unofficially to discuss with them the propriety of extending their scheme and seeing whether the whole of British America could not be included in one government.

The Conference was accordingly organized without us, but that being done we were formally invited to be present and were presented in great style to the Conference. Having gone through the shake elbow and the how dyedo and the fine weather—the Conference adjourned to the next morning at 10 then to meet for the serious despatch of business. In the evening the Governor, Mr. Dundas, gave a large Dinner party to as many of the party as he could conveniently receive—I being one. . . .

On Friday we met in Conference and Canada opened her batteries—John A. and Cartier exposing the general arguments in favour of Confederation—and this occupied the time until the hour of adjournment at three. At four o'clock Mr. Pope gave us a grand *déjeuner à la fourchette.* . . .

On Saturday the Conference resumed its deliberations and Mr. Galt occupied the sitting in opening up the financial aspects of the Federation and the manner in which the financial disparities and requirements of the several Provinces ought to be arranged. When the Conference adjourned, we all proceeded on board our steamer and the members were entertained at luncheon in princely style. Cartier and I made eloquent speeches—of course—and whether as the result of our eloquence or of the goodness of our champagne, the ice became completely broken, the tongues of the delegates wagged merrily, and the banns of matrimony between all the Provinces of BNA having been formally proclaimed and all manner of persons duly warned their [*sic*] and then to speak or forever after to hold their tongues—no man appeared to forbid the banns and the union was thereupon formally completed and proclaimed! In the evening, Col. Gray gave a grand dinner party at his beautiful mansion. . . .

On Monday the Conference resumed its sittings, when I addressed the members on the Constitutional aspects of the question—the manner in which the several governments general and local should be constructed—and the Judiciary should be constituted—what duties should be ascribed to the general and local legislatures respectively—and so forth. My speech occupied the whole sitting. . . .

On Tuesday the Conference resumed its deliberations—earnestly discussing the several details of the scheme. The Canadians this day closed their case, and left the Conference to decide what course it would take on their propositions. At four o'clock Mr. Palmer, Attorney-General, gave the delegates a grand luncheon at his residence. . . .

On Wednesday, the Conference gave the Canadian Delegates their answer—that they were unanimous in regarding Federation of all the Provinces to be highly desirable, *if the terms of union could be made satisfactory*—and that they were prepared to waive their own more limited questions until the details of our scheme could be more fully considered and matured. It was agreed that the Conference should stand adjournd until Monday the 12th Sept. then to meet at Halifax. . . .

IX:4 PRINCE EDWARD ISLAND'S PROBLEMS AT QUEBEC, 1864

The major issue at the Quebec Conference was representation in the proposed Parliament. After four days' wrangling over Maritime representation in the Upper House, the Conference found that Prince Edward Island was no happier over the proposals for representation in the Lower House. These excerpts from the minutes of the proceedings illustrate the difficulties that caused Prince Edward Island initially to reject Confederation.

Colonel Gray (Prince Edward Island): I am instructed by my co-delegates to say that the provision of five members is unsatisfactory. Prince Edward Island is divided longitudinally into three counties, each returning ten members. But they are always opposed to change of representation. We cannot divide the three counties into the five members.

Mr. Brown: Every Province must revise its own electoral divisions to suit the number of its representation.

Mr. Coles: Mr. Galt had proposed six members for Prince Edward Island. I approved that rather than Mr. Brown's motion, because it allows us to give to our three counties two members each.

Mr. Pope: I was absent last night. I was under the impression that it had been clearly laid down at Charlottetown that representation by population was to form the basis of the Lower House. I could not, therefore, have argued for a greater number than our population entitled us to get. I agree in all that has been said by Colonel Gray and Mr. Coles. But the circumstances of Prince Edward Island are such that I hope the Conference will agree to give us such a number as we can divide amongst our three constituencies. Nature, as well as the original settlement of the Island, has made three counties, and it would give rise to much difficulty if we had to adjust five members to the three counties. I cannot ask it as a matter of right, but one of expediency, as one without which it is impossible for us to carry the measure in Prince Edward Island. I, therefore, ask for six members.

Mr. Haviland: I fully agree with Mr. Pope. It would be an insuperable difficulty to us if we had not six members.

Mr. Brown: To give Prince Edward Island five members the total properly should be 205. It is obvious we cannot depart from representation by population. The only thing to do would be to take Prince Edward Island as the basis which would give a House of 230, altogether too large. Give one member to each county and let the whole Island elect the other two, and keep the number five intact; or let the whole Island elect five. We should have to add thirty-eight members to the House in order to give Prince Edward Island six, as the basis of representation by population.

Mr. A. A. Macdonald: We are not bound by the principle of representation by population laid down at Charlottetown. Our constituents will say and will speak of the increased representation of the Lower Provinces.

Mr. Galt: There is no use in asking the Conference to depart from the principle laid down. We could not justify it. If the principle is good it is the same for all, and we could not defend the action of giving 13,000 in Prince Edward Island a member where it requires 17,000 in any other Province for that purpose. It would be indefensible. The difficulty is of a purely local nature. It is impossible for the Conference to depart from the rule of population being the basis of representation. . . .

Mr. Dickey: Give one member to each county in Prince Edward Island, one to Charlottetown, and one elected by the whole Island. Members elected for the Federal Legislature would not be elected for local purposes, but are representatives of the whole Island. It is a question for Canada. We (Nova Scotia) would concede the six members though it would place us in difficulty.

Mr. Haviland: There is no solution in the above proposition. . . .

Mr. Fisher: I came here convinced that representation by population was settled as the basis upon which the Provinces were to be asked to confederate.

Mr. Coles: Whatever may be the result of this matter, Prince Edward Island should submit. The question has been settled. Let us go on with the business, and let Prince Edward Island settle for themselves when the question comes before them.

IX:5 GREAT BRITAIN AND CONFEDERATION

Great Britain was remarkably open to the Confederation scheme—so much so that she applied considerable pressure on the reluctant Maritime colonies. The reasoning behind the British attitude is shown in selection (a), part of an 1862 editorial from the London *Times*, which mirrors perfectly the "Little England" sentiment of the 1860's. Selection (b) is the conclusion of the Earl of Carnarvon's speech in favour of Confederation during the debate on the British North America Act in the House of Lords. It represents British statesmanship and foresight at its best.

a. British Opinion, 1862

Great Britain cannot protect Canada without any aid on her part. Such an opinion is founded on a mistake both of our power and of our will. It is not in our power to send forth from this little island a military force sufficient to defend the frontier of Canada against the numerous armies which have learned arms and discipline in the great school of the present civil war. Our resources are unequal to so large a concentration of force on a single point; our empire is too vast, our population too small, our antagonist too powerful. But if we had the power it is quite certain that we should not have the will. Opinion in England is perfectly decided that in the connexion between the mother country and the colony the advantage is infinitely more on the side of the child than of the parent. We no longer monopolize the trade of the colonies; we no longer job their patronage. We cannot hope from them any assistance for defending our own shores while we are bound to assist in protecting theirs. We cannot even obtain from this very colony, Canada, reasonably fair treatment for our manufacturers, which are taxed twenty-five per cent on their value to increase a revenue which the colonies will not apply to our or even to their defence. There is little reciprocity in such a relation. Should the colony wish to put an end to it, we would never draw the sword to defend it; and if Canada will not fight to protect its independence from foreign invasion, neither will England. . . . If they are to be defended at all, they must make up their minds to bear the greater part of the burden of their own defence. This will be the case if they separate from us. This will be the case if they remain by us.

b. The Earl of Carnarvon on Confederation

. . . We are laying the foundation of a great State—perhaps one which at a future day may even overshadow this country.

But, come what may, we shall rejoice that we have shown neither indifference to their wishes nor jealousy of their aspirations, but that we honestly and sincerely, to the utmost of our power and knowledge, fostered their growth, recognising in it the conditions of our own greatness. We are in this measure setting the crown to the free institutions which more than a quarter of a century ago we gave them, and therein we remove, as I firmly believe, all possibilities of future jealousy or misunderstanding — *"Magna sub ingenti Matris se subjicit umbrâ."*

X. The Debate On Confederation: The Supporters

X:1 FRENCH CANADIAN SUPPORT

For more than five weeks in the winter of 1865 the Canadian Parliament debated the Quebec Resolutions. Fortunately for historians they published the debates. The Confederation debates contain almost every possible point of view on Confederation. The French Canadian arguments in favour of Confederation were best presented in the speeches of the Premier, Sir E. P. Taché, and the chief Quebec leader, George Etienne Cartier. Selection (a) is from Taché's speech and selection (b) from Cartier's. Cartier's speech is especially interesting for the light it sheds on the racial agreement that was involved in Confederation.

a. Sir E. P. Taché

. . . He would, then, first address himself to what he considered the intrinsic merits of the scheme of Confederation, and he would therefore say that if we were anxious to continue our connection with the British Empire, and to preserve intact our institutions, our laws, and even our remembrances of the past, we must sustain the measure. If the opportunity which now presented itself were allowed to pass by unimproved, whether we would or would not, we would be forced into the American Union by violence, and if not by violence, would be placed upon an inclined plain which would carry us there insensibly. In either case the result would be the same. . . .

. . . Lower Canada had constantly refused the demand of Upper Canada for representation according to population, and for the good reason that, as the union between them was legislative, a preponderance to one of the sections would have placed the other at its mercy. It would not be so in a Federal Union, for all questions of a general nature would be reserved for the General Government, and those of a local character to the local governments, who would have the power to manage their domestic affairs as they deemed best. If a Federal Union were obtained it would be tantamount to a separation of the provinces, and Lower Canada would thereby preserve its autonomy together with all the institutions it held so dear, and over which they could exercise the watchfulness and surveillance necessary to preserve them unimpaired. [The honourable member repeated this portion of his speech in French, for the express purpose of conveying his meaning in the clearest and most forcible manner to his fellow-members for Lower Canada, who might not have apprehended so well the English.] . . .

b. G. E. Cartier

. . . Objection had been taken to the scheme now under consideration, because of the words "new nationality." Now, when we were united together, if union were attained, we would form a political nationality with which neither the national origin, nor the religion of any individual, would interfere. It was lamented by some that we had this diversity of races, and hopes were expressed that this distinctive feature would cease. The idea of unity of races was utopian—it was impossible. Distinctions of this kind would always exist. Dissimilarity, in fact, appeared to be the order of the physical world and of the moral world, as well as in the political world. But with regard to the objection based on this fact, to the effect that a great nation could not be formed because Lower Canada was in great part French and Catholic, and Upper Canada was British and Protestant, and the Lower Provinces were mixed, it was futile and worthless in the extreme. Look, for instance, at the United Kingdom, inhabited as it was by three great races. (Hear, hear.) Had the diversity of race impeded the glory, the progress, the wealth of England? Had they not rather each contributed their share to the greatness of the Empire? . . . In our own Federation we should have Catholic and Protestant, English, French, Irish and Scotch, and each by his efforts and his success would increase the prosperity and glory of the new Confederacy. (Hear, hear.) He viewed the diversity of races in British North America in this way: we were of different races, not for the purpose of warring against each other, but in order to compete and emulate for the general welfare. (Cheers.) We could not do away with the distinctions of race. We could not legislate for the disappearance of the French Canadians from American soil, but British and French Canadians alike could appreciate and understand their position relative to each other. . . . It was a benefit rather than otherwise that we had a diversity of races. . . .

X:2 GEORGE BROWN ON THE ADVANTAGES OF CONFEDERATION

In the Confederation debates George Brown summarized both the reasons why Confederation would benefit the Province of Canada and why it would benefit all of British North America.

. . . Look, sir, at the map of the continent of America, and mark that island (Newfoundland) commanding the mouth of the noble river that almost cuts our continent in twain. Well, sir, that island is equal in extent to the kingdom of Portugal. Cross the straits to the main land, and you touch the hospitable shores of Nova Scotia, a country as large as the kingdom of Greece. Then mark the sister Province of New Brunswick— equal in extent to Denmark and Switzerland combined. Pass up the river St. Lawrence to Lower Canada—a country as large as France. Pass on to Upper Canada—twenty thousand square miles larger than Great Britain and Ireland put together. Cross over the continent to the shores of the Pacific, and you are in British Columbia, the land of golden promise,—equal in extent to the Austrian Empire. I speak not now of the vast Indian Territories that lie between—greater in extent than the whole soil of Russia—and that will ere long, I trust, be opened up to civilization under the auspices of the British American Confederation. (Cheers.) Well, sir, the bold scheme in your hands is nothing less than to gather all these countries into one—to organize them all under one government, with the protection of the British flag, and in heartiest sympathy and affection with our fellow-subjects in the land that gave us birth. (Cheers.) Our scheme is to establish a government that will seek to turn the tide of European emigration into this northern half of the American continent—that will strive to develope its great natural resources—and that will endeavour to maintain liberty, and justice, and christianity throughout the land. . . .

. . . We imagine not that such a structure can be built in a month or in a year. What we propose now is but to lay the foundations of the structure—to set in motion the governmental machinery that will one day, we trust, extend from the Atlantic to the Pacific. And we take especial credit to ourselves that the system we have devised, while admirably adapted to our present situation, is capable of gradual and efficient expansion in future years to meet all the great purposes contemplated by our scheme. . . .

. . . There is one consideration, Mr. Speaker, that cannot be banished from this discussion, and that ought, I think, to be remembered in every word we utter; it is that the constitutional system of Canada cannot remain as it is now. (Loud cries of hear, hear.) Something must be done. We cannot stand still. We cannot go back to chronic, sectional hostility and discord—to a state of perpetual Ministerial crises. The events of the last eight months cannot be obliterated; the solemn admissions of men of all parties can never be erased. The claims of Upper Canada for justice must be met, and met now. I say, then, that every one who raises his voice in hostility to this measure is bound to keep before him, when he speaks, all the perilous consequences of its rejection,—I say that no man who has a true regard for the well-being of Canada, can give a vote against this scheme, unless he is prepared to offer, in amendment, some better remedy for the evils and injustice that have so long threatened the peace of our country. (Hear, hear.) . . .

. . . Mr. Speaker, there are two views in which this scheme may be regarded, namely, the existing evils it will remedy, and the new advantages it will secure for us as a people. Let us begin by examining its remedial provisions.

First, then, it applies a complete and satisfactory remedy to the injustice of the existing system of parliamentary representation. (Hear, hear.) The people of Upper Canada have bitterly complained that though they numbered four hundred thousand souls more than the population of Lower Canada, and though they have contributed three or four pounds to the general revenue for every pound contributed by the sister province, yet the Lower Canadians send to Parliament as many representatives as they do. Now, sir, the measure in your hands brings this injustice to an end;—it sweeps away the line of demarcation between the two sections on all matters common to the whole province; it gives representation according to numbers wherever found in the House of Assembly; and it provides a simple and convenient system for readjusting the representation after each decennial census. (Cheers.) . . .

But, Mr. Speaker, the second feature of this scheme as a remedial measure is, that it removes, to a large extent, the injustice of which Upper Canada has complained in financial matters. We in Upper Canada have complained that though we paid into the public treasury more than three-fourths of the whole revenue, we had less control over the system of taxation and the expenditure of the public moneys than the people of Lower Canada. Well, sir, the scheme in your hand remedies that. The absurd line of separation between the provinces is swept away for general matters; we are to have seventeen additional members in the house that holds the purse; and the taxpayers of the country, wherever they reside, will have their just share of influence over revenue and expenditure. (Hear, hear.) We have also complained that immense sums of public money have been systematically taken from the public chest for local purposes of Lower Canada, in which the people of Upper Canada had no interest whatever, though compelled to contribute three-fourths of the cash. Well, sir, this scheme remedies that. All local matters are to be banished from the General Legislature; local governments are to have control over local affairs, and if our friends in Lower Canada choose to be extravagant, they will have to bear the burden of it themselves. (Hear, hear.) . . .

. . . But, Mr. Speaker, there is another great evil in our existing system that this scheme remedies; it secures to the people of each province full control over the administration of their own internal affairs. We in Upper Canada have complained that the minority of our representatives, the party defeated at the polls of Upper Canada, have been, year after year, kept in office by Lower Canada votes, and that all the local patronage of our section has been dispensed by those who did not possess the confidence of the people. Well, sir, this scheme remedies that. The local patronage will be under local control, and the wishes of the majority in each section will be carried out in all local matters. (Hear, hear.) . . .

. . . Viewed then, Mr. Speaker, from a merely Canadian stand-point—viewed solely as a remedial measure—I fearlessly assert that the scheme in your hands is a just and satisfactory remedy for the evils and injustice that have so long distracted the province—(cheers)—and so strongly do I feel this, that were every word of objection urged against our union with the Maritime Provinces just and true to the very letter, I would not hesitate to adopt the union as the price of a measure of constitutional reform in Canada, so just and so complete as now proposed. . . .

. . . I think I can present unanswerable arguments to show that this union of all British America should be heartily and promptly accepted by all the provinces. (Cheers.) Mr. Speaker, I am in favor of a union of the British American Colonies, first, because it will raise us from the attitude of a number of inconsiderable colonies into a great and powerful people. (Cheers.) The united population of Canada, Nova Scotia, New Brunswick, Newfoundland and Prince Edward Island, is at this moment very close on four millions of souls. Now, there are in Europe forty-eight Sovereign States, and out of that number there are only eleven having a greater population than these colonies united. . . .

. . . I am persuaded that this union will inspire new confidence in our stability, and exercise the most beneficial influence on all our affairs. I believe it will raise the value of our public securities, that it will draw capital to our shores, and secure the prosecution of all legitimate enterprises; . . .

. . . But secondly, Mr. Speaker, I go heartily for the union, because it will throw down the barriers of trade and give us the control of a market of four millions of people. (Hear, hear.) . . . If a Canadian goes now to Nova Scotia or New Brunswick, or if a citizen of these provinces comes here, it is like going to a foreign country. The customs officer meets you at the frontier, arrests your progress, and levies his imposts on your effects. But the proposal now before us is to throw down all barriers between the provinces—to make a citizen of one, citizen of the whole; the proposal is, that our farmers and manufacturers and mechanics shall carry their wares unquestioned into every village of the Maritime Provinces; and that they shall with equal freedom bring their fish, and their coal, and their West India produce to our three millions of inhabitants. The proposal is, that the law courts, and the schools, and the professional and industrial walks of life, throughout all the provinces, shall be thrown equally open to us all. (Hear, hear.)

But, thirdly, Mr. Speaker, I am in favor of a union of the provinces because—and I call the attention of honorable gentlemen opposite to it—because it will make us the third maritime state of the world. (Hear, hear.) When this union is accomplished, but two countries in the world will be superior in maritime influence to British America—and those are Great Britain and the United States. (Hear, hear.) . . .

But, in the fourth place, Mr. Speaker, I go for a union of the provinces, because it will give a new start to immigration into our country. It will bring us out anew prominently before the world—it will turn earnest attention to our resources, and bring to our shores a stream of immigration greater, and of a better class, than we ever had before. . . .

. . . But, fifthly, Mr. Speaker, I am in favor of a union of these provinces, because it will enable us to meet, without alarm, the abrogation of the American Reciprocity Treaty, in case the United States should insist on its abolition. (Hear, hear.) I do not believe that the American Government is so insane as to repeal that treaty. But it is always well to be prepared for contingencies—and I have no hesitation in saying that if they do repeal it, should this union of British America go on, a fresh outlet for our commerce will be opened up to us quite as advantageous as the American trade has ever been. . . .

. . . But, sixthly, Mr. Speaker, I am in favor of the union of the provinces, because, in the event of war, it will enable all the colonies to defend themselves better, and give more efficient aid to the Empire, than they could do separately. . . . it must be admitted—and there is no use of closing our eyes to the fact—that this question of defence has been placed, within the last two years, in a totally different position from what it ever occupied before. The time has come—it matters not what political party may be in power in England—when Britain will insist on a reconsideration of the military relations which a great colony, such as Canada, ought to hold to the Empire. And I am free to admit that it is a fair and just demand. . . . I have no belief that the Americans have the slightest thought of attacking us. I cannot believe that the first use of their new-found liberty will be the invasion, totally unprovoked, of a peaceful province. I fancy that they have had quite enough of war for a good many years to come—and that such a war as one with England would certainly be, is the last they are likely to provoke. But, Mr. Speaker, there is no better mode of warding off war when it is threatened, than to be prepared for it if it comes. The Americans are now a warlike people. They have large armies, a powerful navy, an unlimited supply of warlike munitions, and the carnage of war has to them been stript of its horrors. The American side of our lines already bristles with works of defence, and unless we are willing to live at the mercy of our neighbors, we, too, must put our country in a state of efficient preparation. War or no war—the necessity of placing these provinces in a thorough state of defence can no longer be postponed. . . .

Never, I venture to assert, was any great measure so thorougly understood, and so cordially endorsed by the people of Canada, as this measure now under consideration. (Hear, hear.)—The British Government approves of it—the Legislative Council approves of it—this House almost unanimously approves of it—the press of all parties approves of it—and though the scheme has already been directly submitted to fifty out of the one hundred constituencies into which Canada is divided, only four candidates ventured to appear at the hustings in opposition to it—all of them in Lower Canada—and but two of them were elected. (Cheers.) And yet, sir, we are to be told that we are stealing a march upon the country; that it is not understood by the people; and that we must dissolve the House upon it, at a vast cost to the exchequer, and at the risk of allowing political partisanship to dash the fruit from our hands at the very moment we are about to grasp it! (Hear, hear.) . . . An appeal to the people of Canada on this measure simply means postponement of the question for a year—and who can tell how changed ere then may be the circumstances surrounding us? Sir, the man who strives for the postponement of this measure on any ground, is doing what he can to kill it almost as effectually as if he voted against it. (Hear, hear.) . . .

X:3 JOHN A. MACDONALD ON THE FEDERAL SYSTEM

These portions of Macdonald's speech during the Confederation debates are exceptionally important in that they give us the clearest picture of the motives underlying our federal system as outlined in the British North America Act.

. . . Now, as regards the comparative advantages of a Legislative and a Federal Union, I have never hesitated to state my own opinions. I have again and again stated in the House, that, if practicable, I thought a Legislative Union would be preferable. (Hear, hear.) I have always contended that if we could agree to have one government and one parliament, legislating for the whole of these peoples, it would be the best, the cheapest, the most vigorous, and the strongest system of government we could adopt. (Hear, hear.) But, on looking at the subject in the Conference, and discussing the matter as we did, most unreservedly, and with a desire to arrive at a satisfactory conclusion, we found that such a system was impracticable. In the first place, it would not meet the assent of the people of Lower Canada, because they felt that in their peculiar position—being in a minority, with a different language, nationality and religion from the majority,—in case of a junction with the other provinces, their institutions and their laws might be assailed, and their ancestral associations, on which they prided themselves, attacked and prejudiced; it was found that any proposition which involved the absorption of the individuality of Lower Canada—if I may use the expression—would not be received with favor by her people. We found too, that though their people speak the same language and enjoy the same system of law as the people of Upper Canada, a system founded on the common law of England, there was as great a disinclination on the part of the various Maritime Provinces to lose their individuality, as separate political organizations, as we observed in the case of Lower Canada herself. (Hear, hear.) Therefore, we were forced to the conclusion that we must either abandon the idea of Union altogether, or devise a system of union in which the separate provincial organizations would be in some degree preserved. . . .

. . . The Conference having come to the conclusion that a legislative union, pure and simple, was impracticable, our next attempt was to form a government upon federal principles, which would give to the General Government the strength of a legislative and administrative union, while at the same time it preserved that liberty of action for the different sections which is allowed by a Federal Union. And I am strong in the belief—that we have hit upon the happy medium in those resolutions, and that we have formed a scheme of government which unites the advantages of both, giving us the strength of a legislative union and the sectional freedom of a federal union, with protection to local interests. In doing so we had the advantage of the experience of the United States. . . . We can now take advantage of the experience of the last seventy-eight years, during which that Constitution has existed, and I am strongly of the belief that we have, in a great measure, avoided in this system which we propose for the adoption of the people of Canada, the defects which time and events have shown to exist in the American Constitution. . . . Ever since the union was formed the difficulty of what is called "State Rights" has existed, and this had much to do in bringing on the present unhappy war in the United States. They commenced, in fact, at the wrong end. They declared by their Constitution that each state was a sovereignty in itself, and that all the powers incident to a sovereignty belonged to each state, except those powers which, by the Constitution, were conferred upon the General Government and Congress. Here we have adopted a different system. We have strengthened the General Government. We have given the General Legislature all the great subjects of legislation. We have conferred on them, not only specifically and in detail, all the powers which are incident to sovereignty, but we have expressly declared that all subjects of general interest not distinctly and exclusively conferred upon the local governments and local legislatures, shall be conferred upon the General Government and Legislature.—We have thus avoided that great source of weakness which has been the cause of the disruption of the United States. We have avoided all conflict of jurisdiction and authority, and if this Constitution is carried out, . . . we will have in fact, as I said before, all the advantages of a legislative union under one administration, with, at the same time the guarantees for local institutions and for local laws, which are insisted upon by so many in the provinces now, I hope, to be united. . . .

. . . any honorable member on examining the list of different subjects which are to be assigned to the General and Local Legislatures respectively, will see that all the great questions which affect the general interests of the Confederacy as a whole, are confided to the Federal Parliament, while the local interests and local laws of each section are preserved intact, and entrusted to the care of the local bodies. As a matter of course, the General Parliament must have the power of dealing with the public debt and property of the Confederation. Of course, too, it must have the regulation of trade and commerce, of customs and excise. The Federal Parliament must have the sovereign power of raising money from such sources and by such means as the representatives of the people will allow. It will be seen that the local legislatures have the control of all local works; and it is a matter of great importance, and one of the chief advantages of the Federal Union and of local legislatures, that each province will have the power and means of developing its own resources and aiding its own progress after its own fashion and in its own way. Therefore all the local improvements, all local enterprizes or undertakings of any kind, have been left to the care and management of the local legislatures of each province. (Cheers.) . . .

. . . With respect to the local governments, it is provided that each shall be governed by a chief executive officer, who shall be nominated by the General Government. As this is to

be one united province, with the local governments and legislatures subordinate to the General Government and Legislature, it is obvious that the chief executive officer in each of
the provinces must be subordinate as well. The General Government assumes towards the local governments precisely the
same position as the Imperial Government holds with respect
to each of the colonies now; so that as the Lieutenant Governor of each of the different provinces is now appointed
directly by the Queen, and is directly responsible, and reports
directly to Her, so will the executives of the local governments
hereafter be subordinate to the Representative of the Queen,
and be responsible and report to him. . . .

. . . In conclusion, I would again implore the House not to
let this opportunity to pass. It is an opportunity that may
never recur. At the risk of repeating myself, I would say, it
was only by a happy concurrence of circumstances, that we
were enabled to bring this great question to its present position. If we do not take advantage of the time, if we show ourselves unequal to the occasion, it may never return, and we
shall hereafter bitterly and unavailingly regret having failed
to embrace the happy opportunity now offered of founding a
great nation under the fostering care of Great Britain, and our
Sovereign Lady, Queen Victoria. (Loud cheers, amidst which
the honorable gentleman resumed his seat).

XI. The Debate On Confederation: The Opponents

XI:1 FRENCH CANADIAN OPPOSITION: JOSEPH PERRAULT

The objections to Confederation raised by the Quebec *Rouges* stemmed from their doubts about French Canada's minority position within the new federation. This brief excerpt from the speech of Joseph Perrault in the Confederation debates is representative of their arguments.

. . . With equality of numbers, and of sectional representation, the two nationalities cannot fall foul of each other; but with Confederation, as we shall be in a great minority in the General Parliament, which has all the important powers in relation to legislation, we shall have to carry on a constant contest for the defence and preservation of our political rights and of our liberty. Under the union the French Canadians are divided in this House into two camps, opposed the one to the other, because they have nothing to fear in regard to their national interests; but under Confederation, as we shall have but forty-eight French members against one hundred and forty-six in the Federal Legislature, those members will have to go together like one man to maintain their influence, and the simple fact of that union of the French Canadians into a solid phalanx will cause the English element to unite on its

124

side to crush and vanquish it. It is because I fear such a strife that I cannot approve of a Constitution which does not secure our political rights, and the working of which will necessarily entail disastrous consequences to our race. (Hear, hear.) . . .

XI:2 NOVA SCOTIA'S OBJECTIONS: JOSEPH HOWE

> Joseph Howe, thirty years before the most eloquent voice in favour of responsible government, now turned his sharp pen against the "Botheration Scheme." Whatever his motives (and historians are still uncertain), his fellow Nova Scotians warmly responded to his arguments. Nova Scotia barely accepted Confederation and its first parliamentary delegation after 1867 was dedicated to procuring Nova Scotia's secession from Canada. The following two selections are from an 1866 pamphlet and an 1867 speech at Dartmouth.

a. Howe in 1866

. . . Let us see what these Canadians desire to do. They are not, as we have shown, a very harmonious or homogeneous community. Two-fifths of the population are French and three-fifths English. They are therefore perplexed with an internal antagonism which was fatal to the unity of Belgium and Holland, and which, unless the fusion of races becomes rapid and complete, must ever be a source of weakness. They are shut in by frost from the outer world for five months of the year. They are at the mercy of a powerful neighbour whose population already outnumbers them by more than eight to one, and who a quarter of a century hence will probably present sixty-eight millions to six millions on the opposite side of a naturally defenceless frontier. Surely such conditions as these ought to repress inordinate ambition or lust of territory on the part of the public men of Canada. The wisdom of Solomon and the energy and strategy of Frederick the Great would seem to be required to preserve

and strengthen such a people, if formed, as it appears they
desire to form themselves, into "a new nationality." While
they discharge their duties as unobtrusive good neighbours
to the surrounding populations, and of loyal subjects of the
empire, Great Britain will protect them by her energy in
other fields should the Province become untenable; but it is
evident that a more unpromising nucleus of a new nation can
hardly be found on the face of the earth, and that any organized communities, having a reasonable chance to do anything better, would be politically insane to give up their
distinct formations and subject themselves to the domination
of Canada. . . .

b. Howe at Dartmouth, 1867

MEN OF DARTMOUTH,—Never, since the Indians came down
the Shubenacadie Lakes in 1750, burnt the houses of the early
settlers, and scalped or carried them captives to the woods,
have the people upon this harbour been called upon to face
circumstances so serious as those which confront them now.
We may truly say, in the language of Burke, that "the high
roads are broken up and the waters are out," and that everything around us is in a state of chaos and uncertainty. . . .

The old men who sit around me, and the men of middle
age who hear my voice, know that thirty years ago we engaged in a series of struggles which the growth of population,
wealth and intelligence rendered inevitable. For what did we
contend? Chiefly for the right of self-government. We won it
from Downing Street after many a manly struggle, and we
exercised and never abused it for a quarter of a century.
Where is it now? Gone from us, and certain persons in Canada
are now to exercise over us powers more arbitrary and excessive than any the Colonial Secretaries ever claimed. Our
Executive and Legislative Councillors were formerly selected
in Downing Street. For more than twenty years we have
appointed them ourselves. But the right has been bartered
away by those who have betrayed us, and now we must be
content with those our Canadian masters give. The batch

already announced shows the principles which are to govern the selection. . . .

But it is said, why should we complain? we are still to manage our local affairs. I have shown you that self-government, in all that gives dignity and security to a free state, is to be swept away. The Canadians are to appoint our governors, judges and senators. They are to "tax us by any and every mode" and spend the money. They are to regulate our trade, control our Post Offices, command the militia, fix the salaries, do what they like with our shipping and navigation, with our sea-coast and river fisheries, regulate the currency and the rate of interest, and seize upon our savings banks. What remains? Listen, and be comforted. You are to have the privilege of "imposing direct taxation, within the Province, in order to the raising of revenue for Provincial purposes." Why do you not go down on your knees and be thankful for this crowning mercy when fifty per cent has been added to your *ad valorem* duties, and the money has been all swept away to dig canals or fortify Montreal. You are to be kindly permitted to keep up your spirits and internal improvements by direct taxation. . . .

XI:3 CHRISTOPHER DUNKIN'S ATTACK ON THE QUEBEC RESOLUTIONS

By far the most perceptive criticism of Confederation was made by Christopher Dunkin, a representative from Canada East, during the Confederation debates. Although some of his criticisms proved unfounded, the reader cannot help being impressed by the foresight of much of what Dunkin had to say.

. . . I say it is a scheme which is as complex and as vast as one can well imagine, and declamation about first principles can be of no real use in its discussion—can avail only to mislead in reference to it. We have to deal with no mere abstract question of a nationality, or of union or disunion, or of a Federal as opposed to a Legislative union. It is idle to talk vaguely about the maintenance of British connection, or to go into magnificent speculations about the probable results of independence, or blindly to urge this scheme as a sure preventative of annexation to the United States. These cheap and easy generalities are thoroughly unreliable. The only question is, how is this plan, in its entirety, going to work? . . .

. . . Such is the way in which this matter was laid before the people. Every possible advantage was given to the people to praise it from every point of view, and nobody got a fair opportunity of saying that he did not like it. The praise was carefully prepared and published, and everything that could possibly be done to prepare the public mind for the scheme before its final announcement was skilfully done. And now what have we? Why, the cry that the whole thing must be passed, "now or never." It will never pass, we are told, if it does not pass now! (Hear, hear.) Was there ever a measure of this magnitude before, on which the heart of a country was set, the whole of which was so wise and good as this scheme is said to be—and yet, that had to be passed (the whole of it) at once, or never? (Hear, hear.) We are even told that it is a positive treaty—made however, by the way, by parties who were never authorized to make any treaty at all. I must say, for one, that I cannot but see in all this precipitancy the unmistakeable admission *de facto*, that the Government themselves know and feel that the feeling they have got up in favor of this scheme is a passing feeling of momentary duration, that they cannot themselves in the least rely upon. (Hear, hear.) . . .

Surely, Mr. Speaker, this Legislative Council, constituted so differently from the Senate of the United States, presided over by a functionary to be nominated by the General Government; having no such functions of a judicial or executive character as attached to that body, and cut off from that minute oversight of the finances which attaches to the Senate of the United States; although it may be a first-rate deadlock; although it may be able to interpose an absolute veto, for no one can say how long, on all legislation, would be no Federal check at all. . . . I do not like the quasi-despotism of this Legislative Council, even though so tempered. Representing no public opinion or real power of any kind, it may hurt the less but it can never tend to good, and it can never last. . . .

. . . But now, if this Executive Council is to have in it, as I am sure it must have, in order to work at all, a representation of the different provinces, all or nearly all of them, let us look for a moment at what will have to be its number. . . . Six members—four, one and one—are just about what you must give to please each section of Lower Canada. Well, sir, if there are to be six for Lower Canada, there must be six or seven for Upper Canada, and you cannot very well leave less than three each for Nova Scotia and New Brunswick, and, as I have said, one each for Newfoundland and Prince Edward Island; and thus you have an Executive Council of twenty or twenty-one members, besides all we might have to add for other provinces; and this, I rather think, is a little too many. . . .

. . . But now, sir, what is the system we are going to adopt according to these resolutions? What are the relations to be established between our general and local governments? We are told to take for granted that no clashing of interest or feeling need be feared; that the Federal union offered us in name will be a legislative union in reality. Yet, whoever dislikes the notion of a legislative union is assured it will be nothing of the sort. Now, sir, I do not believe that you can have all the advantages of these two systems combined in one. (Hear, hear.) A Legislative union is one thing; a Federal union is another. The same system cannot be both at once. You cannot devise a system that shall have all the advantages of the one and of the other; but it is quite possible that you may devise one that will combine the chief disadvantages of both, and that is, I fear, pretty much what this system does. (Hear, hear). . . .

If this permission of disallowance rests on a presumption that the legislation of our provinces is going to be unjust or unwise, it may be needed; but under that idea, one might have done better either not to allow, or else to restrict within narrower limits, such legislation. If the promised non-exercise of the power to disallow rests on a presumption that all will be done justly and wisely in the provincial legislatures, the legislative power is well given; but then there is no need, on the other hand, for the permission to disallow. (Hear, hear.) . . . And the plain truth is, that the Federal system is simply inconsistent with the first principles that must prevail in a properly organized British responsible central government. (Hear, hear.) Indeed, aside even from Federalism, the British system and the republican are antagonist in principle; neither of them will work mixed up with the other. You must be content with one or other, and must not commit the folly of attempting any new, untried, mongrel system, or compound of the two—such as nobody can shew to be capable of being worked at all. . . .

But there is another result, about which there can be no question. With one accord, . . . in all the provinces —the provincial governments will, in a quiet way, want money, and the provincial legislators and people will want it yet more; grants for roads and bridges, for schools, for charities, for salaries, for contingencies of the legislative body —for all manner of ends they will be wanting money, and where is it to come from? . . . Gentlemen will go to their constituents with an easy conscience, telling them: "True, we had not much to do in the Provincial Legislature, and you need not ask very closely what else we did; but I tell you what, we got the Federal Government to increase the subvention to our province by five cents a head, and see what this gives you— $500 to that road—$1000 to that charity—so much here, so much there. That we have done; and have we not done well?" (Hear, hear.) I am afraid in many constituencies the answer would be; "Yes, you have done well; go and do it again." I am afraid the provincial constituencies, legislatures and executives will all show a most calf-like appetite for the milking of this one most magnificent government cow. . . .

   . . . the moment you tell Lower Canada that the large-sounding powers of your General Government are going to be handed over to a British-American majority, decidedly not of the race and faith of her majority, that moment you wake up the old jealousies and hostility in their strongest form. By the very provisions you talk of for the protection of the non-French and non-Catholic interests, you unfortunately countenance the idea that the French are going to be more unfair than I believe they wish to be. For that matter, what else can they well be? They will find themselves a minority in the General Legislature, and their power in the General Government will depend upon their power within their own province and over their provincial delegations in the Federal Parliament. They will thus be compelled to be practically aggressive, to secure and retain that power. They may not, perhaps, wish to be; they may not, perhaps, be aggressive in the worst sense of the term.—I do not say that they certainly will be; but whether they are or not, there will certainly be in this system the very strongest tendencies to make them practically aggressive upon the rights of the minority in language and faith, and at the same time to make the minority most suspicious and resentful of aggression. . . .

As it is, I have but to say in conclusion, while warmly thanking the House for the attention and patience with which it has for so many hours listened to me, that I have said nothing but what I firmly believe, and felt myself bound to say, and that I trust the sober good sense of the people of these provinces, after full reflection and discussion, will decide rightly upon this the largest question by far that has ever been before them for decision. (Cheers.)

XII. Confederation Achieved

XII:1 THE BRITISH NORTH AMERICA ACT, 1867

The terms of the British North America Act correspond quite closely with the Quebec Resolutions. The Act was passed by the British Parliament without significant debate; it received royal assent on March 29, 1867, and came into effect on July 1, 1867.

The various amendments to the British North America Act which have been passed since 1867 may be found in any of the more comprehensive collections of constitutional documents.

An Act for the Union of Canada, Nova Scotia, and New Brunswick, and the Government thereof; and for Purposes connected therewith

Whereas the Provinces of Canada, Nova Scotia, and New Brunswick have expressed their Desire to be federally united into One Dominion under the Crown of the United Kingdom of Great Britain and Ireland, with a Constitution similar in Principle to that of the United Kingdom:

And Whereas such a Union would conduce to the Welfare of the Provinces and promote the Interests of the British Empire: . . .

Be it therefore enacted and declared by the Queen's Most Excellent Majesty, by and with the advice and Consent of the Lords Spiritual and Temporal, and Commons, in this present Parliament assembled, and by the Authority of the same, as follows:

I. PRELIMINARY

1. This Act may be cited as the British North America Act, 1867.

II. UNION

3. It shall be lawful for the Queen, by and with the Advice of Her Majesty's Most Honourable Privy Council, to declare by Proclamation that, on and after a Day therein appointed, not being more than Six Months after the passing of this Act, the Provinces of Canada, of Nova Scotia, and New Brunswick shall form and be One Dominion under the name of Canada; and on and after that Day those Three Provinces shall form and be One Dominion under that Name accordingly.

5. Canada shall be divided into Four Provinces, named Ontario, Quebec, Nova Scotia, and New Brunswick.

6. The Parts of the Province of Canada (as it exists at the passing of this Act) which formerly constituted respectively the Provinces of Upper Canada and Lower Canada shall be deemed to be severed, and shall form two separate Provinces. The Part which formerly constituted the Province of Upper Canada shall constitute the Province of Ontario; and the Part which formerly constituted the Province of Lower Canada shall constitute the Province of Quebec.

7. The Provinces of Nova Scotia and New Brunswick shall have the same Limits as at the passing of this Act.

III. EXECUTIVE POWER

9. The Executive Government and authority of and over Canada is hereby declared to continue and be vested in the Queen.

11. There shall be a Council to aid and advise in the Government of Canada, to be styled the Queen's Privy Council for Canada; and the Persons who are to be Members of that

Council shall be from time to time chosen and summoned by the Governor General and sworn in as Privy Councillors, and Members thereof may be from time to time removed by the Governor General.

16. Until the Queen otherwise directs the Seat of Government of Canada shall be Ottawa.

IV. LEGISLATIVE POWER

17. There shall be One Parliament for Canada, consisting of the Queen, an Upper House styled the Senate, and the House of Commons.

The Senate

21. The Senate shall, subject to the Provisions of this Act, consist of Seventy-two Members, who shall be styled Senators.

22. In relation to the Constitution of the Senate, Canada shall be deemed to consist of Three Divisions:

1. Ontario;
2. Quebec;
3. The Maritime Provinces, Nova Scotia and New Brunswick; which Three Divisions shall (subject to the Provisions of this Act) be equally represented in the Senate as follows: Ontario by Twenty-four Senators; Quebec by Twenty-four Senators; and the Maritime Provinces by Twenty-four Senators, Twelve thereof representing Nova Scotia, and Twelve thereof representing New Brunswick. . . .

24. The Governor General shall from time to time, in the Queen's Name, by instrument under the Great Seal of Canada, summon qualified Persons to the Senate; and, subject to the Provisions of this Act, every Person so summoned shall become and be a Member of the Senate and a Senator.

26. If at any time, on the Recommendation of the Governor General, the Queen thinks fit to direct that Three or Six Members be added to the Senate, the Governor General may by Summons to Three or Six qualified Persons (as the Case

may be), representing equally the Three Divisions of Canada, add to the Senate accordingly.

29. A Senator shall, subject to the Provisions of this Act, hold his Place in the Senate for Life.

The House of Commons

37. The House of Commons shall, subject to the Provisions of this Act, consist of One hundred and eighty-one Members, of whom Eighty-two shall be elected for Ontario, Sixty-five for Quebec, Nineteen for Nova Scotia, and Fifteen for New Brunswick.

50. Every House of Commons shall continue for Five Years from the Day of the Return of the Writs for choosing the House (subject to be sooner dissolved by the Governor General), and no longer.

52. The Number of Members of the House of Commons may be from time to time increased by the Parliament of Canada, provided the proportionate Representation of the Provinces prescribed by this Act is not thereby disturbed.

Money Votes; Royal Assent

53. Bills for appropriating any Part of the Public Revenue, or for imposing any Tax or Impost, shall originate in the House of Commons.

55. Where a Bill passed by the Houses of Parliament is presented to the Governor General for the Queen's Assent, he shall declare, according to his Discretion, but subject to the Provisions of this Act and to Her Majesty's Instructions, either that he assents thereto in the Queen's Name, or that he withholds the Queen's Assent, or that he reserves the Bill for the Signification of the Queen's Pleasure.

Legislative Power

90. The following Provisions of this Act respecting the Parliament of Canada, namely, — the Provisions relating to Appropriation and Tax Bills, the Recommendation of Money

Votes, the Assent to Bills, the Disallowance of Acts, and Signification of Pleasure on Bills reserved, — shall extend and apply to the Legislatures of the several Provinces. . . .

VI. DISTRIBUTION OF LEGISLATIVE POWERS

Powers of the Parliament

91. It shall be lawful for the Queen, by and with the Advice and Consent of the Senate and House of Commons, to make Laws for the Peace, Order, and good Government of Canada, in relation to all Matters not coming within the Classes of Subjects by this Act assigned exclusively to the Legislatures of the Provinces; and for greater Certainty, but not so as to restrict the Generality of the foregoing Terms of this Section, it is hereby declared that (notwithstanding anything in this Act) the exclusive Legislative Authority of the Parliament of Canada extends to all Matters coming within the Classes of Subjects next hereinafter enumerated; that is to say,—

1. The Public Debt and Property.

2. The Regulation of Trade and Commerce.

3. The raising of Money by any Mode or System of Taxation.

4. The borrowing of Money on the Public Credit.

5. Postal Service.

6. The Census and Statistics.

7. Militia, Military and Naval Service, and Defence.

8. The fixing of and providing for the Salaries and Allowances of Civil and other Officers of the Government of Canada.

9. Beacons, Buoys, Lighthouses, and Sable Island.

10. Navigation and Shipping.

11. Quarantine and the Establishment and Maintenance of Marine Hospitals.

12. Sea Coast and Inland Fisheries.

13. Ferries between a Province and any British or Foreign Country or between Two Provinces.

14. Currency and Coinage.
15. Banking, Incorporation of Banks, and the Issue of Paper Money.
16. Savings Banks.
17. Weights and Measures.
18. Bills of Exchange and Promissory Notes.
19. Interest.
20. Legal Tender.
21. Bankruptcy and Insolvency.
22. Patents of Invention and Discovery.
23. Copyrights.
24. Indians and Lands reserved for the Indians.
25. Naturalization and Aliens.
26. Marriage and Divorce.
27. The Criminal Law, except the Constitution of Courts of Criminal Jurisdiction, but including the Procedure in Criminal Matters.
28. The Establishment, Maintenance, and Management of Penitentiaries.
29. Such Classes of Subjects as are expressly excepted in the Enumeration of the Classes of Subjects by this Act assigned exclusively to the Legislatures of the Provinces.

And any Matter coming within any of the Classes of Subjects enumerated in this Section shall not be deemed to come within the Class of Matters of a local or private Nature comprised in the Enumeration of the Classes of Subjects by this Act assigned exclusively to the Legislatures of the Provinces.

Exclusive Powers of Provincial Legislatures

92. In each Province the Legislature may exclusively make Laws in relation to Matters coming within the Classes of Subjects next hereinafter enumerated; that is to say,—

1. The Amendment from time to time, notwithstanding anything in this Act, of the Constitution of the Province, except as regards the Office of Lieutenant-Governor.

2. Direct Taxation within the Province in order to the Raising of a Revenue for Provincial Purposes.

3. The borrowing of Money on the sole Credit of the Province.

4. The Establishment and Tenure of Provincial Offices and the Appointment and Payment of Provincial Officers.

5. The Management and Sale of the Public Lands belonging to the Province and of the Timber and Wood thereon.

6. The Establishment, Maintenance, and Management of Public and Reformatory Prisons in and for the Province.

7. The Establishment, Maintenance, and Management of Hospitals, Asylums, Charities, and Eleemosynary Institutions in and for the Province, other than Marine Hospitals.

8. Municipal Institutions in the Province.

9. Shop, Saloon, Tavern, Auctioneer, and other Licences in order to the raising of a Revenue for Provincial, Local, or Municipal Purposes.

10. Local Works and Undertakings other than such as are of the following Classes:—

    (a) Lines of Steam and other Ships, Railways, Canals, Telegraphs, and other Works and Undertakings connecting the Province with any other or others of the Provinces, or extending beyond the Limits of the Province:

    (b) Lines of Steam Ships between the Province and any British or Foreign Country:

    (c) Such Works as, although wholly situate within the Province, are before or after their Execution declared by the Parliament of Canada to be for the general Advantage of Canada or for the Advantage of Two or more of the Provinces.

11. The Incorporation of Companies with Provincial Objects.

12. The Solemnization of Marriage in the Province.

13. Property and Civil Rights in the Province.

14. The Administration of Justice in the Province, including the Constitution, Maintenance, and Organization of Provincial Courts, both of Civil and of Criminal Jurisdiction, and including Procedure in Civil Matters in those Courts.

15. The Imposition of Punishment by Fine, Penalty, or Imprisonment for enforcing any Law of the Province made in relation to any Matter coming within any of the Classes of Subjects enumerated in this Section.

16. Generally all Matters of a merely local or private Nature in the Province.

Education

93. In and for each Province the Legislature may exclusively make Laws in relation to Education, subject and according to the following Provisions:—

(1) Nothing in any such Law shall prejudicially affect any Right or Privilege with respect to Denominational Schools which any Class of Persons have by Law in the Province at the Union:

(2) All the Powers, Privileges, and Duties at the Union by Law conferred and imposed in Upper Canada on the Separate Schools and School Trustees of the Queen's Roman Catholic Subjects shall be and the same are hereby extended to the Dissentient Schools of the Queen's Protestant and Roman Catholic Subjects in Quebec:

(3) Where in any Province a System of Separate or Dissentient Schools exists by Law at the Union or is thereafter established by the Legislature of the Province, an Appeal shall lie to the Governor General in Council from any Act or Decision of any Provincial Authority affecting any Right or Privilege of the Protestant or Roman Catholic Minority of the Queen's Subjects in relation to Education:

(4) In case any such Provincial Law as from time to time seems to the Governor General in Council requisite for

the due Execution of the Provisions of this Section is not made, or in case any Decision of the Governor General in Council on any Appeal under this Section is not duly executed by the proper Provincial Authority in that Behalf, then and in every such Case, and as far only as the Circumstances of each Case require, the Parliament of Canada may make remedial Laws for the due Execution of the Provisions of this Section and of any Decision of the Governor General in Council under this Section.

Agriculture and Immigration

95. In each Province the Legislature may make Laws in relation to Agriculture in the Province, and to Immigration into the Province; and it is hereby declared that the Parliament of Canada may from time to time make Laws in relation to Agriculture in all or any of the Provinces, and to Immigration into all or any of the Provinces; and any Law of the Legislature of a Province relative to Agriculture or to Immigration shall have effect in and for the Province as long and as far only as it is not repugnant to any Act of the Parliament of Canada.

VIII. REVENUES; DEBTS; ASSETS; TAXATION

111. Canada shall be liable for the Debts and Liabilities of each Province existing at the Union.

118. The following Sums shall be paid yearly by Canada to the several Provinces for the Support of their Governments and Legislatures:

	Dollars
Ontario	Eighty thousand.
Quebec	Seventy thousand.
Nova Scotia	Sixty thousand.
New Brunswick	Fifty thousand.

Two hundred and sixty thousand;

and an annual Grant in aid to each Province shall be made, equal to Eighty Cents per Head of the Population as ascertained by the Census of One thousand eight hundred and sixty-one, and in the Case of Nova Scotia and New Brunswick, by each subsequent Decennial Census until the Population of each of those two Provinces amounts to Four hundred thousand Souls, at which Rate such Grant shall thereafter remain. Such Grants shall be in full Settlement of all future Demands on Canada, and shall be paid half-yearly in advance to each Province; but the Government of Canada shall deduct from such Grants, as against any Province, all Sums chargeable as Interest on the Public Debt of that Province in excess of the several Amounts stipulated in this Act.

119. New Brunswick shall receive by half-yearly Payments in advance from Canada for the period of Ten years from the Union an additional Allowance of Sixty-three thousand Dollars per Annum; but as long as the Public Debt of that Province remains under Seven million Dollars, a Deduction equal to the interest of Five per Centum per Annum on such Deficiency shall be made from that Allowance of Sixty-three thousand Dollars.

121. All articles of the Growth, Produce, or Manufacture of any one of the Provinces shall, from and after the Union, be admitted free into each of the other Provinces.

IX. MISCELLANEOUS PROVISIONS

133. Either the English or the French Language may be used by any Person in the Debates of the House of the Parliament of Canada and of the Houses of the Legislature of Quebec; and both those Languages shall be used in the respective Records and Journals of those Houses; and either of those Languages may be used by any Person or in any Pleading or Process in or issuing from any Court of Canada established under this Act, and in or from all or any of the Courts of Quebec.

The Acts of the Parliament of Canada and of the Legislature of Quebec shall be printed and published in both those Languages.

X. INTERCOLONIAL RAILWAY

145. Inasmuch as the Provinces of Canada, Nova Scotia, and New Brunswick have joined in a Declaration that the Construction of the Intercolonial Railway is essential to the Consolidation of the Union of British North America, and to the Assent thereto of Nova Scotia and New Brunswick, and have consequently agreed that Provision should be made for its immediate Construction by the Government of Canada: Therefore, in order to give effect to that Agreement, it shall be the Duty of the Government and Parliament of Canada to provide for the Commencement within Six Months after the Union, of a Railway connecting the River St. Lawrence with the City of Halifax in Nova Scotia, and for the Construction thereof without Intermission, and the Completion thereof with all practicable Speed.

XI. ADMISSION OF OTHER COLONIES

146. It shall be lawful for the Queen, by and with the Advice of Her Majesty's Most Honourable Privy Council, on Addresses from the Houses of the Parliament of Canada, and from the Houses of the respective Legislatures of the Colonies or Provinces of Newfoundland, Prince Edward Island, and British Columbia, to admit those Colonies or Provinces, or any of them, into the Union, and on Address from the Houses of the Parliament of Canada to admit Rupert's Land and the North-western Territory, or either of them, into the Union, on such Terms and Conditions in each Case as are in the Addresses expressed and as the Queen thinks fit to approve, subject to the Provisions of this Act; and the Provisions of any Order in Council in that Behalf shall have effect as if they had been enacted by the Parliament of the United Kingdom of Great Britain and Ireland. . . .

XIII. Macdonald's Nation Building

XIII: 1 FAILURE: THE PACIFIC SCANDAL

After Canada's expansion to the Pacific, Sir John A. Macdonald's main task was to tie together the diverse provinces and territories into an economic whole. The binding cord was to be a transcontinental railway. The first attempt to form a company, however, destroyed Macdonald's Government. It was found that Cartier and other Conservatives, including Macdonald, had accepted huge campaign donations from Sir Hugh Allan, to whom the Government had promised the presidency of the new company. Cartier, badly in need of money for his campaign in Montreal East, had drawn Macdonald and the Government into his negotiations with Allan. Cartier, who died just after the scandal broke, may have made commitments to Allan that have never been revealed; even with Allan's support he had lost his seat in the election.

Selection (a) is a crucial, incriminating telegram to Allan from Macdonald requesting funds. Macdonald defends his Government in selection (b), a memorandum to the Governor General, Lord Dufferin. Selection (c), Dufferin's reply to Macdonald, is still one of the fairest assessments of the Government's role in the scandal.

a. The Incriminating Telegram

I must have another ten thousand; will be the last time of calling; do not fail me; answer today.

b. Macdonald's Defence

Sir Hugh Allan and Mr. Macpherson came to Parliament each with a railway Bill of his own. The Government did not desire to evince any preference for one company over the other. They therefore announced that they would not oppose the incorporation of any bodies of capitalists, for the purpose of building the railway, and accordingly Sir Hugh Allan's company, called, "The Canada Pacific Railway Company," and Mr. Macpherson's company, called "The Interoceanic Company," received Acts of incorporation. . . .

So soon as Parliament was prorogued the Government endeavoured to procure the amalgamation of the two incorporated companies. It was felt to be impossible to give the work to either to the exclusion of the other. To have done so would have aroused against the measure, and against the Government, the hostility of the province whose company was excluded.

Sir Hugh Allan always expressed his desire for amalgamation, but the Interoceanic and Mr. Macpherson objected. Mr. Macpherson professed to dread the influence of the Americans through Sir Hugh Allan, and, although the latter had pledged himself to the Government and to Parliament that all connection with the Americans had been severed by him, such assurance was not satisfactory to Mr. Macpherson. It afterwards proved that Mr. Macpherson's suspicions were not without foundation, as the private correspondence published between Sir Hugh Allan and his American friends showed that he was still keeping up a connection with them, in the hope that he would be able to overcome the feeling against them. The real and principal reason, however, for Mr. Macpherson's objection was a rivalry as to who should be the president of the company, both being desirous of connecting themselves in that position with the great work. . . .

The general elections were to commence in July, and I was naturally very anxious to go to the country with a completed scheme. I spared no effort, therefore, to effect an amalgamation, and on several occasions had nearly succeeded.

As to the presidency, my own opinion was that it was really of little consequence who should be the figure-head, but that, as between the two, Sir Hugh Allan, from his infinitely greater wealth, and from the fact of his having been the first to take up the subject, as well as his having largely connected himself with other railway lines which would be auxiliary to and in effect connect the Pacific Railway with the Atlantic Ocean, should have the preference.

The feeling in the province of Quebec on the subject had become intense. Sir Hugh Allan had put himself at the head of several railway enterprises, and was selected by the voice of the whole province as their representative man. He was especially and pecuniarily interested in all these lines of railway from his position as a ship-owner.

The Montreal Ocean Steamship Company, in which he has the chief interest, had practically the control of the Canadian freight and passenger trade to Europe.

An opposition steamship line was announced as being about to be formed under the auspices of the Grand Trunk Railway of Canada, which railway, as you know, is the great artery of trade and transport through the two Canadas to the sea. Sir Hugh Allan felt that his steamship line would get no fair play from the Grand Trunk Railway Company, but that all its efforts would be directed to sending the current of freight and passengers by the new line. He therefore took up warmly the Northern Colonization Road, which is intended to connect Montreal with Ottawa. He encouraged the North Shore Railway, which is the one to connect Montreal and Quebec, and he also became party to a project for building a railway from Ottawa to Toronto by an interior route, thus establishing a rival line to the Grand Trunk Railway from Toronto to Quebec.

His connection with these lines made him, as I have said, the representative man in Lower Canada, and his support was of great consequence to Sir George Cartier and the French Canadian wing of the Government.

A coolness had arisen between them, as Sir George was believed, justly or unjustly, not to favour the Northern Colonization Road. He had, from its inception, been intimately connected, professionally and otherwise, with the Grand Trunk Railway, and was charged by his countrymen with throwing cold water on all rival schemes. Sir George, however, finally agreed to give his influence and countenance to the Northern Colonization Railway, and the other roads with which Sir Hugh Allan had, as I have mentioned, connected himself.

These roads, it must be remembered, did not form portion of the Pacific Railway scheme, and the Canadian Government had no connection with them. The Northern Colonization Railway was incorporated by an Act of the Legislature of the province of Quebec, and Sir Hugh Allan was naturally anxious to obtain the powerful support and influence of Sir George, with the Government and Legislature of that province, in order to obtain aid in money and lands.

This being understood between them, Sir Hugh gave his strong support, as he had done previously for many years, to Sir George Cartier and his friends at the general election.

While this matter was being arranged at Montreal, I was at Toronto pressing the amalgamation, with good hope of success, and Mr. Abbott came up from Montreal, as agent for Sir Hugh Allan, to negotiate the details. Mr. Macpherson and he nearly came to terms, the only question really in difference between them being the presidency.

Such being the case, I considered that the amalgamation would be carried out, but, as the elections were then going on, it was felt to be impossible to enter into the details until they were finished.

And now as to the expenditure of money at the elections. In Canada, as in England, elections cannot be conducted without expenditure of money. There are legitimate expenses which must be incurred by those candidates who are resolved in no way to infringe the law; and the legal expenditure in the rural constituencies, which are of large area, with bad roads and a sparse and scattered population, is necessarily large.

In addition to strictly legal disbursements, there is a cause of expense which, though against the letter of the law, has by all parties been considered necessary, and the law is in this particular a dead letter—that is, the conveyance of voters to the polls. By universal consent this seems to have been considered so necessary, that never in my experience of twenty years has the hiring of carriages for that purpose been pressed before a committee on controverted elections. At every general election in Canada, therefore, political parties have always created funds for the purpose of assisting their candidates. At this particular election we had every reason to expect a stern contest, especially in the province of Ontario. . . .

As Your Excellency has perhaps had an opportunity of knowing, I had been for some time desirous of quitting official life, believing that I required, and had earned, a night of rest. My colleagues, however, as one man, stated that they would not go into the contest without me, and I nerved myself for the struggle.

From my point of view, I considered that on the result of the elections depended the continuance of Confederation. I may be wrong, but my opinion then was, and still is, that in the hands of the present Opposition, connected with and supported, as they are, by the "alien," "annexation," and "independent" elements, Confederation would not last ten years.

We had, amidst great difficulties, administered the affairs of Canada for five years, under the new constitution, with less friction than could have been anticipated. We had soothed provincial jealousies and ambitions, and conciliated the recalcitrant provinces, but still the embers of disunion were hot. I thought that with five years more over our heads we might safely consider that the gristle had hardened into bone, and the union been thoroughly cemented.

When, therefore, Sir George Cartier and I parted at Ottawa, he to go to Montreal, and I to Toronto, I asked him to do what he could with our friends in his province in the way of getting us pecuniary subscriptions to our central fund at Toronto. . . . Sir Hugh's name was, of course, mentioned, as being the richest man in Canada, and the one most interested in procuring the return of members in favour of the large, I may say, the Imperial policy which had characterized our administration. Aid had come to the fund from Montreal from several quarters, and I was not surprised to receive a communication from Sir Hugh Allan, that he would contribute twenty-five thousand dollars to the Ontario fund.

As regards myself, I was made the medium through which the subscriptions were paid, but it might, had he so chosen, have been remitted through any other channel.

I did not consider it at all an unusually large subscription from a man of his wealth. Others, with not a twentieth part of his means, subscribed from five to ten thousand dollars. . . .

I may say here, that no portion of the election fund, whether subscribed by Sir Hugh Allan or any one else, was used in my own election. I paid all the expenses of that contest, which was a severe, and, for a small constituency, a costly one.

I had forgotten to state, in the first part of my narrative, that it was not until the 26th July, 1872, when my own election was going on at Kingston, that I gave up the idea of effecting an amalgamation between the two companies before the conclusion of the election.

On that day I saw Mr. Macpherson, and the consequence of our conversation was, that I sent to Sir George Cartier the following telegram:—

"Have seen Macpherson. He has no personal ambition, but cannot, in justice to Ontario, concede any preference to Quebec in the matter of the presidency, or in any other particular. He says the question about the presidency should be left to the Board. Under these circumstances I authorize you to assure Allan that the influence of the Government will be exercised to secure him the position of president, the other terms to be as agreed upon between Macpherson and Abbott, and the whole matter to be kept quiet until after the election, then the two gentlemen to meet the Privy Council at Ottawa and settle the terms of a provisional agreement. This is the only practical solution of the difficulty, and should be accepted at once by Allan. Answer."

On the 30th, I received a letter from Sir Hugh Allan, stating that he had, on that day, made an arrangement with Sir George Cartier respecting the position of his company with respect to the Pacific Railway, to the effect, among other things, that, if the attempts at amalgamation failed, the construction of the railway should be confided to the Canadian Pacific Railway Company, of which he was the head. He did not send me a copy of his arrangement with Sir George, but merely stated what he considered its purport.

I at once saw that, if Sir George had entered into any such arrangement, he had made a grievous mistake, which the Government could not too soon repudiate. I immediately telegraphed him that I could not agree to any such arrangement, and that I would go down to Montreal the following night and see him on the subject.

On receiving my message, Sir George communicated it to Sir Hugh Allan, and it was then agreed that the arrangement should be considered as waste paper, and that the whole matter should stand over until after the elections, and be considered as resting on the basis of my telegram of the 26th.

I may say here, *par parenthèse,* that, on reference to the arrangement which Sir George made, he did not profess to bind the Government, but merely stated that he would use his influence to have it carried out. He, of course, had no power to make an arrangement on behalf of the Government, not having been authorized to do so.

It is too evident, however, from the evidence that has come out before the Commissioners, that Sir Hugh Allan took undue advantage of the failing health and waning mental faculties of Sir George.

After this, on securing my own election, I went to Toronto for the purpose of aiding my friends. The contest over the whole province, as was anticipated, proved to be severe in the extreme, and we were getting the worst of it. Every member of the Ontario Government went into the field, either as a candidate or a political agent, and its whole power was used to defeat my friends. . . .

Among others, I wrote to Sir George Cartier to procure from Sir Hugh Allan ten thousand dollars more, and again to Mr. Abbott. In writing to Sir George, I was quite unaware of the extent to which he had committed himself in Montreal. His persistence in offering for East Montreal, against all advice, was most distressing. It was known that, if elected at all, it must be after an enormously expensive contest, and I pressed him to take a rural constituency, where he would have been returned by acclamation.

Not until after his death, and the evidence was produced, were any of his colleagues aware of his insane course. As I have already said, it showed too clearly that mind had broken down as well as body. Of course, I can only say this to you, as I would rather suffer any consequences than cast any reflections on his memory before the public, or say anything that would have even the appearance of an attempt to transfer any blame that may attach to these transactions to one who is no longer here to speak for himself.

No member of the Government here knew or had any suspicion of the nature of the arrangement made between Sir George and Sir Hugh Allan, or of the papers signed by the former, until they were recently published. I certainly did not. . . .

Sir Hugh Allan . . . knew, before he subscribed or paid any money, the extent of the interest which his company would have in the road. It would be neither more nor less than that agreed upon between Mr. Abbott on his behalf, and Mr. Macpherson as the representative of the other company.

Sir Hugh Allan's position with regard to the Pacific Railway was, therefore, assured beyond a doubt, if the construction of the line went on at all. His danger was that, if the Opposition carried the country at the elections, they would reverse the whole railway policy of Canada. . . . if the construction of the Pacific Railway were abandoned or even postponed, the detriment to Sir Hugh Allan's interest would have been enormous. . . . but, if the Pacific Railway were once constructed, there would be ample work for both in the future, as well as for Sir Hugh's fleet of steamships.

It was, therefore, of importance, to his interests and the undertaking with which he had so connected himself, that a Parliament favourable to such enterprises, and to the development of the country thereby, should be elected, and, as a man of business, he expended his money accordingly. And it suited the purposes of the Ministerial party to accept his subscription, as well as the subscriptions of others.

The Conservative party in England does not repudiate the action of the brewers and distillers and the Association of Licensed Victuallers in electing candidates in their interests, and we did not repudiate or reject the influence of the railway interest. Our misfortune was that, by the base betrayal of these private communications, the names of certain members of the Government, including myself, were mixed up in the obtaining of these subscriptions. Had this betrayal not taken place, it would have been only known that Sir Hugh Allan, and the railways with which he had been connected, had taken a decided line in supporting one party in preference to another, by their influence and money.

c. Lord Dufferin's Assessment

. . . What I feel is simply this—that although it has been distinctly proved that in numerous respects you have been the victim of the most atrocious calumnies—that your personal honour is as stainless as it has ever been—that in spite of many inducements to the contrary, in spite of Cartier's weakness, you have religiously protected the interests of Canada both against the American speculators who addressed you, and against the approaches of Sir Hugh Allan—that although it has evidently never entered into your thoughts to make a single illegitimate concession in consideration of the support and assistance you expected on other grounds to receive from Allan—it is still an indisputable and patent fact that you and some of your colleagues have been the channels through which extravagant sums of money—derived from a person with whom you were negotiating on the part of the Dominion—were distributed throughout the constituencies of Ontario and Quebec, and have been applied to purposes forbidden by the statutes.

This circumstance carries with it the further ill effect of rendering the arbitrament of Parliament itself untrustworthy.

In acting as you have, I am well convinced that you have only followed a traditional practice, and that probably your political opponents have resorted with equal freedom to the same expedients, but as Minister of Justice, and the official guardian and protector of the laws, your responsibilities are exceptional, and your immediate and personal connection with what has occurred, cannot but fatally affect your position as a minister.

I need not say what distress I experience in making this communication to you. Independent of the personal attachment I feel towards you, I have always had and still have the greatest faith and confidence in your ability, patriotism, integrity and statesmanship. I believe there is no one in the country capable of administering its affairs to greater advantage than yourself. It is to you in fact that Canada owes its existence, and your name will be preserved in history as the father and founder of the Dominion. But no considerations of this kind are sufficient, I fear, to affect the present situation, controlled, as it is, by a special and immediate necessity. . . .

XIII:2 SUCCESS: THE CANADIAN PACIFIC RAILWAY CHARTER, 1880

Macdonald made no mistakes after being given a second chance by the voters in 1878. An agreement was made in 1880 with an experienced, largely Canadian group of railway men to build the line. The charter was granted early in 1881 and construction began immediately. On November 7, 1885, the last spike was driven in the Canadian Pacific Railway.

It was one of the greatest achievements in Canadian history, but not solely the work of private enterprise. These excerpts from the charter indicate the extreme generosity of the federal government in its eagerness to assure the project's success.

7. The Railway constructed under the terms hereof shall be the property of the Company: and pending the completion of the Eastern and Central sections, the Government shall transfer to the Company the possession and right to work and run the several portions of the Canadian Pacific Railway already constructed or as the same shall be completed. And upon the completion of the Eastern and Central sections, the Government shall convey to the Company, with a suitable number of station buildings and with water service (but without equipment), those portions of the Canadian Pacific Railway constructed or to be constructed by the Government which shall then be completed; and upon completion of the remainder of the portion of railway to be constructed by the Government, that portion shall also be conveyed to the Company, and the Canadian Pacific Railway shall become, and be thereafter the absolute property of the Company. And the Company shall thereafter and forever efficiently maintain, work and run the Canadian Pacific Railway.

9. In consideration of the premises, the Government agree to grant to the Company a subsidy in money of $25,000,000, and in land of 25,000,000 acres, for which subsidies the construction of the Canadian Pacific Railway shall be completed and the same shall be equipped, maintained and operated, the said subsidies respectively to be paid and granted as the work of construction shall proceed, in manner and upon the conditions following, . . .

10. In further consideration of the premises the Government shall also grant to the Company the lands required for the roadbed of the railway, and for its stations, station grounds, workshops, dock ground and water frontage at the termini on navigable waters, buildings, yards, and other appurtenances required for the convenient and effectual con-

struction and working of the railway, in so far as such land shall be vested in the Government. And the Government shall also permit the admission free of duty, of all steel rails, fish plates and other fastenings, spikes, bolts and nuts, wire, timber and all material for bridges, to be used in the original construction of the railway, and of a telegraph line in connection therewith, and all telegraphic apparatus required for the first equipment of such telegraph line. And will convey to the Company, at cost price, with interest, all rails and fastenings bought in or since the year 1879, and other materials for construction in the possession of or purchased by the Government at a valuation; such rails, fastenings and materials not being required by it for the construction of the said Lake Superior and Western sections.

11. The grant of land hereby agreed to be made to the Company, shall be so made in alternate sections of 640 acres each, extending back 24 miles deep, on each side of the railway, from Winnipeg to Jasper House, in so far as such lands shall be vested in the Government, the Company receiving the sections bearing uneven numbers. But should any of such sections consist in a material degree of land not fairly fit for settlement, the Company shall not be obliged to receive them as part of such grant, and the deficiency thereby caused and any further deficiency which may arise from the insufficient quantity of land along the said portion of railway, to complete the said 25,000,000 acres, or from the prevalence of lakes and water stretches in the sections granted (which lakes and water stretches shall not be computed in the acreage of such sections), shall be made up from other portions to be selected by the Company in the tract known as the Fertile Belt, that is to say the land lying between parallels 49 and 57 degrees of north latitude or elsewhere at the option of the Company by the grant therein of similar alternate sections extending back 24 miles deep on each side of any branch line or lines of railway to be located by the Company, . . .

13. The Company shall have the right subject to the approval of the Governor in Council to lay out and locate the

line of the railway hereby contracted for, as they may see fit, preserving the following terminal points, namely: from Callander station to the point of junction with the Lake Superior section; and from Selkirk to the junction with the Western section at Kamloops by way of the Yellow Head Pass.

15. For 20 years from the date hereof, no line of railway shall be authorised by the Dominion Parliament to be constructed South of the Canadian Pacific Railway, from any point at or near the Canadian Pacific Railway except such line as shall run South West, or to the Westward of South West: nor to within fifteen miles of Latitude 49. And in the establishment of any new Province in the North-West Territories, provision shall be made for continuing such prohibition after such establishment until the expiration of the said period.

16. The Canadian Pacific Railway, and all stations and station grounds, workshops, buildings, yards and other property, rolling stock and appurtenances required and used for the construction and working thereof, and the capital stock of the Company shall be forever free from taxation by the Dominion, or by any Province hereafter to be established or by any Municipal Corporation therein, and the lands of the Company, in the North-West Territories, until they are either sold or occupied, shall also be free from such taxation for 20 years after the grant thereof from the Crown. . . .

XIII:3 MACDONALD INTRODUCES THE NATIONAL POLICY, 1878

Nationalist economic policies for Canada were a logical consequence of 1867's decision to build a nation. As early as 1870 the Conservative party was beginning to discuss tariff protection. In the face of the depression of the 1870's, coupled with the failure of all efforts to renew the reciprocity agreement with the United States, protection became a burning issue in Canada. In 1878, while still leader of the Opposition, Macdonald introduced the new Conservative

policy. In this excerpt from his speech he explains the
benefits Canada could expect from a "National
Policy," and at the same time tries to evade charges
that he intends a drastic change in the tariff. The
National Policy was put into effect in 1879 and has
been accepted in principle by most subsequent Canadian Governments.

I move: That . . . this House is of the opinion that
the welfare of Canada requires the adoption of a National
Policy, which, by a judicious readjustment of the Tariff, will
benefit and foster the agricultural, the mining, the manufacturing and other interests of the Dominion; that such a policy
will retain in Canada thousands of our fellow countrymen
now obliged to expatriate themselves in search of the employment denied them at home, will restore prosperity to our
struggling industries, now so sadly depressed, will prevent
Canada from being made a sacrifice market, will encourage
and develop an active interprovincial trade, and moving (as
it ought to do) in the direction of a reciprocity of tariffs with
our neighbours, so far as the varied interests of Canada may
demand, will greatly tend to procure for this country,
eventually, a reciprocity of trade.

. . . I say then that, if our manufacturers had a reasonable
protection, if they had a hold upon our four millions of
people in the same way as the manufacturers in the United
States, then there would be a basis whereby they might be
enabled to go in by degrees and develop their resources like
those of the United States, who, as I have pointed out, can
compete with and undersell England in every part of the
world. The consequence of carrying out the principle of
Free-trade to its utmost extent will prevent capital from being
generated to any appreciable degree. As John Stuart Mill
said in the celebrated passage so often quoted: the very fact
that a nation commenced a particular industry first gives
them a control over that industry. By getting the start in this
way, capital is generated and a system of manufacture is
formed which will prevent any rivals from successfully com-

peting with them. So long as we have a Free-trade system, we can only have substantially one description of industry, and that is—agriculture. . . . But no nation has arisen which had only agriculture as its industry. There must be a mixture of industries to bring out the national mind and the national strength and to form a national character. . . .

. . . We must, by every reasonable means, employ our people, not in one branch of industry, not merely as farmers, as tillers of the soil, but we must bring out every kind of industry, we must develop the minds of the people and their energies. Every man is not fitted to be a farmer, to till the soil; one man has a constructive genius, another is an artist, another has an aptitude for trade, another is a skilful mechanic—all these men are to be found in a nation, and, if Canada has only one branch of industry to offer them, if these men cannot find an opportunity in their own country to develop the skill and genius with which God has gifted them, they will go to a country where their abilities can be employed, as they have gone from Canada to the United States.

Having said so much about a National Policy, I will call the attention of the House to what that policy is. It should consist of a judicious readjustment of the tariff which would benefit and foster the agricultural, the mining, the manufacturing, and other interests of the Dominion; a judicious readjustment of the tariff will mean, to a certain extent, an increased duty upon certain articles; upon those articles which we can produce ourselves, which this country is fit to produce, which our clime can produce, which our people are able to manufacture. . . .

XIV. The West And Louis Riel

XIV: 1 RED RIVER REBELS, 1870

The basic cause of the Red River Rebellion of 1870 was the total failure of the parties negotiating the sale of the West to Canada—the Hudson's Bay Company, the Imperial government, the Canadian government—to discuss the change of government with the settlers in Red River.

The Métis "nation" in Red River, anxious to maintain its language, religion and land holdings, was organized by Louis Riel to oppose the establishment of the new government. The new governor, William McDougall, was barred by the Métis from crossing the border, but nevertheless, proclaimed his authority over the West on December 1, 1869. In response, Riel organized a Provisional Government and issued the following *Declaration of the People of Rupert's Land and the North-West* to justify the action.

Whereas, it is admitted by all men, as a fundamental principle, that the public authority commands the obedience and respect of its subjects. It is also admitted, that a people, when it has no Government, is free to adopt one form of Government, in preference to another, to give or to refuse allegiance to that which is proposed. In accordance with the above first principle, the people of this country had obeyed and respected the authority to which the circumstances surrounding its infancy compelled it to be subject. . . .

. . . this people, ever actuated by the above-mentioned principles, had generously supported the aforesaid Government [the Hudson's Bay Company] and gave to it a faithful allegiance, when, contrary to the law of nations, in March, 1869, that said Government surrendered and transferred to Canada all the rights which it had, or pretended to have, in this Territory, by transactions with which the people were considered unworthy to be made acquainted.

And, whereas, it is also generally admitted that a people is at liberty to establish any form of government it may consider suited to its wants, as soon as the power to which it was subject abandons it, or attempts to subjugate it, without its consent to a foreign power; and maintain, that no right can be transferred to such foreign power. Now, therefore, first, we, the representatives of the people, in Council assembled in Upper Fort Garry, on the 24th day of November, 1869, after having invoked the God of Nations, relying on these fundamental moral principles, solemnly declare, in the name of our constituents, and in our own names, before God and man, that, from the day on which the Government we had always respected abandoned us, by transferring to a strange power the sacred authority confided to it, the people of Rupert's Land and the North-West became free and exempt from all allegiance to the said Government. Second. That we refuse to recognize the authority of Canada, which pretends to have a right to coerce us, and impose upon us a despotic form of government still more contrary to our rights and interests as British subjects, than was that Government to which we had subjected ourselves, through necessity, up to a recent date. Thirdly. That, by sending an expedition on the 1st of November, ult., charged to drive back Mr. William McDougall and his companions, coming in the name of Canada, to rule us with the rod of despotism, without previous notification to that effect, we have acted conformably to that sacred right which commands every citizen to offer energetic opposition to prevent this country from being enslaved. Fourth. That we continue, and shall continue, to oppose, with all our strength, the establishing of the Canadian authority in our country, under the announced form; . . . and, furthermore, we do declare and proclaim, in the name of the people of Rupert's Land and the North-West, that we have, on the said 24th day of November, 1869, above mentioned, established a Provisional Government, and hold it to be the only and lawful authority now in existence in Rupert's Land and the North-West which claims the obedience and respect of the people; that, meanwhile, we hold ourselves in readiness to enter in such negotiations with the Canadian Government as may be favourable for the good government and prosperity of this people. In support of this declaration, relying on the protection of Divine Providence, we mutually pledge ourselves, on oath, our lives, our fortunes, and our sacred honor, to each other.

Issued at Fort Garry, this Eighth day of December, in the year of our Lord One thousand eight hundred and sixty-nine.

JOHN BRUCE, Pres.
LOUIS RIEL, Sec.

XIV:2 THE METIS' "LIST OF RIGHTS"

The demands of the Métis, as shown in this "List of Rights," to be used in bargaining with Canada, indicate both the fears that had led them to rebel and their determination to win solid guarantees for the future. Revised to include denominational schools, this list was substantially accepted by the Canadian government, and Red River entered Confederation as the Province of Manitoba.

I. THAT the Territories heretofore known as Rupert's Land and the North-West, shall not enter into the Confederation of the Dominion of Canada, except as a Province; to be styled and known as the Province of Assiniboia, and with all the rights and privileges common to the different Provinces of the Dominion.

II. THAT we have two Representatives in the Senate, and four in the House of Commons of Canada, until such time as an increase of population entitle the Province to a greater Representation.

IV. THAT the sum of Eighty Thousand (80,000) dollars be paid annually by the Dominion Government to the local Legislature of this Province.

V. THAT all properties, rights and privileges engaged [sic: enjoyed] by the people of this Province, up to the date of our entering into the Confederation, be respected; and that the arrangement and confirmation of all customs, usages and privileges be left exclusively to the local Legislature.

VII. THAT a sum of money equal to eighty cents per head of the population of this Province, be paid annually by the Canadian Government to the local Legislature of the said Province; until such time as the said population shall have reached six hundred thousand.

X. THAT the bargain of the Hudson's Bay Company with respect to the transfer of the Government of this country to the Dominion of Canada, be annulled; so far as it interferes with the rights of the people of Assiniboia, and so far as it would affect our future relations with Canada.

XI. THAT the local Legislature of the Province of Assiniboia shall have full control over all the public lands of the Province . . .

XIII. THAT treaties be concluded between Canada and the different Indian tribes of the Province of Assiniboia, by and with the advice and cooperation of the local Legislature of this Province.

XIV. THAT an uninterrupted steam communication from Lake Superior to Fort Garry be guaranteed, to be completed within the space of five years.

XV. THAT all public buildings, bridges, roads and other public works, be at the cost of the Dominion Treasury.

XVI. THAT the English and French languages be common in the Legislature and in the Courts, and that all public documents, as well as all acts of the Legislature be published in both languages.

XVII. THAT whereas the French and English speaking people of Assiniboia are so equally divided as to number, yet so united in their interests and so connected by commerce, family connections and other political and social relations, that it has, happily, been found impossible to bring them into hostile collision,—although repeated attempts have been made by designing strangers, for reasons known to themselves, to bring about so ruinous and disastrous an event;—and whereas after all the troubles and apparent dissentions of the past, —the result of misunderstanding among themselves; they have —as soon as the evil agencies referred to above were removed, —become as united and friendly as ever;—therefore, as a means to strengthen this union and friendly feeling among all classes, we deem it expedient and advisable,—That the Lieutenant-Governor, who may be appointed for the Province of Assiniboia, should be familiar with both the French and English languages.

XVIII. THAT the Judge of the Supreme Court speak the English and French languages.

XIX. THAT all debts contracted by the Provisional Government of the Territory of the North-West, now called Assiniboia, in consequence of the illegal and inconsiderate measures adopted by Canadian officials to bring about a civil war in our midst, be paid out of the Dominion Treasury; and that none of the members of the Provisional Government, or any of those acting under them, be in any way held liable or responsible with regard to the movement, or any of the actions which led to the present negotiations. . . .

XIV: 3 ONTARIO'S REACTION

The biggest mistake of Riel's career was his "execution" of a troublesome, Ontario Protestant, Thomas Scott, on March 4, 1870. At the time it was an effective show of strength in Red River, but Scott's death made Riel the object of Ontario's undying hatred. The outcry led directly to Riel's long exile (his amnesty finally came into effect in 1880) and indirectly to his execution in 1885. The impact of Scott's execution on Ontario opinion is shown in this excerpt from a speech by Malcolm Cameron, a Member of Parliament, at the Toronto meeting held to celebrate the return of several English Canadian settlers from Red River.

Hon. M. C. Cameron: after a few introductory remarks, said:
. . . He never could understand how those free men of the North-West, who claimed a right to enjoy their liberties and institutions untrammelled, expected to hold them by trampling on the rights of others; and it did seem to him to be the most gross sort of impudence on the part of these men led by Riel to resort to arms, to control the affairs in Red River, to set the British Government and the people of Canada at defiance, and to take the life of a man who endeavoured to remain true to his colours and allegiance, and who asked merely the rights for himself that Mr. Riel claimed. (Cheers)
. . . Riel at first assumed to stand up for what was termed the attainment of the rights of the settlers of Red River Territory—though the act displayed a great deal of folly, yet at the same time it showed that he and his followers had something of the spirit of men to assert that they had rights and were prepared to take up arms to defend them. But the very moment he went from that position and, instead of standing merely in defence of their rights and property that they might have thought, no matter how foolishly, was being assailed, he overstepped the bounds of reason and showed himself a black-hearted and cruel traitor. (Cheers) It was a

matter of regret, and he was sure every heart in the crowd before him would swell with indignation at the thought, that a man who had connections in the city of Toronto—that a courageous, manly, noble-hearted fellow should have been taken out in cold blood while in the heighth and heigh-day of life, to be shot like a dog for asserting the very rights and freedom that Mr. Riel claimed he had a right to maintain. (Cheers) . . .

The act which Riel had committed, if it had been done in our midst would have been considered a cold and cruel murder, and it was none the less murder because it was committed in Red River Territory. This man Riel asserted that he had risen in protection of the rights of the people; but instead he despoiled the people of their freedom, seized and confiscated the property of the Hudson Bay Company, and in every respect acted in a manner which, if done here, would consign him to a dungeon as a felon for whom none would feel sympathy.

If he could only see those who were present at this meeting, he would see that there were enough there to sweep the people of Red River from one end of the Territory to the other— (Cheers)—and if he understood that we had in Ontario a body of men feeling as this meeting did, intense indignation for his bloody act, he would understand that his reign was short, and his rule in Red River of but a temporary character.

[The meeting ended by resolving:]

That this meeting expresses the strongest indignation at the cold-blooded murder of poor Scott, and sympathizes deeply with his relatives and friends, and considers that it would be a gross injustice to the loyal inhabitants of Red River, humiliating to our national honour and contrary to British traditions for our Government to receive, negotiate, or treat with the emissaries of those who have robbed, imprisoned and murdered loyal Canadians, whose only fault was zeal for British institutions, whose only crime was devotion to the old flag.

XIV:4 THE CAUSES OF THE NORTH-WEST REBELLION, 1885

> Three factors combined to produce the agitation that led to the North-West rebellion of 1885—Indian misery, Métis discontent, and the hard times suffered by English settlers in the North-West. The problems of these groups are all illustrated in this petition sent to Ottawa in December, 1884, by white and Métis settlers in the North-West.

To His Excellency the Governor General of Canada, in Council.

We, the undersigned, your humble petitioners, would respectfully submit to Your Excellency-in-Council, the following as our grievances:

1. that the Indians are so reduced that the settlers in many localities are compelled to furnish them with food, partly to prevent them from dying at their doors, partly to preserve the peace of the territory;

2. that the Half-breeds of the territory have not received 240 acres of land each, as did the Manitoba Half-breeds;

3. that the Half-breeds who are in possession of tracts of land have not received patents therefor;

4. that the old settlers of the N.W.T. [North-West Territories] have not received the same treatment as the old settlers of Manitoba;

5. that the claims of settlers on odd numbers, prior to survey, and on reserves, prior to the proclamation of such reserves, are not recognized;

8. that settlers are charged dues on lumber, rails, and firewood required for home use;

9. that customs duties are levied on the necessaries of life;

14. that no effective measures have yet been taken to put the people of the North-West in direct communication with the European markets, via Hudson's Bay;

15. that settlers are exposed to coercion at elections, owing to the fact that votes are not taken by ballot;

17. . . . (h) that the N.W.T., although having a population of 60,000, are not yet granted responsible government, as was Manitoba when she had less than 12,000 of a population; (i) that the N.W.T. and its Premier Province [Manitoba] are not yet represented in the Cabinet, as are the Eastern Provinces; (j) that the North-West is not allowed the administration of its resources as are the eastern provinces and British Columbia. . . .

In conclusion, your petitioners would respectfully state that they are treated neither according to their privileges as British subjects nor according to the rights of people and that consequently as long as they are retained in those circumstances, they can be neither prosperous nor happy.

Your humble petitioners are of opinion that the shortest and most effectual methods of remedying these grievances would be to grant the N.W.T. responsible government with control of its own resources and just representation in the Federal Parliament and Cabinet.

Wherefor your petitioners humbly pray that Your Excellency in Council would be pleased to cause the introduction, at the coming session of Parliament, of a measure providing for the complete organization of the District of Saskatchewan as a province, and that they be allowed as in '70, to send delegates to Ottawa with their Bill of Rights; whereby an understanding may be arrived at as to their entry into confederation, with the constitution of a free province. . . .

XIV:5 LOUIS RIEL ON TRIAL

When the newly returned Riel assumed leadership of the disturbance, his moderate supporters fell away, leaving the Métis and the Indians to attempt to re-create 1870. This time the rebellion quickly became violent, and was vigorously suppressed. At Riel's trial his lawyers pleaded insanity. But Riel damaged his own defence by the relative coherence of his testimony before the court. These excerpts from his lengthy speech contain the major points of his own defence.

The six English Protestant jurors found him guilty of treason; the judge sentenced him to death. (For Quebec's reaction to Riel's execution see document XVII:3 on page 192.)

Your Honors, Gentlemen of the Jury: It would be easy for me to-day to play insanity, because the circumstances are such as to excite any man and under the natural excitement of what is taking place to-day (I cannot speak English very well, but I am trying to do so because most of those here speak English). Under the excitement which my trial causes me would justify me not to appear as usual, but with my mind out of its ordinary condition. I hope, with the help of God, I will maintain calmness and decorum as suits the Honorable Court, this Honorable Jury. . . .

Your Honors, Gentlemen of the Jury: If I was a man of to-day perhaps it would be presumptuous to speak in that way, but the truth is good to say, and it is said in a proper manner, and it is not without presumption, it is not because I have been libelled for 15 years that I do not believe myself something. I know that through the grace of God I am the founder of Manitoba; I know that though I have no open road for my influence, I have big influence concentrated, as a big amount of vapour in an engine. I believe by what I suffered for 15 years, by what I have done for Manitoba and the people of the North-West that my words are worth something, if I give offence I do not speak to insult. . . .

As to religion what is my belief? What is my insanity about that? My insanity, Your Honors, Gentlemen of the Jury, is that I wish to leave Rome aside inasmuch as it is the cause of division between the Catholics and Protestants. I did not wish to force my views because, in Batoche, to the Half-breeds that followed me I used the word *Carte blanche*. If I have any influence in the New World it is to help in that way and even if it takes two hundred years to become practical, then after my death that will bring out practical results, and then my children will shake hands with the Protestants of the New World in a friendly manner. I do not wish those evils which exist in Europe to be continued as much as I can influence it, among the Half-breeds. I do not wish that to be repeated in America, that work is not the work of some days or some years it is the work of hundreds of years.

My condition is helpless, so helpless that my good lawyers and they have done it with conviction (Mr. Fitzpatrick in his beautiful speech has proved he believed I was insane), my condition seems to be so helpless that they have recourse to try and prove insanity to try and save me that way. If I am insane, of course I don't know it, it is a property of insanity to be unable to know it. But what is the kind of mission that I have? Practical results. It is said that I had myself acknowledged as a prophet by the Half-breeds. The Half-breeds have some intelligence. Capt. Young who has been so polite and gentle during the time I was under his care, said that what was done at Batoche from a military point of view was nice, that the line of defence was nice, that showed some intelligence. It is not to be supposed that the Half-breeds acknowledge me as a prophet if they had not seen that I could see something into the future. If I am blessed without measure I can see something into the future, we all see into the future more or less. As what kind of a prophet would I come? Would it be a prophet who could all the time have a stick in his hand and threatening, a prophet of evil? If the Half-breeds have acknowledged me as a prophet, if on the other side priests come and say that I am polite, if there are general officers, good men, come into this box and prove that I am polite, prove that I am decent in my manners, in combining all together you have a decent prophet. . . .

I am glad that the Crown have proved that I am the leader of the Half-breeds in the North-West. I will perhaps be one day acknowledged as more than a leader of the Half-breeds, and if I am I will have an opportunity of being acknowledged as a leader of good in this great country. . . .

. . . If it is any satisfaction to the doctor to know what kind of insanity I have, if they are going to call my pretentions insanity, I say, humbly, through the grace of God I believe I am the prophet of the New World. . . .

The only things I would like to call your attention to, before you retire to deliberate, are: 1st. That the House of Commons, Senate, and ministers of the Dominion who make laws for this land and govern it are no representation whatever of the people of the North-West.

2ndly. That the North-West Council generated by the federal Government has the great defect of its parent.

3rdly. The number of members elected for the Council by the people make it only a sham representative legislature and no representative Government at all.

British civilisation, which rules today the world, and the British constitution has defined such Government as this is which rules the North-West Territory as irresponsible Government, which plainly means that there is no responsibility, and by the science which has been shown here yesterday you are compelled to admit it, there is no responsibility, it is insane.

Good sense combined with scientific theories lead to the same conclusion.

By the testimony laid before you during my trial, witnesses on both sides made it certain that petition after petition has been sent to the Federal Government, and so irresponsible is that Government to the North-West, that in the course of several years beside doing nothing to satisfy the people of this great land, it has even hardly been able to answer once or to give a single response. That fact would indicate absolute lack of responsibility and therefore insanity complicated with paralysis.

The ministers of an insane and irresponsible Government and its offspring the North-West Council made up their mind to answer my petitions by surrounding me slyly and by attempting to jump upon me suddenly and upon my people in the Saskatchewan. Happily when they appeared and showed their teeth to devour, I was ready; that is what is called my crime of high treason and for which they hold me today. Oh, my good Jurors, in the name of Jesus Christ the only one who can save and help me, they have tried to tear me to pieces.

If you take the plea of the defence, that I am not responsible for my acts, acquit me completely, since I have been quarrelling with an insane and irresponsible Government. If you pronounce in favour of the Crown, which contends that I am responsible, acquit me all the same. You are perfectly justified in declaring that having my reason and sound mind I have acted reasonably and in self-defence, while the Government, my accuser, being irresponsible and consequently insane, cannot but have acted wrong, and if high treason there is, it must be on its side and not on my part. . . .

XIV: 6 RIEL'S PLANS FOR THE NEW WORLD

> Was Riel insane? Possibly today he would have been acquitted on that ground. Always intensely religious, Riel had fallen more and more into grandiose mystical delusions after 1875. In 1876-77 he spent 20 months in mental asylums. In one of his stages of religious fervour while in prison in 1885, he wrote this letter to Archbishop Taché, his lifelong spiritual guide. The letter contains Riel's vision of his "divine" mission. Of course, the Church had by this time often denounced his views. After his trial, however, Riel renounced all of these heresies and died a faithful Roman Catholic.

. . . By the simple lights even of common sense, it is reasonable to suppose that the jealous spirit of God has been unable to remain in Rome, after the latter had been finally doomed to the prostitution of the anti-religious ideas which unfortunately are raging through Italy and France today. Rome is to Jesus Christ like unto a ravished bride. On another side how could the fullness of the gifts of the Papacy be satisfied to remain in a bishop attached to the area of Rome? Even if the pope were, quite apart from that, personally entirely holy, the mere fact of his residence in the midst of the abominations of desolation naturally seems contrary to the good pleasure of God. But just as a person in good health cannot remain in an unhealthy place without being infected himself, thus in the present condition of things which surround him, the bishop of Rome cannot prevent his moral state from being gravely affected and damaged. . . .

The comforting Holy Spirit of Jesus Christ has chosen another vicar for himself. He had dwelt in Bishop Ignace Bourget from 8 December, 1875. It is pleasing to God that we should consider the holy Archbishop as the first successor of St. Peter in spirit and in truth, in the New World. This is what Divine Providence in its mercy helped me to proclaim with the Métis in Saskatchewan.

But since the death of the good Archbishop Bourget, God has cast the eyes of his unutterable goodness upon you. He wants to reward you before the whole world and to render unto you an hundredfold the worldly goods which you have sacrificed for him these forty years, to serve and to please him. You are by divine election the true successor of Archbishop Bourget. And yet while you were rendering the last honours to the mortal remains of this great servant of God, you became yourself for the happiness of many and for the despair of none, the vicar of Jesus Christ on earth. God has wished that I, captured in a terrible war of defence, and in the midst of the greatest dangers, should proclaim, assisted by his gracious succour and by the good faith of the Métis, the Pontificate of Ignace Bourget. In its mercy Providence has spared me, my wife, and my children from death, wounds, and misfortunes of all kinds. Providence has miraculously saved Gabriel Dumont and the existence of the Métis as a population. Let us render unto God eternal thanksgiving for this.

Now that I am imprisoned, accused of High Treason, with no means to defend myself, with no chance of having my witnesses and in such a situation that my best witnesses have fallen out with me, I entrust myself to this paternal providence of God who cares for everything and everyone: *and this day the 24 July, 1885,* I proclaim humbly from the confines of this padlocked prison of Regina that you are the Pontiff elected by God, to instruct, console, comfort, lead, bless and save through the grace of Jesus Christ, the New World.

The day that the Holy Pontifical Spirit adopted Archbishop Bourget, He deigned to choose at the same time Ville-Marie as the religious capital of this continent and the French Canadian people for his sacerdotal people. Today when this divine Spirit of consolation dwells in you, the Holy Spirit deigns to choose in advance the French Canadian Métis for his sacerdotal people and St-Boniface for his present city. After you, the Papacy will go back to Ville-Marie, to remain there fifteen months and a week of years, that is, 457 years, beginning 8 December, 1875. Then it will come back to continue the thread of your succession in Manitoba and will be there one thousand eight hundred and sixty-seven years.

Carte Blanche is granted to any Catholic to leave Rome. Having to proclaim this truth, it was fitting that I should have the courage of my faith and give the example. For this reason I have separated from Rome and have besought the Métis to do as I, if they so wished. It is also to forge onward, in deed as well as in word, that I have incited my brethren, the Métis of Saskatchewan, to recognize Archbishop Ignace Bourget as pontiff of the New World. . . .

. . . Our conditions would be that Canada with the Population living therein would take for itself one-seventh of the extent of the territory; and that for the remainder, it would agree to found a new Italy, a new Bavaria, a new Ireland, a new Poland, . . . Belgium is a country in which good principles find remarkable support. Would it not be lovely to see it reproduced, surrounded by the waters of the Pacific, in the cheerful island of Vancouver? And would it not be charming to see on the mainland across from it a new Judea arise, a Judea for the Jews who would agree to recognize Jesus Christ as the only Messiah, and to recognize you, Monseigneur, as the lawful guide of the faith? So that our brethren, the Protestant Christian, would not object to the sight of so many

Catholic establishments, the Swedes, the Norwegians, the Danes would have as well the pleasure of emigrating to English Columbia and of establishing there a new Sweden, a new Norway, and a new Denmark. . . .

While England and the English of Canada would be developing their great emigration and would be sending the immigrants in waves in every direction in British North America, your Eminence, sitting in the papal seat of the two Americas, would give the Catholic nations of Europe the signal to depart for the New World. The good Christians of France to whom the Faith remains dear and who daily experience greater and greater tribulation in the practice of their religion would leave for Canada. They would swell the provinces of Quebec and Manitoba. The Federal Power would become one of the most prosperous centres of the world; thanks to God, thanks to the Catholic Church of the New World, Apostolic and vital. . . .

The will of God is that Leo XIII himself grants you Full Power along with Rome; that he will come himself for a time, for some months, to Ville-Marie; that he will assemble at Ville-Marie the American episcopate; that he will have you recognized as their Archbishop of Universal Jurisdiction; that he will himself assist you in inviting the Catholic nations of Europe and in directing the flow of their precious emigration from this side of the Atlantic. . . .

Louis Riel

XV. The Rise Of The Provinces

XV:1 TWO CONCEPTS OF FEDERALISM

Canada's federal system was designed as a compromise between the vital need for a strong central authority and the equal necessity of preserving local autonomy (see document X:3 on page 120). Almost immediately after Confederation the two levels of government began to quarrel over their respective spheres of authority. These two selections present the two radically conflicting views of provincial status within the federal system held by the chief protagonists, the Macdonald government and Oliver Mowat's Ontario administration. Selection (a) is from a letter of Macdonald's and selection (b) is from a Toronto *Globe* editorial.

a. Sir John A. Macdonald

. . . I fully concur with you as to the apprehension that a conflict may, ere long, arise between the Dominion and the "States Rights" people. We must meet it however as best we may. By a firm yet patient course, I think the Dominion must win in the long run. The powers of the General Government are so much greater than those of the United States, in its relations with the local Governments, that the central power must win. . . .

My own opinion is that the General Government or

Parliament should pay no more regard to the status or position of the Local Governments than they would to the prospects of the ruling party in the corporation of Quebec or Montreal. . . .

b. The "Compact" Theory of Confederation

The Confederation has its origin in a bargain between certain Provinces, in which bargain the Provinces agreed to unite for certain purposes and to separate or continue separated for others. The Provinces party to the bargain were at the time of the compact independent nations in the sense that they enjoyed self-government subject to the Imperial veto upon their legislation, to the Imperial appointment of the Governor-General, and to the Queen's command of the forces. The Dominion was the creation of these Provinces; or, in other words, was created by the British Parliament at the request of the Provinces. The Dominion being non-existent at the time the bargain was made, was plainly not a party to the bargain. It cannot then, be a party to the revision of the bargain. The power to revise the created body must lie in the hands of those who created that body. The overwhelming majority of those who created the Dominion being in favour of the revision of the Confederation compact, the British Parliament is not entitled to look any further or to consult the wishes of the Dominion Government in the matter.

XV:2 THE PRIVY COUNCIL AND PROVINCIAL RIGHTS

As the final court of appeal for Canada until 1949, the Judicial Committee of the British Privy Council has played the key role in interpreting the British North America Act. Most experts agree that the Privy Council has strengthened the role of the provinces in the federal system far beyond the intent or the wording of the British North America Act. The three decisions below represent the most significant of the early cases. In *Russell v. the Queen* (a) the Council apparently supported the broad use of federal power under the "peace, order, and good government" provision of section 91. But a year later, in *Hodge v. the Queen* (b), the wording of the decision amounted to a recognition of the sovereign powers of the provinces within their own sphere. Finally, in the Local Prohibition case (c), the Council apparently reversed *Russell v. the Queen* by making the "peace, order, and good government" provision almost completely subordinate to the sphere of provincial authority.

a. Russell *v.* the Queen (1882)

. . . Few, if any, laws could be made by Parliament for the peace, order and good government of Canada which did not in some incidental way affect property and civil rights; and it could not have been intended, when assuring to the provinces exclusive legislative authority on the subjects of property and civil rights, to exclude the Parliament from the exercise of this general power whenever any such incidental interference would result from it. The true nature and character of the legislation in the particular instance under discussion must always be determined, in order to ascertain the class of subject to which it really belongs. . . .

b. Hodge *v.* the Queen (1883)

. . . It appears to their Lordships, however, that the objection thus raised by the appellants is founded on an entire misconception of the true character and position of the provincial legislatures. They are in no sense delegates of, or acting under any mandate from, the Imperial Parliament. When the British North America Act enacted that there should be a legislature for Ontario and that its legislative assembly should have exclusive authority to make laws for the province, and for provincial purposes in relation to the matters enumerated in section 92, it conferred powers not in any sense to be exercised by delegation from, or as agents of, the Imperial Parliament, but authority as plenary and as ample within the limits prescribed by section 92, as the Imperial Parliament, in the plenitude of its power, possessed and could bestow. Within these limits of subjects and area the local legislature is supreme, and has the same authority as the Imperial Parliament, or the Parliament of the Dominion. . . .

c. The Local Prohibition Case (Attorney-General for Ontario v. Attorney-General for Canada et al., 1896)

. . . The general authority given to the Canadian Parliament by the introductory enactments of section 91 is "to make laws for the peace, order and good government of Canada in relation to all matters not coming within the classes of subjects by this Act assigned exclusively to the legislatures of the provinces;" and it is declared, but not so as to restrict the generality of these words, that the exclusive authority of the Canadian Parliament extends to all matters coming within the classes of subjects which are enumerated in the clause. There may, therefore, be matters not included in the enumeration, upon which the Parliament of Canada has power to legislate because they concern the peace, order and good government of the Dominion. But to those matters which are not specified among the enumerated subjects of legislation, the exception from section 92, which is enacted by the concluding words of section 91, has no application, and, in legislating with regard to such matters the Dominion Parliament has no authority to encroach upon any class of subjects which is exclusively assigned to provincial legislatures by section 92. These enactments appear to their Lordships to indicate that the exercise of legislative power by the Parliament of Canada in regard to all matters not enumerated in section 91 ought to be strictly confined to such matters as are unquestionably of Canadian interest and importance and ought not to trench upon provincial legislation with respect to any of the classes of subjects enumerated in section 92. To attach any other construction to the general power which, in supplement of its enumerated powers, is conferred upon the Parliament of Canada by section 91 would, in their Lordships' opinion, not only be contrary to the intendment of the Act, but would practically destroy the autonomy of the provinces. If it were once conceded that the Parliament of Canada has authority to make laws applicable to the whole Dominion in relation to matters which, in each province, are substantially of local or private interest, upon the assumption that these matters also concern the peace, order and good government of the Dominion, there is hardly a subject enumerated in section 92 upon which it might not legislate, to the exclusion of the provincial legislatures. . . .

XV: 3 THE INTERPROVINCIAL CONFERENCE OF 1887

The constant strife between federal and provincial governments came to a head in 1887 when the Premiers of Ontario, Quebec, Nova Scotia, New Brunswick (all Liberals), and Manitoba met at Quebec in the first interprovincial conference. Their resolutions called for a major revision of the British North America Act. The following excerpt contains the most important of the resolutions, as well as a clear statement of the provinces' sense of their new power. Naturally, the Macdonald government ignored the resolutions.

Whereas, in framing the British North America Act 1867, and defining therein the limits of the Legislative and Executive powers and functions of the Federal and Provincial Legislatures and Governments, the authors of the Constitution performed a work, new, complex and difficult, and it was to be anticipated that experience in the working of the new system would suggest many needed changes: that twenty years' practical working of the Act has developed much friction between the Federal and Provincial Governments and Legislatures, has disclosed grave omissions in the provisions of the Act, and has shewn (when the language of the Act came to be judicially interpreted) that in many respects what was the common understanding and intention had not been expressed, and that important provisions in the Act are obscure as to their true intent and meaning; and whereas the preservation of Provincial autonomy is essential to the future well-being of Canada; and if such autonomy is to be maintained, it has become apparent that the Constitutional Act must be revised and amended; therefore the representatives and delegates of the Provinces of Ontario, Quebec, Nova Scotia, New Brunswick and Manitoba, duly accredited by their respective Governments, and in Conference assembled, believing that they express the views and wishes of the people of Canada, agree upon the following Resolutions as the basis upon which the Act should be amended; subject to the approval of the several Provincial Legislatures:

1. That by the British North America Act exclusive authority is expressly given to the Provincial Legislatures in relation to subjects enumerated in the 92nd section of the Act; that a previous section of the Act reserves to the Federal Government the legal power of disallowing at will all Acts passed by a Provincial Legislature; that this power of disallowance may be exercised so as to give to the Federal Government arbitrary control over legislation of the Provinces within their own sphere; and that the Act should be amended by taking away this power of disallowing Provincial Statutes, leaving to the people of each Province, through their representatives in the Provincial Legislature, the free exercise of their exclusive right of legislation on the subjects assigned to them subject only to disallowance by Her Majesty in Council as before Confederation; the power of disallowance to be exercised in regard to the Provinces upon the same principles as the same is exercised in the case of Federal Acts;

4. That a leading purpose of the Senate was to protect the interests of the respective Provinces as such; that a Senate to which the appointments are made by the Federal Government, and for life, affords no adequate security to the Provinces; and that, in case no other early remedy is provided, the British North America Act should be so amended as to

limit the term for which Senators hold office, and to give the choice, as vacancies occur, to the Province to which the vacancy belongs, until, as to any Province, one half of the members of the Senate representing such Province are Senators chosen by the Province; that thereafter the mode of selection be as follows: if the vacancy is occasioned by the death, resignation or otherwise of a Senator chosen by a Province, that Province to choose his successor; and if the vacancy is occasioned by the death, resignation or otherwise of any other Senator, the vacancy to be filled as now provided by the Act, but only for a limited term of years; . . .

XVI. The Problem
Of Canada's Destiny

XVI: 1 EDWARD BLAKE SUGGESTS INDEPENDENCE

Canada was still very much a British colony at Confederation. It was not long, however, before voices were heard demanding greater Canadian autonomy. This was one of the goals of the Canada First Movement. In this portion of his famous Aurora speech (1874), Edward Blake, the most brilliant of the Liberal party's leaders, seemed to support the Canada First position.

Let me turn to another question which has been adverted to on several occasions, as one looming in the not very distant future. I refer to the relations of Canada to the Empire. . . . Matters cannot drift much longer as they have drifted hitherto. The Treaty of Washington produced a very profound impression throughout this country. It produced a feeling that at no distant period the people of Canada would desire that they should have some greater share of control than they now have in the management of foreign affairs; that our Government should not present the anomaly which it now presents—a Government the freest, perhaps the most democratic in the world with reference to local and domestic matters, in which you rule yourselves as fully as any people in the world, while in your foreign affairs, your relations with other countries, whether peaceful or warlike, commercial or financial, or otherwise, you may have no more voice than the people of Japan. This, however, is a state of things of which you have no right to complain, because so long as you do not choose to undertake the responsibilities and burdens which attach to some share of control in these affairs, you cannot fully claim the rights and privileges of free-born Britons in such matters.

But how long is this talk in the newspapers and elsewhere, this talk which I find in very high places, of the desirability, aye, of the necessity of fostering a national spirit among the people of Canada, to be mere talk? . . .

. . . the time will come when that national spirit which has been spoken of will be truly felt among us, when we shall realize that we are four millions of Britons who are not free, when we shall be ready to take up that freedom, and to ask what the late Prime Minister of England assured us we should not be denied—our share of national rights. . . .

XVI: 2 GOLDWIN SMITH ADVOCATES UNION WITH THE UNITED STATES

As the grandiose plans for Canadian development languished toward the end of the 1880's, the old annexationist spirit was revived, part of it flowing into the movement for commercial union with the United States. The most articulate exponent of union in any form with the United States was Goldwin Smith, an English journalist and professor who had immigrated to Canada. At first Smith was a supporter of Canadian independence, but by 1891 he was convinced that Canada could not escape the magnetic pull of the United States. He set out his case in his book, *Canada and the Canadian Question*.

. . . That a union of Canada with the American Commonwealth, like that into which Scotland entered with England, would in itself be attended with great advantages cannot be questioned, whatever may be the considerations on the other side or the reasons for delay. It would give to the inhabitants of the whole Continent as complete a security for peace and immunity from war taxation as is likely to be attained by any community or group of communities on this side of the Millenium. Canadians almost with one voice say that it would greatly raise the value of property in Canada; in other words, that it would bring with it a great increase of prosperity. The writer has seldom heard this seriously disputed, while he has heard it admitted in the plainest terms by men who were strongly opposed to Union on political or sentimental grounds, and who had spent their lives in the service of Separation. The case is the same as that of Scotland or Wales in relation to the rest of the island of which they are parts, and upon their union with which their commercial prosperity depends. The Americans, on the other hand, would gain in full proportion as England gains by her commercial union with Wales and Scotland. These inducements are always present to the minds of the Canadian people, and they are specially present when the trade of Canada, with the rest of her Continent, is barred by such legislation as the M'Kinley Act, when her security is threatened by the imminence of war in Europe, or when from internal causes she happens to be acutely feeling the commercial atrophy to which her isolation condemns her. Canadians who live on the border, and who from the shape of the country form a large proportion of the population, have always before their eyes the fields and cities of a kindred people, whose immense prosperity they are prevented from sharing only by a political line, while socially, and in every other respect, the identity and even the fusion is complete. . . .

. . . There is something to be said in favour of recognising destiny without delay. The reasoning of Lord Durham with regard to French Canada holds good in some measure with regard to Canada altogether in its relation to the Anglo-Saxon Continent. He thought it best to make the country at once that which after the lapse of no long time it must be.

And this reminds us of another reason for not putting off the unification of the English-speaking race, since it is perfectly clear that the forces of Canada alone are not sufficient to assimilate the French element or even to prevent the indefinite consolidation and growth of a French nation. Either the conquest of Quebec was utterly fatuous or it is to be desired that the American Continent should belong to the English tongue and to Anglo-Saxon civilisation. . . .

There is a conflict of forces, and we must judge each for himself which are the primary forces and likely to prevail. Prevail the primary forces will in the end, however long their action may be suspended by a number of secondary forces arrayed against them. In the case of German and in that of Italian unity the number and strength of the secondary forces arrayed against the event were such, and the action of the great forces was so long suspended by them, that it seemed even to sagacious observers as if the event would never come. It came, irresistible and irreversible, and we see now that Bismarck and Cavour were the ministers of destiny.

In the present case there are, on one side, geography, commerce, identity of race, language, and institutions, which with the mingling of population and constant intercourse of every kind, acting in ever-increasing intensity, have brought about a general fusion, leaving no barriers standing but the political and fiscal lines. On the other side, there is British and Imperial sentiment, which, however, is confined to the British, excluding the French and Irish and other nationalities, and even among the British is livelier as a rule among the cultivated and those whose minds are steeped in history than among those who are working for their bread; while to set against it there is the idea, which can hardly fail to make way, of a great continent with an almost unlimited range of production forming the home of a united people, shutting out war and presenting the field as it would seem for a new and happier development of humanity. . . .

XVI:3 SIR JOHN A. MACDONALD UPHOLDS THE BRITISH CONNECTION

By far the strongest feeling among Canadians, including Canadian nationalists, was their attachment to British institutions. For the 1891 election the Liberal Party adopted a policy of unrestricted reciprocity with the United States. Accusing the Liberals of "veiled treason" (because unrestricted reciprocity had annexationist implications), Macdonald won his last and perhaps most important victory by appealing to Canadian loyalties. This selection is an excerpt from his last major election speech.

. . . For a century and a half this country has grown and flourished under the protecting ægis of the British Crown. The gallant race who first bore to our shores the blessings of civilization passed by an easy transition from French to English rule, and now form one of the most law-abiding portions of the community. These pioneers were speedily recruited by the advent of a loyal band of British subjects, who gave up everything that men most prize, and were content to begin life anew in the wilderness rather than forego allegiance to their Sovereign. To the descendants of these men, and of the multitude of Englishmen, Irishmen, and Scotchmen who emigrated to Canada, that they might build up new homes without ceasing to be British subjects—to you Canadians I appeal, and I ask you what have you to gain by surrendering that which your fathers held most dear? Under the broad folds of the Union Jack, we enjoy the most ample liberty to govern ourselves as we please, and at the same time we participate in the advantages which flow from association with the mightiest Empire the world has ever seen. Not only are we free to manage our domestic concerns, but, practically, we possess the privilege of making our own treaties with foreign countries, and, in our relations with the outside world, we enjoy the prestige inspired by a consciousness of the fact that behind us towers the majesty of England. The question which you will shortly be called upon to determine resolves itself into this; shall we endanger our possession of the great heritage bequeathed to us by our fathers, and submit ourselves to direct taxation for the privilege of having our tariff fixed at Washington, with a prospect of ultimately becoming a portion of the American Union? I commend these issues to your determination, and to the judgment of the whole people of Canada, with an unclouded confidence that you will proclaim to the world your resolve to show yourselves not unworthy of the proud distinction that you enjoy, of being numbered among the most dutiful and loyal subjects of our beloved Queen.

As for myself, my course is clear. A British subject I was born—a British subject I will die. With my utmost effort, with my latest breath, will I oppose the "veiled treason" which attempts by sordid means and mercenary proffers to lure our people from their allegiance. During my long public service of nearly half a century, I have been true to my country and its best interests, and I appeal with equal confidence to the men who have trusted me in the past, and to the young hope of the country, with whom rests its destinies for the future, to give me their united and strenuous aid in this, my last effort, for the unity of the Empire and the preservation of our commercial and political freedom.

XVII. Race, Religion And Liberalism

XVII:1 ULTRAMONTANISM: THE "CATHOLIC PROGRAMME"

After Confederation the Liberal Party in Quebec was hampered not only by the strength of the old Conservative-*Bleu* alliance, but by the Roman Catholic Church's suspicions that Canadian Liberals were as anti-clerical as their European counterparts. Bishop Bourget of Montreal led the dominant ultramontane wing of the Church which held that the Church was superior to the state and that the slightest hint of political anti-clericalism was to be condemned without qualification. In effect Quebec ultramontanism led to a tacit political alliance between the Roman Catholic Church and the Conservative party. One of the most extreme statements of the ultramontane position was made in 1871 by a group of Roman Catholic laymen who, with Bishop Bourget's approval, drew up the following "Catholic Programme."

We belong in principle to the Conservative Party, that is to that party which proclaims itself defender of the social order. In the political situation of our country, the Conservative Party being the only one which offers serious guarantees to religious interests, we consider it a duty to support its leadership loyally.

But this loyal support must be subordinated to religious interests of which we must never lose sight. If then there exist in our laws some gaps, some ambiguities, or some provisions which jeopardize Catholic interests, we must require of our candidates a formal promise to work to eliminate these flaws in our legislation.

. . . It is the duty of the electors to give their votes only to those who will comply entirely with the teachings of the Church on these matters.

Let us conclude then by adopting the following general rules in certain given circumstances.

1. If the contest occurs between two Conservatives, it goes without saying that we shall support the one who will accept the programme that we have just set forth.

2. If on the other hand it occurs between any shade of Conservative and a follower of the Liberal school, our active sympathies will be given to the former.

3. If the only candidates who offer themselves in a constituency are all Liberals or oppositionists, we must choose the one who will agree to our conditions.

4. Finally, in the situation where the contest is between a Conservative rejecting our programme and an oppositionist who accepts it, the situation would be most delicate. To vote for the first man would be putting us in contradition with the doctrine that we have just expounded. To vote for the second man would be to jeopardize the Conservative Party which we wish to see powerful. Which decision should we take between the two dangers? In this instance we would advise the abstention of Catholic electors.

XVII:2 WILFRID LAURIER DEFENDS POLITICAL LIBERALISM

Although Papal intervention was finally necessary to silence the ultramontanes, the young Wilfrid Laurier made himself a national figure as a result of this 1877 speech defending Liberalism in Quebec.

. . . I know that, in the eyes of a large number of my fellow countrymen, the Liberal party is a party composed of men of perverse doctrines and dangerous tendencies, pressing knowingly and deliberately towards revolution. I know that, in the eyes of a portion of my fellow countrymen, the Liberal party is a party of men with upright intentions, perhaps, but victims and dupes of principles which are leading them unconsciously, but fatally, towards revolution. In fine, I know that, in the eyes of another, and not the least considerable portion, perhaps, of our people, Liberalism is a new form of evil, a heresy carrying with it its own condemnation. . . .

I maintain that there is not one thing less understood in this country by its assailants than Liberalism and there are several reasons for this.

It is only yesterday that we were initiated into representative institutions. The English element understand the working of these institutions in some way by instinct, as well as by long experience. On the other hand, our people hardly understand them yet. Education is only beginning to spread amongst us and, in the case of the educated, our French education leads us naturally to study the history of modern liberty, not in the classic land of liberty, not in the history of old England, but among the peoples of the continent of Europe, of the same origin and faith as ourselves. And there, unfortunately, the history of liberty has been written in letters of blood on the most harrowing pages which the annals of the human race, perhaps, contain. In all classes of educated society may be seen loyal souls, who, frightened by these mournful pages, regard with terror the spirit of liberty, imagining that it must produce here the same disasters and the same crimes as in the countries I have just referred to. In the eyes of such well meaning people, the very word "Liberalism" is fraught with national calamity. . . .

[Laurier then quotes with approval Macaulay's definition of Liberals and Conservatives.]

". . . Everywhere there is a class of men who cling with fondness to whatever is ancient and who, even when convinced by overpowering reasons that innovation would be beneficial, consent to it with many misgivings and forebodings. We find also everywhere another class of men sanguine in hope, bold in speculation, always pressing forward, quick to discern the imperfection of whatever exists, disposed to think lightly of the risks and inconveniences which attend improvements and disposed to give every change credit for being an improvement." . . .

Now, I ask: between these two ideas which constitute the basis of parties, can there be a moral difference? Is the one radically good and the other radically bad? Is it not evident that both are what are termed in moral philosophy *indifferents,* that is to say, that both are susceptible of being appreciated, pondered and chosen? Would it not be as unfair as it would be absurd to condemn or to approve either the one or the other as absolutely bad or good?

Both are susceptible of much good, as they are also of much evil. The Conservative, who defends his country's old institutions may do much good, as he also may do much evil, if he be obstinate in maintaining abuses, which have become intolerable. The Liberal, who contends against these abuses and who, after long efforts, succeeds in extirpating them, may be a public benefactor, just as the Liberal who lays a rash hand on hallowed institutions may be a scourge not only for his own country, but for humanity at large. . . .

It is true that there is in Europe, in France, in Italy and in Germany, a class of men, who give themselves the title of Liberals, but who have nothing of the Liberal about them but the name and who are the most dangerous of men. These are not Liberals; they are revolutionaries: in their principles they are so extravagant that they aim at nothing less than the destruction of modern society. With these men, we have nothing in common; but it is the tactic of our adversaries to always assimilate us to them. Such accusations are beneath our notice and the only answer we can with dignity give them is to proclaim our real principles and to so conduct ourselves that our acts will conform with our principles. . . .

I have too much respect for the opinion of my adversaries to ever insult them; but I reproach them with understanding neither their time nor their country. I accuse them of judging the political situation of the country, not according to what is happening in it, but according to what is happening in France. I accuse them of wanting to introduce here ideas, which are impossible of application in our state of society. I accuse them of laboriously and, by misfortune, too efficaciously working to degrade religion to the simple proportions of a political party. . . .

You wish to organize a Catholic party. But have you not considered that, if you have the misfortune to succeed, you will draw down upon your country calamities of which it is impossible to foresee the consequences?

You wish to organize all the Catholics into one party, without other bond, without other basis, than a common religion; but have you not reflected that, by the very fact, you will organize the Protestant population as a single party and that then, instead of the peace and harmony now prevailing between the different elements of the Canadian population, you throw open the door to war, a religious war, the most terrible of all wars?

Once more, Conservatives, I accuse you in the face of Canada of not understanding either your country or your time. . . .

But, while reproaching us with being friends of liberty our adversaries further reproach us, with an inconsistency which would be serious, if the charge were well founded, with denying to the Church the freedom to which it is entitled. They reproach us with seeking to silence the administrative body of the Church and to prevent it from teaching the people their duties as citizens and electors. They reproach us with wanting to hinder the clergy from meddling in politics and to relegate them to the sacristy.

In the name of the Liberal party and of Liberal principles, I repel this assertion.

I maintain that there is not one Canadian Liberal who

wants to prevent the clergy from taking part in political affairs, if they wish to do so.

. . . No, let the priest speak and preach, as he thinks best; such is his right and no Canadian Liberal will dispute that right. . . .

This right, however, is not unlimited. We have no absolute rights amongst us. The rights of each man, in our state of society, end precisely at the point where they encroach upon the rights of others.

The right of interference in politics finishes at the spot where it encroaches on the elector's independence. . . .

XVII: 3 HONORE MERCIER ON RIEL'S DEATH

The execution of Louis Riel was a vital turning point in Liberal fortunes in Quebec. French Canadian re-action to Riel's death and the decision of the Cabinet ministers from Quebec to side with Macdonald is typified in this speech by the nationalist leader Honoré Mercier at the mass meeting on the Champ de Mars in Quebec City on November 22, 1885. (At the same meeting Laurier said, "If I had been on the banks of the Saskatchewan, I, too, would have shouldered my musket.") Within two years Mercier was Premier of Quebec and the Quebec Liberals had managed to equal Quebec Conservative representa-tion in the federal House of Commons.

Mr. Chairman—

Riel, our brother, is dead, the victim of his devotion to the cause of the Métis of whom he was the leader, the victim of fanaticism and treason—of the fanaticism of Sir John and some of his friends, of the treason of three of our own, who, to keep their portfolios, have sold their brother.

Riel has died upon the scaffold, as did the patriots of 1837, as a good Christian. By giving over his head to the executioner, like de Lorimier, he gave his heart to his country. Like Christ he forgave his murderers.

He mounted the gallows with a firm and steady step; not one muscle of his face twitched; his soul, strengthened by martyrdom, knew not the faintness of death.

By killing Riel Sir John has not only struck our race at the heart, but he has grossly struck the cause of justice and humanity which, represented by all languages and hallowed by all religions, asked mercy for the prisoner of Regina, our poor brother of the North-West.

The expiring breath of Riel has echoed sorrowfully over the whole world; it has been drowned out by the heart-rending cry coming from the souls of all civilized nations; and this cry has had the same effect on the Minister [Macdonald] as on the executioner; both of them, their hands stained with blood, have gone to hide their shame: one in an Orange Lodge to hear the shrieks of a glutted fanaticism; the other on the sea, to avoid hearing the curses of a mourning nation.

As fifty thousand free citizens we are gathered here under the protective aegis of the constitution, in the name of a humanity crying out for vengance, in the name of all lovers of the justice which has been trampled underfoot, in the name of two million grieving Frenchmen, to pronounce to the fleeing Minister a last curse which, echoing along the banks of our great river, will reach him at the moment he loses sight of the shores of Canada, which he has defiled with a legal murder.

As for those who remain; as for those three who represent the province of Quebec in the federal government and who no longer represent there anything but treachery, let us bow our heads before their weakness and bemoan their sad fate; for the stain of blood which they bear on their foreheads will remain a permanent mark of their cowardice. They will share the fate of their brother Cain; their memory will be cursed like his; and like the sons of Abel who fled into the wilderness to avoid the world's first fratricide, our children will turn away their heads to avoid seeing Canada's three fraticides.

In the face of this crime, in the presence of this weakness, what is our duty? We have three things to accomplish: to unite in order to punish the guilty; to sever the alliance which our elected representatives have made with Orangeism and to seek in a more natural and less dangerous alliance the protection of our national interests.

To unite! Oh! with what ease I pronounce those words! These twenty years have I sought the union of all the forces of our nation. These twenty years I have besought my brethren to sacrifice on the altar of the endangered fatherland, the hatreds which were blinding us and the divisions which were killing us. And what reply has been given to this rallying cry of a patriotic heart? Abuse, recrimination, calumny. It took a national disaster which we now bewail, it took the death of one of our own blood for this rallying cry to be understood. . . .

. . . it is not a racially-based war which we seek; it is not an exclusively French party which we ask, but rather the union of all friends of justice and humanity whose holy cause has suffered the outrage of Riel's death.

This death which was a crime among our enemies will become a rallying sign and a means of salvation for us.

Our duty is thus to unite in order to punish the guilty; may this unon be hallowed by this people and let us swear before God and before men to oppose, with all our strength and with all our soul and with every means the constitution permits us, the treachery of Sir John's government, the three traitors who have dishonoured our race, and all who would be so cowardly as to imitate or excuse their crime. . . .

XVII: 4 ONTARIO'S CHAUVINISM

1885 was the beginning of ten years of unprecedented racial bitterness in Canada—bitterness which disrupted the Conservative coalition and further strengthened the sense of national solidarity in Quebec. This 1885 editorial from the Toronto *Evening News* is representative of the incredibly violent language that was often commonplace in Orange-dominated Ontario—and often reciprocated in Quebec.

FRENCH AGGRESSION

Ontario is proud of being loyal to England.

Quebec is proud of being loyal to sixteenth century France.

Ontario pays about three-fifths of Canada's taxes, fights all the battles of provincial rights, sends nine-tenths of the soldiers to fight the rebels, and gets sat upon by Quebec for her pains.

Quebec, since the time of Intendant Bigot, has been extravagant, corrupt and venal, whenever she could with other people's money, and has done nothing for herself or for progress with her own earnings.

Quebec now gets the pie.

Ontario gets the mush, and pays the piper for the Bleu carnival. . . .

Hundreds of thousands of dollars are spent in maintaining the French language in an English country.

Ontario is getting sick of it.

Ontario taxpayers are about to take a tumble.

An anti-French party is springing up in all the Provinces except Quebec.

As the Republicans said, after the war of secession, "if we are to have a solid South, we must have a solid North."

If we in Canada are to be confronted with a solid French vote, we must have a solid English vote.

If Quebec is always to pose as a beggar in the Dominion soup kitchen, she must be disfranchised as a vagrant.

If she is to be a traitor in our wars, a thief in our treasury, a conspirator in our Canadian household, she had better go out.

She is no use in Confederation.

Her representatives are a weakness in Parliament, her cities would be nothing but for the English speaking people, and to-day Montreal would be as dead as the city of Quebec but for Anglo-Saxons, who are persecuted and kept down by the ignorant French. . . .

We are sick of the French Canadians with their patriotic blabber and their conspiracies against the treasury and the peace of what without them might be a united Canada. . . .

With Quebec holding the balance of power Canada isn't safe a moment.

The constitution, or the British North America Act, which is our alleged constitution, must be altered so as to deprive these venal politicians of their powers or else Confederation will have to go.

As far as we are concerned, and we are concerned, and we are as much concerned for the good of Canada as any one else, Quebec could go out of the Confederation to-morrow and we would not shed a tear except for joy.

If Ontario were a trifle more loyal to herself she would not stand Quebec's monkey business another minute.

XVII:5 THE MANITOBA SCHOOLS CRISIS, 1896

The Conservative government, badly hurt by depression, scandal, and weak leadership after Macdonald's death, was destroyed in 1896 by the Manitoba Schools issue. The Manitoba Liberal government had abolished the educational rights of Roman Catholics in that province in 1890. After much hesitation the federal Conservatives prepared to restore separate schools in Manitoba by remedial legislation under Section 93 of the British North America Act. In opposing remedial legislation, Wilfrid Laurier made the most daring stand of his career, for the Church hierarchy in Quebec was solidly in favour of the remedial bill. In selection (a) Sir Charles Tupper explains the Government's position to the House of Commons. Selection (b) is a statement of Laurier's "sunny way" policy for dealing with Manitoba. His counter-arguments against Tupper and the Roman Catholic bishops are contained in selection (c), also from the Commons debate on remedial legislation.

a. Sir Charles Tupper on Remedial Legislation

. . . If there be any man to be found in Canada who from any narrow, any selfish, any exclusive, any bigoted, or any fanatical sentiment would yield for a single moment to a disposition to advance his own race, religion or sect at the sacrifice of the interest and the conscience of others: if there be any such man, I ask him to look back at the deplorable condition into which Canada had sunk when she yielded to that sentiment, and when we had in this country a great party fomenting a war of races and a war of creeds. I ask such a one to look back upon Canada at that unhappy period, and I ask him to raise his eyes to the present proud position that our country occupies. I ask him to inquire from himself as to the reason for all this progress, all this prosperity, all this high position that we have obtained throughout the civilized world—for it is not extravagant to use that term in regard to Canada. I ask such an one if he is prepared to re-open a war of races, and a war of creeds, because he wishes to deny to a small and helpless Roman Catholic minority in the province of Manitoba the rights which the Imperial statute and the law under which Manitoba came into the union have guaranteed to them should be preserved. . . .

He may be acting from the highest and most conscientious principles. He may regard, as many do regard, that this is a question of separate schools, and that he is opposed to separate schools, and consequently he may wish to defeat this measure that is now proposed to the Parliament of Canada. But, Sir, no man who takes the trouble to examine this question can for a single moment consider that the question of separate schools is at issue at all. It is not a question of separate schools, it is a question of the constitution of the country. The progress and the prosperity and the future development of Canada depends upon that constitution being sacredly maintained, and that all the rights that are guaranteed under it, whether to the central or the provincial governments, shall be sacredly guarded. . . .

I put it to any intelligent man who recognizes the fact that within this wide Dominion you have got over 41 per cent of the population Roman Catholics; I put it to gentlemen who may hold—and I think some have without due consideration held—rather narrow views on the subject; I put it to them:

whether for any object that was not of the most transcendent importance it would be right for this Government to refuse, or right for this Parliament to refuse, to grant redress in a case such as is presented on the present occasion, and to leave rankling in the minds of over 41 per cent of the entire population of the Dominion of Canada the sentiment that a Roman Catholic cannot, in the Parliament of this country, obtain the same just consideration that he would obtain if he were a Protestant. . . .

There is no coercion so far as the Dominion Government is concerned. There is not a line of coercion to be found in the Bill from beginning to end. There is a simple, a most easy and natural provision, to meet the interests of these people whose consciences deprive them from the opportunity of making use of such schools in Manitoba as they are now taxed to sustain. Under these circumstances, the Government have been compelled to adopt the policy which they have adopted. I need not say that they have adopted this policy in the face of great difficulty, because it is always an extremely unpleasant thing for any government to find itself in a position in which there is even a single member of their party that does not see eye to eye with them. In the face of even this difficulty, the Government have felt compelled, in justice to their own position, and in regard to their duty to the country as imposed by the Imperial Act, the Government have felt obliged to take the step they have taken. They have taken that step in the most moderate and temperate manner that was possible to be devised, and even down to the present hour they have been open to any suggestion by which the responsibility which is imposed upon them under the circumstances could be removed. They are still open to any suggestion, from any quarter, of any means which will remove the necessity of their being compelled to take action of this kind. . . .

b. Laurier's Policy

. . . I ask you now, would it not have been more fair, more just, more equitable, more statesmanlike, at once to investigate the subject, and to bring the parties together to hear them, to have the facts brought out so as to see whether a case had been made out for interference or not? . . .

. . . If it were in my power, I would try the sunny way. I would approach this man Greenway with the sunny way of patriotism, asking him to be just and to be fair, asking him to be generous to the minority, in order that we may have peace among all the creeds and races which it has pleased God to bring upon this corner of our common country. Do you not believe that there is more to be gained by appealing to the heart and soul of men rather than by trying to compel them to do a thing? . . .

c. Laurier on Remedial Legislation and the Church

. . . Now, again, I am sorry to say, we can hear the roar coming upon us of another wave of agitation and civil commotion in this country. The demon of discord is in the land, blowing the wind of strife over all and in all directions, awakening slumbering passions, arousing old prejudices. You can follow the trace of its passage in our cities, towns and country villages, nay, in the backwoods settlements where the rude toil and the anxious days of the pioneer do not save him from its evil suggestions. . . . If religious war is to brought in this country, by whose action will it be brought but by the action of this Government, which, although it had the methods of persuasion in its hands, has chosen to take the methods of coercion in order to redress a wrong.

. . . The Government say to-day that they are bound to bring in this measure, because the Manitoba government have refused to come to any terms. I take complete issue with the Government on this point. The government of Manitoba never was approached in a proper spirit upon the point. It was approached with threatening hands. It was threatened with the strong arm of this Government unless it would do what it was ordered to do. . . .

I admit that this is a most crucial question, but it is all the more crucial that it has been bungled from first to last by the

Government. There are men in this House, who are against separate schools, but who would have no objection to the re-establishment of separate schools in Manitoba, provided they were re-established by the province of Manitoba itself. There are men in this House who are in favour of separate schools, but who think very strongly that it would not be advisable to interfere with the legislation of Manitoba at all until all means of conciliation had been exhausted. Sir, in face of this perilous position, I maintain to-day, and I submit it to the consideration of gentlemen on both sides, that the policy of the Opposition . . . is the only policy which can satisfactorily deal with this question—the only policy which can remedy the grievance of the minority, while, at the same time, not violently assaulting the right of the majority and thereby, perhaps, creating a greater wrong. . . .

Sir, I cannot forget at this moment that the policy which I have advocated and maintained all along has not been favourably received in all quarters. Not many weeks ago I was told from high quarters in the church to which I belong that unless I supported the school Bill, which was then being prepared by the Government, and which we have now before us, I would incur the hostility of a great and powerful body. Sir, this is too grave a phase of this question for me to pass it by in silence. . . . I am here the acknowledged leader of a great party composed of Roman Catholics and Protestants as well, in which Protestants are in the majority, as Protestants must be in the majority in every part in Canada. Am I to be told, I, occupying such a position, that I am to be dictated the course I am to take in this House, by reasons that can appeal to the consciences of my fellow Catholic members, but which do not appeal as well to the consciences of my Protestant colleagues? No. So long as I have a seat in this House, so long as I occupy the position I do now, whenever it shall become my duty to take a stand upon any question whatever, that stand I will take not upon grounds of Roman Catholicism, not upon grounds of Protestantism, but upon grounds which can appeal to the consciences of all men, irrespective of their particular faith, upon grounds which can be occupied by all men who love justice, freedom and toleration.

So far as this Bill is concerned I have given you my views. I know, I acknowledge, that there is in this Government the power to interfere, there is in the Parliament the power to interfere; but that power should not be exercised until all the facts bearing upon the case have been investigated and all means of conciliation exhausted. . . .

XVIII. The Laurier Years: Expansion

XVIII:1 CLIFFORD SIFTON ON THE ROLE OF THE WEST

The major failure in Macdonald's policy of nation
building had been the sparse settlement of the Canadian West. In the late 1890's, for numerous reasons,
settlers finally began to pour into Canada. Clifford
Sifton, Laurier's Minister of the Interior, directed a
skillful and extensive campaign to attract settlers to
Canada. In this 1904 speech Sifton outlines his vision
of the West's place in the Canadian nation.

What do we expect this great west to accomplish for itself
and for its people? We know now that there is no place known
to civilization, where the poor man with willing and strong
hands, and a mind disposed to success, may find a more certain
reward for his labour; where he is more assured by reasonable
diligence and frugality of social advancement and prosperity
to himself and his family. And we know that the home-seekers
of the world, at present, are aware of this fact, and are coming
to cast their destinies amongst us. And therefore, sir, we look
in the near future to see upon these western plains, and in this
western province and territories, a great population; great not
only in numbers, but in other respects; not depressed by
poverty, but a population characterized in its social conditions
by a high degree of comfort and prosperity.

We look forward to other things. We look forward to the

production of natural wealth of all kinds. In this great country we expect to see the wealth of the field, of the forest and of the mine exploited in vast quantities, furnishing remunerative occupation to large numbers of our people. We expect to see cities and towns springing up, in which the comforts and refinements of civilization will be within the reach of all. We expect to see a creditable system of education amongst our people, in which intellectual advancement and intellectual culture will go hand in hand with material progress. . . .

I have to say a word as to what we expect western Canada will do for itself. But it will not be enough that it shall do only for itself. It is a portion of Canada. Canada is a national entity. Canada is an organism, and you cannot develop a single part of an organism satisfactorily. Each and all parts must contribute to the vitality of the whole. What then will western Canada do for the Canadian organism? Sir, it will give a vast and profitable traffic to its railways and steamship lines. It will give remunerative employment to tens of thousands of men, to keep the permanent way in order, to man the trains and ships, and to engage in the multitude of occupations which gather around the great system of transportation. It will do more. It will build up our Canadian seaports. It will create a volume of ocean traffic which shall place Canada in a short time in its proper position as a maritime nation. It will furnish a steady and remunerative business to the manufacturers of eastern Canada, giving assured prosperity where uncertainty now exists. These are things which the west will do for the east. In a word, I may say it will send a flood of new blood from one end of this great country to the other, through every artery of commerce. . . .

XVIII: 2 SIFTON ON THE QUALITY OF IMMIGRANTS

Many of the ideals and methods of the Laurier government's immigration policy are illustrated in this excerpt from an article written by Sifton in 1922.

. . . People who do not know anything at all about the policy which was followed by the department of the Interior under my direction quite commonly make the statement that my policy for Immigration was quantity and not quality. As a matter of fact that statement is the direct opposite of the fact. In those days settlers were sought from three sources; one was the United States. The American settlers did not need sifting; they were of the finest quality and the most desirable settlers. In Great Britain we confined our efforts very largely to the North of England and Scotland, and for the purpose of sifting the settlers we doubled the bonuses to the agents in the North of England, and cut them down as much as possible in the South. The result was that we got a fairly steady stream of people from the North of England and from Scotland and they were the very best settlers in the world. I do not wish to suggest that we did not get many very excellent people from the more southerly portions of England, but they were people who came on their own initiative largely, which was the best possible guarantee of success.

Our work was largely done in the North. Then, came the continent—where the great emigrating center was Hamburg. Steamships go there to load up with people who are desirous of leaving Europe. The situation is a peculiar one. If one should examine twenty people who turn up at Hamburg to emigrate he might find one escaped murderer, three or four wasters and ne'er-do-wells, some very poor shop-keepers, artisans or laborers and there might be one or two stout, hardy peasants in sheep-skin coats. Obviously the peasants are the men that are wanted here. Now, with regard to these twenty men, no one knows anything about them except the shipping agents. These men are sent in from outlying local agencies all over Europe. They arrive at Hamburg and the booking agents have their names and full descriptions of who they are and where they come from. No one else has this information.

We made an arrangement with the booking agencies in Hamburg, under which they winnowed out this flood of people, picked out the agriculturalists and peasants and sent them to Canada, sending nobody else. We paid, I think, $5 per head for the farmer and $2 per head for the other members of the family. . . .

When I speak of quality I have in mind, I think, something that is quite different from what is in the mind of the average writer or speaker upon the question of Immigration. I think a stalwart peasant in a sheep-skin coat, born on the soil, whose forefathers have been farmers for ten generations, with a stout wife and a half-dozen children, is good quality. A Trades Union artisan who will not work more than eight hours a day and will not work that long if he can help it, will not work on a farm at all and has to be fed by the public when work is slack is, in my judgment, quantity and very bad quality. I am indifferent as to whether or not he is British born. It matters not what his nationality is; such men are not wanted in Canada and the more of them we get the more trouble we shall have. . . .

XVIII:3 ANGLO-SAXON RESERVATIONS ABOUT IMMIGRATION

British Canadians were not uniformly delighted by the way in which their country was at last being populated. This 1914 article from the *Canadian Courier,* entitled "Canadianizing the Newcomer," is quite representative of their reservations about immigration.

. . . So long as Britons and northwestern Europeans constitute the vast majority there is not so much danger of losing our national character. To healthy Britons of good behaviour our welcome is everlasting; but to make this country a dumping ground for the scum and dregs of the old world means transplanting the evils and vices that they may flourish in a new soil.

Since 1882 the immigration flowing into the United States has changed from the progressive and enlightened people of northwestern Europe to those of the south and east. Nearly

80 per cent of the immigration of the United States consists of peasantry, scarcely a generation removed from serfdom, and comes from Austria-Hungary, Italy, Poland and Russia. More than one-half their total population is foreign born, and the very foundations of their civilization are threatened with destruction. The United States has long ceased to be British in sentiment or ideals. These are facts that Canadians should ponder seriously. When the United States finally close their gates against the immigrant, as they are certain to do soon, Canada will face the deluge. . . .

A state cannot accept an excessive influx of people without injury. . . . What has happened in the United States during a century appears likely to happen in Canada in a few short years. We are introducing into our population elements that are wholly at variance with the people who have made this Dominion what it is. Fortunately 75 per cent of the newcomers speak English, but the remainder presents a problem with which we must grapple or we shall find the language question alone a menace to our future peace. The non-English-speaking immigrants are in most cases illiterate, and have minds that are unresponsive to Canadian sentiment. Their tendency is to form colonies and establish on Canadian soil their own customs, methods and traditions.

The granting of the franchise to these groups only serves to encourage corruption in political matters, endangering the interests of good government. The serious character of the problem may be stated thus: if we do not Canadianize and Christianize the new-comer, he will make us foreigners and heathen on our own soil and under our own flag. If British institutions mean anything they stand for the championship of Christian civilization. If the foundation principles underlying our institutions are to be ignored and set aside by the illiterate foreigner who has no conception of the character or purpose of the ideals governing our race, we are taking hazardous risks. Material prosperity may be desirable, but are we not making too great a sacrifice to bring it about? It seems that Canada is undertaking to solve a problem that has never been successfully worked out by any people heretofore. We must not only Canadianize the new-comer, but we must check the tide of immigration until we are better prepared to deal with it. . . .

XVIII:4 LAURIER ON THE NEED FOR NEW RAILWAYS

Although railway expansion was obviously necessary to keep pace with western expansion, it was scarcely necessary for the government to sponsor two new transcontinental railways (the Canadian Northern and the Grand Trunk Pacific). These excerpts from Laurier's speech introducing the Grand Trunk Pacific scheme in the House of Commons show some of both the practical and the emotional factors behind the decision.

. . . To those who urge upon us the policy of tomorrow, and tomorrow, and tomorrow; to those who tell us, Wait, wait, wait; to those who advise us to pause, to consider, to reflect, to calculate and to inquire, our answer is: No, this is not a time for deliberation, this is a time for action. The flood tide is upon us that leads on to fortune; if we let it pass it may never recur again. If we let it pass, the voyage of our national life, bright as it is today, will be bound in shallows. We cannot wait, because time does not wait; we cannot wait because, in these days of wonderful development, time lost is doubly lost; we cannot wait, because at this moment there is a transformation going on in the conditions of our national life which it would be folly to ignore and a crime to overlook; we cannot wait, because the prairies of the North-west, which for countless ages have been roamed over by the wild herds of the bison, or by the scarcely less wild tribes of red men, are now invaded from all sides by the white race. They came— last year 100,000—and still they come in still greater numbers. Already they are at work opening the long dormant soil; already they are at work sowing, harvesting and reaping. We say that today it is the duty of the Canadian government, it is the duty of the Canadian parliament, it is the duty of all those who have a mandate from the people to attend to the needs and requirements of this fast growing country, to give heed to that condition of things. We consider that it is the duty of all those who sit within these walls by the will of the people, to provide immediate means whereby the products of those new settlers may find an exit to the ocean at the least possible cost, and whereby, likewise, a market may be found in this new region for those who toil in the forests, in the fields, in the mines, in the shops of the older provinces. Such is our duty; it is immediate and imperative. It is not of tomorrow, but of this day, of this hour and of this minute. Heaven grant that it be not already too late; heaven grant that whilst we tarry and dispute, the trade of Canada is not deviated to other channels, and that an ever vigilant competitor does not take to himself the trade that properly belongs to those who acknowledge Canada as their native or their adopted land. Upon this question we feel that our position is absolutely safe and secure; we feel that it corresponds to the beating of every Canadian heart. . . .

XVIII: 5 A POST-MORTEM ON LAURIER'S RAILWAYS

Not until the middle of World War I, with both railways in desperate financial condition, did Canadians realize the consequences of their optimism. The chairman of the Royal Commission which investigated the plight of the railways summarized and evaluated former policy.

. . . It is unfortunate that Canada did not have a policy of regulation in this period which could have prevented needless duplication of lines and facilities. Competing lines have been built where effective regulaton could have saved a large part of the investment, while completely satisfying every reasonable and proper need for service. Instead of co-ordination and conservation under government supervision, railways were permitted to duplicate plant in fields not yet productive enough to support the one; the Government, on the other hand, was, in one way or another, aiding both projects, if it had not indeed itself promoted either or both projects. Very naturally, it has not and could not have obtained the benefit which should have followed a correct programme of government aid. The policy of government aid makes the need for regulation of railway building more necessary even than where private capital is depended upon, for in the latter case the proposal must at least have a promise of commercial success before capital can be induced to come in and give it support. To the absence of such regulation must be charged responsibility for no small part of the railway problem today.

We may well inquire here as to the effect of this policy upon the three principal systems. The Grand Trunk Railway Company, feeling no doubt that its own traffic field had been invaded by the government-aided Canadian Pacific, desired in turn to enter the promising western territory. Accordingly, it proposed to build a line from North Bay to the Pacific coast. Public aid was required and granted in a way to ensure the building of the road. If any serious thought was given to co-ordinating existing or proposed roads, and to utilizing them for the public good, it did not find public expression in any constructive way. The Grand Trunk Railway Company evidently felt confident in the success of its plans, for it pledged its own credit in aid of the extension, and entered into contracts which it now finds quite beyond its ability to carry out.

Canadian Northern interests, directed by Mackenzie, Mann & Co., who since an early date had been operating local lines in Manitoba, seized the opportunity afforded them for expansion and rapidly extended their rails throughout the Prairie region. The records show that the Canadian Northern had a large mileage on the prairies before the projection of the Grand Trunk Pacific; so that when the extension plans of the Grand Trunk became a part of the national policy, as they did become, the Canadian Northern was added to the number of those who wanted to own a transcontinental system and one as fully complete and self-contained as was that of the Canadian Pacific. Hence, we find two new companies, both built largely upon public credit, striving for first place in a field which, as for transcontinental transportation, or even as for connecting Eastern and Western Canada, was already occupied. Besides having the Great Lakes waterway, there could have been barely enough business to support one additional line, and that only by the exercise of economy in operation and prudence in investment.

The Canadian Pacific, enjoying splendid credit, with adequate powers and resources, and keenly alive to the possibilities of losing business to competitors challenging its supremacy everywhere, then entered the contest by undertaking to build new lines in an effort to protect its sources of revenues.

The stimulation felt throughout the country by the influx of settlers and by the importation of so much new capital not only created a boom, but it quite naturally affected prices for labour and materials, sending these soaring; the increased prices in turn contributed largely to the higher costs which are now reflected in the construction accounts of the new roads.

This brings us fairly to a recognition of the fact that while the policy of public aid to railways had originally been founded on the urgent need for transportation to open up a new country, to develop its resources, and to unify Canada commercially and politically, it was carried far beyond the limits warranted by the original exigency. It appears to me that the responsibility is as much the Government's as the private companies'. Without enabling legislation and the extension of Government credit from which all received their essential support, the companies could not have expanded and overbuilt. . . .

XIX. The Laurier Years: Canada and the Empire

XIX: 1 JOSEPH CHAMBERLAIN PROPOSES IMPERIAL FEDERATION

The movement for imperial federation—some form of confederation of Britain and her Dominions into a "super" state—had been simmering since the 1880's. It became a major issue after 1895 when Joseph Chamberlain became Colonial Secretary and made imperial unity a dominant theme of British policy. In this speech before the Colonial Conference of 1902 Chamberlain repeats his proposals and indicates the chief reasons why Britain favoured imperial federation.

. . . Gentlemen, we do want your aid. We do require your assistance in the administration of the vast Empire which is yours as well as ours. The weary Titan staggers under the too vast orb of its fate. We have borne the burden for many years. We think it is time that our children should assist us to support it, and whenever you make the request to us, be very sure that we shall hasten gladly to call you to our Councils. If you are prepared at any time to take any share, any proportionate share, in the burdens of the Empire, we are prepared to meet you with any proposal for giving to you a corresponding voice in the policy of the Empire. And the object, if I may point out to you, may be achieved in various ways. Suggestions have been made that representation should be given to the Colonies in either, or in both, Houses of Parliament. There is no objection in principle to any such proposal. If it comes to us, it is a proposal which His Majesty's Government would certainly feel justified in favourably considering, but I have always felt myself that the most practical form in which we could achieve our object, would be the establishment or the creation of a real Council of the Empire to which all questions of Imperial interest might be referred, and if it were desired to proceed gradually, as probably would be our course—we are all accustomed to the slow ways in which our Constitutions have been worked out—if it be desired to proceed gradually, the Council might in the first instance be merely an advisory council. . . . But although that would be a preliminary step, it is clear that the object would not be completely secured until there had been conferred upon such a Council executive functions, and perhaps also legislative powers, and it is for you to say, gentlemen, whether you think the time has come when any progress whatever can be made in this direction. . . .

. . . If an Imperial Council were established, it is clear that the two subjects which would immediately call for its attention are those which I have already mentioned—of Imperial defence and commercial relations. And we invite your special attention to these two subjects on the present occasion.

Imperial Defence

As regards Imperial defence, I propose to lay before you, for your information, a paper which will show the comparative amount of the ordinary naval and military expenditure of the United Kingdom and of the different self-governing Colonies. . . . At the present moment the Estimates for the present year for naval and military expenditure in the United Kingdom—not including the extraordinary war expenses, but the normal Estimates—involve an expenditure per head of the population of the United Kingdom of 29s. 3d.—29s. 3d. per head per annum. . . .

In Canada the same items involve an expenditure of only

2s. per head of the population, about one-fifteenth of that incurred by the United Kingdom. In New South Wales—I have not the figures for the Commonwealth as a whole, but I am giving those as illustrations—and I find that in New South Wales the expenditure is 3s. 5d.; in Victoria, 3s. 3d.; in New Zealand, 3s. 4d.; and in the Cape and Natal, I think it is between 2s. and 3s. Now, no one, I think, will pretend that that is a fair distribution of the burdens of Empire. No one will believe that the United Kingdom can, for all time, make this inordinate sacrifice. While the Colonies were young and poor, in the first place they did not offer anything like the same temptation to the ambitions of others, and, in the second place, they were clearly incapable of providing large sums for their own defence, and therefore it was perfectly right and natural that the mother country should undertake the protection of her children. But now that the Colonies are rich and powerful, that every day they are growing by leaps and bounds, their material prosperity promises to rival that of the United Kingdom itself, and I think it is inconsistent with their position—inconsistent with their dignity as nations —that they should leave the mother country to bear the whole, or almost the whole, of the expense. . . . And I would beg of you in this relation to bear in mind that you are not asked— your people are not asked—to put upon their own shoulders any burden for the exclusive advantage of the mother country. On the contrary, if the United Kingdom stood alone, as a mere speck in the northern sea, it is certain that its expenditure for these purposes of defence might be immensely curtailed. It is owing to its duties and obligations to its Colonies throughout the Empire; it is owing to its trade with those Colonies, a trade in which of course they are equally interested with ourselves, that the necessity has been cast upon us to make these enormous preparations. . . .

Commercial Relations

Our first object then, as I say, is free trade within the Empire. We feel confident—we think that it is a matter which demands no evidence or proof, that if such a result were feasible it would enormously increase our inter-imperial trade; that it would hasten the development of our Colonies; that it would fill up the spare places in your lands with an active, intelligent, and industrious, and, above all, a British, population; that it would make the mother country entirely independent of foreign food and raw material. . . .

XIX: 2 STEPHEN LEACOCK CALLS FOR IMPERIAL UNITY

Many Canadians of British descent vigorously supported the imperial federation movement. Among the more notable Canadian imperialists was Stephen Leacock, who, in these excerpts from a pamphlet entitled *Greater Canada: An Appeal,* turns from humour to exuberant patriotism in presenting the imperialist case.

Now, in this month of April, when the ice is leaving our rivers, the ministers of Canada take ship for this the fourth Colonial Conference at London. What do they go to do? Nay, rather what shall we bid them do? We—the six million people of Canada, unvoiced, untaxed in the Empire, unheeded in the councils of the world,—we, the six million colonials sprawling our over-suckled infancy across a continent,—what shall be our message to the motherland? Shall we still whine of our poverty, still draw imaginary pictures of our thin herds shivering in the cold blasts of the North, their shepherds huddled for shelter in the log cabins of Montreal and Toronto? . . . Or, shall we say to the people of England, "The time has come; we know and realize our country. We will be your colony no longer. Make us one with you in an Empire, Permanent and Indivisible."

This last alternative means what is commonly called Imperialism. It means a united system of defence, an imperial navy for whose support somehow or other the whole Empire shall properly contribute, and with it an imperial authority in whose power we all may share. To many people in Canada this imperialism is a tainted word. It is too much associated with a truckling subservience to English people and English ideas and the silly swagger of the hop-o'-my-thumb junior officer. But there is and must be for the true future of our country, a higher and more real imperialism than this—the imperialism of the plain man at the plough and the clerk in the counting house, the imperialism of any decent citizen that demands for this country its proper place in the councils of the Empire and in the destiny of the world. In this sense, imperialism means but the realization of a Greater Canada, the recognition of a wider citizenship.

I, that write these lines, am an Imperialist because I will not be a Colonial. This Colonial status is a worn-out, by-gone thing. The sense and feeling of it has become harmful to us. It limits the ideas, and circumscribes the patriotism of our people. It impairs the mental vigour and narrows the outlook of those that are reared and educated in our midst. . . .

. . . Our politics, our public life and thought, rise not to the level of our opportunity. The mud-bespattered politicians of the trade, the party men and party managers, give us in place of patriotic statecraft the sordid traffic of a tolerated jobbery. For bread, a stone. Harsh is the cackle of the little turkey-cocks of Ottawa, fighting the while as they feather their own mean nest of sticks and mud, high on their river bluff. Loud sings the little Man of the Province, crying his petty Gospel of Provincial Rights, grudging the gift of power, till the cry spreads and town hates town and every hamlet of the country-side shouts for its share of plunder and of pelf. This is the tenor of our politics, carrying as its undertone the voice of the black-robed sectary, with narrow face and shifting eyes, snarling still with the bigotry of a by-gone day. This is the spirit that we must purge. This is the demon we must exorcise; this is the disease, the canker-worm of corruption, bred in the indolent security of peace, that must be burned from us in the pure fire of an Imperial patriotism that is no theory but a passion. This is our need, our supreme need of the Empire—not for its ships and guns, but for the greatness of it, the soul of it, aye for the very danger of it. . . .

Nor is it ever possible or desirable that we in Canada can form an independent country. The little cry that here and there goes up among us is but the symptom of an aspiring discontent, that will not let our people longer be colonials. 'Tis but a cry forced out by what a wise man has called the growing pains of a nation's progress. Independent, we could not survive a decade. Those of us who know our country realize that beneath its surface smoulder still the embers of racial feud and of religious bitterness. Twice in our generation has the sudden alarm of conflict broken upon the quiet of our prosperity with the sound of a fire-bell in the night. Not thus our path. Let us compose the feud and still the strife of races, not in the artificial partnership of an Independent Canada, but in the joint greatness of a common destiny.

Nor does our future lie in Union with those that dwell to the Southward. The day of annexation to the United States is passed. Our future lies elsewhere. Be it said without concealment and without bitterness. They have chosen their lot; we have chosen ours. Let us go our separate ways in peace. Let them still keep their perennial Independence Day, with its fulminating fireworks and its Yankee Doodle. We keep our Magna Carta and our rough and ready Rule Britannia, shouting as lustily as they! The propaganda of Annexation is dead. Citizens we want, indeed, but not the prophets of an alien gospel. To you who come across our western border we can offer a land fatter than your Kansas, a government better than Montana, a climate kinder than your Dakota. Take it, Good Sir, if you will: but if, in taking it, you still raise your little croak of annexation, then up with you by the belt and out with you, breeches first, through the air, to the land of your origin! This in all friendliness.

Not Independence then, not annexation, not stagnation: nor yet that doctrine of a little Canada that some conceive,— half in, half out of the Empire, with a mimic navy of its own; a pretty navy this,—poor two-penny collection, frollicking on its little way strictly within the Gulf of St. Lawrence, a sort of silly adjunct to the navy of the Empire, semi-detached, the better to be smashed at will. As well a Navy of the Province, or the Parish, home-made for use at home, docked every Saturday in Lake Nipigon! . . .

Thus stands the case. Thus stands the question of the future of Canada. Find for us something other than mere colonial stagnation, something sounder than independence, nobler than annexation, greater in purpose than a little Canada. Find us a way. Build us a plan, that shall make us, in hope at least, an Empire Permanent and Indivisible.

XIX: 3 HENRI BOURASSA REJECTS BRITISH IMPERIALISM

In the dispute over Canada's participation in the Boer War, Henri Bourassa emerged as the new leader of French Canadian nationalism. For the next generation Bourassa ran the gamut from impeccable reasoning to irresponsible emotionalism in his fight to preserve Canadian and French Canadian freedom of action. These excerpts from a 1902 pamphlet, *Great Britain and Canada*, illustrate both techniques.

. . . British Imperialism—as opposed to British democracy, to British traditions, to British grandeur—is a lust for land-grabbing and military dominion. Born of the overgrowth of British power, bred by that stupid and blatant sense of pride known as *Jingoism*, it delights in high-sounding formulas:— *"Britannia, rule the waves!"* . . . *"Britons never shall be slaves!"* . . . *"Trade follows the Flag"* . . . *"What we have, we hold!"* . . .

Having undertaken more responsibilities than she is able to stand, surrounded as she is by hostile or indifferent nations, the new Britain of Mr. Chamberlain is in sore need of soldiers and sailors to prop the fabric raised by her frantic ambition. Being actually denuded of troops at home, she turns in distress to her colonies. Realising as they do that without practising evasion they cannot possibly achieve their purpose, British rulers of to-day resort to deceit and bribery with colonial states-men; they lull the credulity and inflame the jingo feelings of the people of the colonies. Under miscellaneous names and variegated uniforms—Royal Rifles, Mounted Infantry, Strath-cona Horse, Yeomanry—they extort from us whatever they may get in the shape of human material for their army; even if they have to dangle before our eyes a few paltry advantages to be thrown as a sop to us whenever we get tired of this deadly game.

In short, MILITARY CONTRIBUTIONS FROM THE COLONIES TO GREAT BRITAIN, in men and treasure, but mainly in men, constitute British Imperialism. . . .

* * *

From the presence of the two races in Canada, there is no reason, I believe, to dread any danger or even any additional troubles, if only our politicians be willing, instead of pander-ing to sectional prejudices, to appeal to the best sentiments of both elements.

A mutual regard for racial sympathies on both sides, and a proper discharge of our exclusive duty to this land of ours, such is the only ground upon which it is possible for us to meet, so as to work out our national problems. There are here neither masters nor valets; there are neither conquerors nor conquered ones: there are two partners whose partnership was entered into upon fair and well defined lines. We do not ask that our English-speaking fellow-countrymen should help us to draw closer to France; but, on the other hand, they have no right to take advantage of their overwhelming majority to infringe on the treaty of alliance, and induce us to assume, however freely and spontaneously, additional burdens in defence of Great Britain.

The Canadian soil, with its blood and its wealth, with its past, its present and its future, in short, our whole national inheritance is ours only to be handed down unimpaired to our descendants. I, for one, respect and admire in my English-speaking fellow-countryman his love for his dear old and glorious motherland;—and I am bound to say that he would be beneath my contempt the man who, in her hours of trial, did not tingle in sympathy with his Mother country. I have a right to expect that he should reciprocate that feeling by showing the same regard for his fellow-countrymen who still keep in their hearts an undying love for France, the land of their origin. But, apart from all such considerations within the province of the heart or of the mind, I say that the only sure way of obviating fatal misunderstandings lies in a determination that we shall, both of us, French and English alike, look at all constitutional and political questions from a purely Canadian standpoint. . . .

XIX: 4 SIR WILFRID LAURIER'S MODERATE POSITION

Despite enormous pressure from all sides, Sir Wilfrid Laurier held firmly to his middle course. He would neither acquiesce in nor flatly reject the points of view of either side. Selection (a) below, a letter to Chamberlain from Lord Minto, the Governor General, is a perceptive assessment of Laurier's attitude. In selection (b) Laurier passionately states his case in in the 1911 election campaign.

a. Lord Minto on Laurier

Sir Wilfrid's own inclination towards an imperial federation of any sort is, in my opininon, extremely doubtful—in fact, though his recent speeches appear to have been taken in England as enthusiastically imperialist, I am convinced they guarantee no such opinion. His speech in the House was very eloquent, and the "call us to your councils" phrase appears to have been accepted as indicating a wish to be called—the very last thing Sir Wilfrid would want, and the speech itself did not justify that interpretation of it. He recognized the strong British devotion to the motherland existent here, and the imperial feeling at home stronger perhaps than here, and got a chance for his great eloquence. But I should say that seriously he is devoid of the British feeling for a united

Empire, that it has no sentimental attraction for him, and that a closer connection with the old country he would consider from a utility point of view and nothing more. He recognizes the fact that his Canadian fellow-countrymen must follow the Anglo-Saxon lead, and will do his best to educate them up to it; but I believe it to be much more with the idea of the welding together of a Canadian nation than of forming part of a great Empire . . . and though he has never actually said so to me, I suspect that he dreams of Canadian independence in some future age. He thinks the arrangement of tariff questions far more likely to bring about imperial unity than any joint system of imperial defence; the former may be made to appear magnanimous in an imperial sense, but it would hardly be advocated by a colonial Government except in a belief in some practical gain to the colony from it, whilst the latter, upon which the safety of trade must depend, probably appears before the public merely as a direct increase in military expenditure to meet an obscure danger not generally realized.

b. Laurier in the 1911 Election

I am branded in Quebec as a traitor to the French, and in Ontario as a traitor to the English. In Quebec I am branded as a Jingo, and in Ontario as a Separatist. In Quebec I am attacked as an Imperialist, and in Ontario as an anti-Imperialist. I am neither. I am a Canadian. Canada has been the inspiration of my life. I have had before me as a pillar of fire by night and a pillar of cloud by day a policy of true Canadianism, of moderation, of conciliation. I have followed it consistently since 1896, and I now appeal with confidence to the whole Canadian people to uphold me in this policy of sound Canadianism which makes for the greatness of our country and of the Empire.

XX. Prewar Canadian Life

XX: 1 PROTESTANTISM IN CANADA

Canadians had always tended to combine their North
American exuberance and vitality with a strict adherence to Victorian codes of morality and religious
observance. In the years before World War I
Canadian Protestantism was at the height of its
political and social influence. These were the years
when the Lord's Day Act banned all commercial
activities on Sundays, when taking a pledge of total
abstinence was a qualification for membership in the
Methodist Church, and when the Women's Christian
Temperance Union was one of the most powerful
pressure groups in the nation. In these passages from
his famous study of Canadian society, *The Race
Question in Canada*, André Siegfried, a French
observer, discusses the religious affiliations and attitudes of English Canadians.

As in all the Anglo-Saxon countries, Protestantism in Canada
is divided into a very small number of large sects and an
infinite variety of small ones. The Methodists, Presbyterians,
Anglicans, and Baptists constitute nearly nine-tenths of the
whole. . . .

The Methodists—it is said of them alike by way of praise
and of blame—represent the respectable bourgeoisie, the class
of people who having made the most of their opportunities in

this world are conscious that they have also made satisfactory provision for their welfare in the next. Throughout Ontario, and especially in Toronto, they occupy a position of importance; they are not the most fashionable people of the town—for there is an Anglican "smart set" which regards itself as very superior in the mundane hierarchy—but they are more solid, more wealthy, they have more prosperous commercial establishments and finer churches. At the same time, they have a very keen sense of their role as Englishmen and Protestants, having carried with them from England the conviction of the inevitable supremacy of their race and the indisputable superiority of their religion.

Such is the twofold patrimony which they guard stoutly in the face of the French Canadians whom Providence has given them for neighbours. Canadian Methodism may be said to form the centre of anti-French, aggressive Protestantism. It is the Methodists who keep up the cry, "No French domination! No Popery!"

The Presbyterian Church, with its 842,000 members, comes next. As everywhere else, it is the Church of the Scots, that prosperous, industrious, and sympathetic race. In Nova Scotia and Manitoba it takes the lead among the Protestant sects, in Ontario it comes after Methodism. Wherever it is to be found predominant it stamps the life and habits of the public with its imprint of somewhat gloomy sternness. Winnipeg, which comes especially under its influence, is one of the most puritanical cities in the Dominion. It is a Western city, overflowing with energy and cosmopolitan to the last degree, yet there is nothing about it of the free, light-hearted tone that characterizes most of the other American cities of mushroom growth. This is particularly noticeable on Sundays.

Apart from their uncompromising morality, the Presbyterians are the most agreeable of companions. Their cordial bearing and their hospitality are proverbial; moreover, they display a special friendliness towards the French, who are quick to respond. England has reason to regard the Presbyterians as the best of her colonists. . . .

... Anglicanism has remained very British. As in the mother country it is especially the religion of people of the world and of the poor. The latter are drawn to its churches by the pomp of its ceremonies and by the fact that no great financial demands are made of them. The former, by the effect of a long tradition, by the memory of England where the Anglican Church is that of the sovereign and the social authorities. One need not believe that this last argument is without appeal to the "society" of Toronto, Montreal, and Victoria. This "society" accords to religious ceremonies an important place among social functions. And one may sense a certain rivalry between the Anglicans, aristocratic and pretentious, and the Methodists, overflowing with money but bourgeois.

The Baptists, to the number of 292,000, have a clearly popular character. Their dogmatic narrowness, their individualism, their democratic and egalitarian sense, make them a church apart, which has its well-marked place among the Methodists, Presbyterians and Anglicans. This is their strength, although "society" often affects to consider the Baptist form of religion as undistinguished, reserved for the lower classes, as Anglicanism is reserved for the aristocracy, Presbyterianism for the Scots, and Methodism for the commercial classes who are well on the way to success. . . .

To all appearance the independence of these churches in regard to the state has been absolutely established in the New World. Perhaps it would not be safe to say quite so positively that the state's independence of the churches, even the Protestant ones, is established to the same degree. The French conception of the lay state would seem never to have penetrated the Anglo-Saxon mind, and they have some difficulty in imagining a state entirely devoid of religious prepossessions. The Protestant clergy do not aim at controlling the government in the ultramontane Catholic fashion, but they do aim at informing it with their spirit. . . . Canada, never having had its 1789, has no real comprehension of the theory of the neutrality of the state. . . .

. . . Even among the poorer classes a man is looked at some-what askance who does not belong to some one denomination; and with the exception of certain mining districts in British Columbia in which the European tone of mind is in the ascendant, the English workmen and labourers are for the most part out-and-out Protestants. The census of 1901 records only 4,181 cases of persons declaring that they belong to no religion, and only 3,613 professed "agnostics," this word being explained in a note as comprising "atheists, free-thinkers, infidels, sceptics, and unbelievers." The Englishman is never really at ease until he is duly catalogued.

In reality, unbelief is frequent in Canada, as everywhere else, though it is not often openly professed. You will hear it admitted in smoking-rooms after a good dinner has given tongues their freedom. . . . But these are remarks which one avoids making outside of fairly intimate circles. Public expression of such sentiments would be severely judged by every-body. It would constitute a scandal, that is to say a sort of revolt against the existing order of things, against British tradition, almost an act of infidelity to the Anglo-Saxon race. It would also be a grave imprudence, for one would have much to lose materially as a result of such freedom. Public opinion would show no mercy. "Society" would find the declaration inelegant. More than one institution would expel you from its midst. In several of the English-Canadian univer-sities which depend partly for support on certain sects, a professor who should express anti-religious views would be severely reprimanded. Not that he is called upon to subscribe formally to any one creed. He is expected merely not to pro-claim his agnosticism. It is the same thing in several of the provinces with the teacher who has to read prayers in the school every morning.

In truth there is here a real hypocrisy, and some violence is done to freedom of speech. But the English do not resent this as Frenchmen would. They find it quite natural, when they belong to a hierarchy, to sacrifice certain prerogatives of their personality. . . .

One would be very wrong to doubt the depth of the anti-Catholic sentiment among Canadian Protestants. Manifestations of outward courtesy between the two religions do not signify much except perhaps a mutual recognition that the belligerents are respectable and worthy to cross swords with each other. In short, anti-Catholicism is much more violent in the Dominion than in Britain because the Roman Church in the colony is more sure of itself, more aggressive, more threatening, because the danger of its victory appears more possible, because, finally, the religious struggle is complicated by the struggle of the races.

Being the majority and, by right of conquest, masters of the country, the Protestants wish to preserve their supremacy. On this point they are uncompromising, and this is for them the primordial purpose. In a manner which is often roundabout and imperceptible, but which is also intransigent and tireless, they pursue this purpose, watching their rivals jealously, noting anxiously and indignantly their slightest progress in the councils of the state. It is thus that they have become accustomed to envisage the public affairs of the nation, from a point of view that is not secular or neutral but essentially confessional. Herein is to be seen a profound cause of the bitterness of the political struggles in Canada.

XX: 2 THE DEVELOPING WORKING CLASS

> Industrialization was just beginning in Canada before 1914; and Canadians were just beginning to notice the new social class that was being created by industrial and urban growth. The following excerpts from Siegfried's *The Race Question in Canada* show both the extent of the Canadian working class in 1906 and the degree to which it had begun to influence national life.

In spite of its growing industrial wealth, the Dominion still remains above all an agricultural country. It is to-day more or less what the United States were thirty or forty years ago, before a movement of expansion beyond all precedent made of them one of the leading manufacturing nations in the world. Consequently the artisan element is infinitely less numerous than the agricultural element.

There are, indeed, very important centres of industrial production, but they are scattered and far apart. First of all, we have in the east of the colony the group of Maritime Provinces, in which the steel works of Sydney (Cape Breton) stand out for notice. In the provinces of Quebec and Ontario must be mentioned the manufacturing regions of Montreal, Toronto, Hamilton, Kingston, and Quebec. It is in these localities that the great manufactories and the great industrial agglomerations are to be found. Proceeding westward, and leaving Sault Ste. Marie on one side, there is nothing to mark this side of the Rocky Mountains except the great camp of Winnipeg, an unfinished city, always in a state of reconstruction and fermentation and marvellous growth—a great agricultural centre, railway junction, and shop—the place whither the immigrants come and whence they go on again: in short, a new Chicago. Then at the other extremity of the continent, on the far side of the mountains, British Columbia, a land apart, distant, out of the way, almost self-governing—a land of fisheries, mines, and forests, with its half Canadian, half Californian mining centres of Crows' Nest Pass (coal), Rossland (iron and copper), Nanaimo, Cumberland, Ladysmith (coal). We must not forget finally an industry that is more important than any and that extends all over the surface of the colony—the vital, essential railway industry which affords employment to a considerable section of the working population.

By reason of this dispersion of a relatively small number of artisans over an enormous expanse of territory, by reason still more of their striking differences of origin, language, and character, there really does not exist, properly speaking, any working class in Canada. Moreover, there is not so wide a gulf between the industrial artisan and the agricultural labourer as exists with us—the distance between them is easily bridged. Thus no one ventures to talk of the "Canadian workman," for this expression does not convey any precise meaning, covering as it does many different types of men with nothing in common but the name.

In the Maritime provinces the industrial workman is generally a native of the country, though the Sydney steel manufactories have imported a good deal of American skilled labour. In this part of the colony, which stands somewhat to one side, the working population is mostly British, stolid, and somewhat slow-going. The more active elements are tempted, as everywhere in America, to go West.

If we pass to the French province, the contrast is remarkable. The French-Canadian artisan is usually a peasant attracted to the factory by the bait of regular wages. He provides an inferior kind of manual labour not exacting high wages, just as is the case in the great factories in New England. The psychology of the Quebec countryman turned artisan undergoes little change. He remains entirely under the control of the clergy, and his new role effaces in no way his national character. Many strikes have been stopped through the influence of the priests, and in many cases the workmen have accepted terms which otherwise they would have rejected, simply because the priests counselled submission. The Church does all it can to keep the French workmen apart from the English—this separation being essential, she feels, to the preservation of their race. Montreal, it should be mentioned, presents an exceptional state of things: the time is perhaps not far distant when the working class of this great city will become emancipated.

In Ontario we find workmen of a more purely Canadian kind. The Toronto artisan, akin to the artisan of the United States, but educated and trained in a very British atmosphere, is pre-eminently Canadian. If one could speak at all of the "Canadian workman," it is certainly in the great English province that it would be necessary to seek the type.

In the West—Manitoba, Alberta, Saskatchewan—American influence is very strong, the number of American immigrants being so considerable. The still greater number of European immigrants of all kinds when assimilated to their surroundings produce a type of workmen very different from those of Eastern Canada.

The province which has become most Americanized is British Columbia. With the exception of Victoria, which is a very English city, the whole of this region resembles most strikingly the neighbouring states of Washington, Idaho, Montana, and Oregon—themselves neighbouring states to California. Indeed, in spite of the Canadian Pacific Railway, British Columbia has more intimate connection with the American Northwest than with Eastern Canada. To the north as to the south of the frontier, you find mushroom cities springing up suddenly in the midst of a wonderful country, with a composite population of British, Americans, Europeans of all kinds, Chinese and Japanese; small wooden shanties, as many bars as dwelling-houses, on one side the trim residences of respectable folk, on the other whole streets given over to prostitution, swarming hives of Chinamen, such is the character of these Western cities, which have nothing in common, not merely with the cities of the East, but even with Winnipeg, Regina, or Calgary. You feel that the everlasting "boom" of California is not far distant.

. . . Employers have not a very well-defined attitude toward their employees. Some are ready to recognize the unions, others take their stand openly for resistance. It would seem that the Canadian working class are not yet sufficiently self-conscious to awaken the fears of the rich. The rich are at the stage where they declare themselves to have at heart the welfare of the workers, while preferring that these should not go too thoroughly into the question for themselves. In this respect the Liberal employers do not seem to differ appreciably from the Conservative.

The workers have begun the work of organizing themselves according to American methods, but have been retarded greatly by all their differences of race, language, moral and material conditions. In imitation of what has been done in the United States, they have established in most of the towns special trade unions for each trade; the different trade unions in each locality take part frequently in Trades and Labour Councils.

There is a general federation of these for the whole of Canada, known as the Trades and Labour Congress, which holds a general convention every year. The majority of the unions belonging to this Congress are affiliated to the American Federation of Labour. The word "general" which I have used is not quite accurate, however, for Nova Scotia, Prince Edward Island, and British Columbia have remained the centres of separate organizations.

These unions have until now devoted themselves principally to professional ends—the securing of higher wages, the reduction of the hours of labour, the improving of the conditions of employment either through their own action or by means of amicable negotiations with employers or through the mediation of the state. However, they have lately shown a tendency to take a larger part in politics, if not actually by asserting themselves at elections, at least in a general sense. The tendency of the Trades and Labour Congress is undoubtedly to exercise influence over the social legislation of the country. Some of the unions, chiefly in British Columbia, are of a distinctly socialistic character, but these are the exception. The others in their manifestoes are content to employ vague formulas by which they do not commit themselves. . . .

Coming now to the political side of the matter, we find that the Canadian workers, in spite of some isolated victories at the polls, have not yet succeeded in constituting themselves a third party. The organization of such a group involves, in truth, numerous difficulties. The agricultural predominance, the scattered condition of manufacturing industries, the absence of marked differences between the social classes, have all combined to prevent the growth of any real class feeling. If such a feeling exists in British Columbia and shows signs of coming into existence in Montreal, it cannot be said to be evident elsewhere. In a new country, prospering and developing rapidly, the general interests of all classes are too interlaced and interdependent for it to be easy to organize a class policy; the policy of national prosperity comes before all else.

XX:3 ELECTIONEERING

> Like so many other aspects of Canadian life, politics
> in the early twentieth century combined the old and
> the new—the "booze and bribes" of the nineteenth
> century and the careful balancing of powerful interest
> groups of the twentieth century. André Siegfried
> draws attention to both facets of Canadian politics
> in this description of a turn-of-the-century election.

Five or six weeks before the voting-day the candidates are
nominated by a local convention held in each constituency.
The siege of the masses has already taken place. What has still
to be done—and it is no small matter—is to hold on to friends
and to make sure of doubtful voters. In this work Canadian
politicians are dangerously expert, with their combination of
Norman shrewdness and Yankee realism.

In each local centre the candidate chooses four or five influential men, who are known in the French districts as chiefs;
according to the amount of money at his disposal, he hands
them sums of $20, $40, or $60, which it is understood that they
are to expend in the interest of the cause. Naturally a portion
of this money stops en route. The candidate is aware of this,
but he shuts his eyes, having need of the co-operation of people
of importance whose opinions are listened to. Besides, when
these have their pockets well lined with dollars, they carry
themselves with more assurance and have more go in them.
Having more confidence in themselves, they inspire more
confidence in others. Their bearing indicates that the party's
coffers are full, and their suggestion of opulence wins many
adherents. . . .

These first preparations having been seen to, the candidate
takes a carriage, a sledge, or a train, and begins a round of
visits and meetings. In the country districts—especially in the
French ones—he goes from locality to locality, following certain
traditional methods, visiting the smaller villages during the
week, and keeping the Sunday for the more populous centres.
It is in these, in the open space in front of the church, that he
delivers his most important addresses. In most of these open

spaces in the province of Quebec there are small wooden tribunes for use on such occasions. In fine weather everything goes off perfectly, but even if it rains or snows the meeting is not abandoned. Umbrellas go up, and those who are cold stamp their feet, while the orator's voice gives out the flowing periods, prefaced always with the words, "Messieurs les Electeurs!"

In the cities there is a different order of procedure. The mass of voters assemble together at monster meetings for a general exposition of the party programme, a public debate, and a visit by some personage of distinction; while smaller meetings are held in different quarters of the town, or for each separate profession.

But public meetings are not enough in themselves. House-to-house canvassing, as the English call it, is also essential. In the French districts the canvassers begin usually with the priest, unless his displeasure has been incurred, which is a grave matter, though not necessarily fatal. Then one proceeds to make the rounds of adherents and opponents, evading dangerous discussion with the latter, and talking rather of the weather, unless some one particular topic should appeal to them. All these ceremonies are carried out most politely, for the country-bred French Canadian is a lover of forms.

Visits of this kind are more difficult in the urban centres. In some of the Western cities, for instance, there are entire quarters inhabited by foreigners who only know a little English, and who are not to be reached by the ordinary posters or addresses. Special posters are made out for their benefit in their own languages, but they are scarcely to be won over otherwise than by personal visits, backed up by promises and presents. These foreigners constitute very important bands of voters, whose presence sometimes dangerously warps the meaning of appeals to the voters.

Meanwhile the great forces whose interests have been solicited and secured are not being inactive. Their co-operation is the result of the negotiations made before the party programme was completed. In return for the promise of a tariff or the withdrawal of some threatened parliamentary bill, the business men make money contributions, the Church puts into play the power of its propaganda.

The Canadian government, not having the Napoleonic bureaucracy at its back, is not able to exercise its influence after the fashion of ours. Its influence is called into action rather by its office-holders, who hold out promises in its name. "Vote for the government, and you shall have such and such a subvention, new railway, or appointment." These are the words you will hear uttered by the ministerialists—no attempt to disguise the nature of the market transaction (as with us). The Opposition, instead of protesting, retaliate with promises of what they will do for their supporters should they come into office. Thus both sides call into play the powers of the state in order to catch votes.

In a country in which the entire population belongs to one or other of two religions, it is inevitable that the voice of the clergy should count for much. It must be said, however, that the Protestant parsons and ministers do not as a rule take an active part in the elections. If they intervene, it is to plead for new laws in defence of morality or to combat existing laws which violate their Protestant idea of morals. They rarely take up a position as a body on the side of either party. As we have seen already, it is quite otherwise with the Catholic clergy.

But the predominant influence, which if a party is bent on victory must be either secured or rendered neutral, is that of the great commercial, industrial, and financial concerns. The resources of the government are to be assessed in money, whether they take the form of office, subventions, or public works. Now, the great concerns are well equipped for a contest with it upon this ground, having great armies of voters dependent upon them, besides having certain public bodies under their control. You hear of gas, water, and electric companies forcing a municipality to carry out their demands; of some huge industrial company, employing thousands of hands, dictating its wishes to a provincial ministry, to whom its support is necessary; of some director of a railway through some region with no other line of communication treating on equal terms with members of the federal government, and sometimes as master of some of its ministers. . . .

On the morning of the great day all available conveyances have been hired, often at exorbitant prices, a practice which reveals a characteristic form of corruption. The chief organizers, taking up a central position, keep in constant touch with the progress of the voting: in such a village, things go well; in such another, electors resident some distance off have failed to record their vote—a carriage is despatched to the scene at once to bring them in. Sometimes just the opposite manœuvre is resorted to with equal success: by some ingenious stratagem the adversary's electors are kept away from the polling booth. A Conservative railway company, for example, despatches Liberal workers miles away to execute some quite unnecessary piece of work!

At the end of the day the excitement has reached its utmost limit. Old men, invalids, cripples, are roped in. Sometimes these just turn the scales, the election being won by 40 or 50 votes out of 3,000 or 4,000. The victory can only go to a party which is perfectly organized. But it can be seen from our remarks that organization is capable of being carried to excess.

XX:4 PORTRAITS OF CANADIAN CITIES

In 1913-14 the as yet unrecognized English poet Rupert Brooke wrote a series of letters to a British newspaper describing his travels in the United States and Canada. The parts of his letters devoted to the Canadian cities he visited combine to form a delightful and basically accurate description of the kaleidoscope of Canadian national life just before World War I. To complete Brooke's survey a description of Vancouver and Victoria has been added from J. A. Hobson's *Canada Today* (published in 1906). The reader will be able to judge for himself how much of its prewar character each city has maintained.

a. Quebec

. . . Is there any city in the world that stands so nobly as Quebec? The citadel crowns a headland, three hundred feet high, that juts boldly out into the St. Lawrence. Up to it, up the side of the hill, clambers the city, houses and steeples and huts, piled one on the other. It has the individuality and the pride of a city where great things have happened, and over which many years have passed. Quebec is as refreshing and as definite after the other cities of this continent as an immortal among a crowd of stockbrokers. She has, indeed, the radiance and repose of an immortal; but she wears her immortality youthfully. When you get among the streets of Quebec, the mediæval, precipitous, narrow, winding, and perplexed streets, you begin to realise her charm. She almost incurs the charge of quaintness (abhorrent quality!) ; but even quaintness becomes attractive in this country. You are in a foreign land, for the people have an alien tongue, short stature, the quick, decided, cinematographic quality of movement, and the inexplicable cheerfulness which mark a foreigner. You might almost be in Siena or some old German town, except that Quebec has her street-cars and grain-elevators to show that she is living.

b. Montreal

. . . The outcome of it all was a vague general impression that Montreal consists of banks and churches. The people of this city spend much of their time in laying up their riches in this world or the next. Indeed, the British part of Montreal is dominated by the Scotch (sic) race; there is a Scotch spirit sensible in the whole place. The rather narrow, rather gloomy streets, the solid, square, grey, aggressively prosperous buildings, the general greyness of the city, the air of dour prosperity. Even the Canadian habit of loading the streets with heavy telephone wires, supported by frequent black poles, seemed to increase the atmospheric resemblance to Glasgow.

But besides all this there is a kind of restraint in the air, due, perhaps, to a state of affairs which, more than any other, startles the ordinary ignorant English visitor. The average man in England has an idea of Canada as a young-eyed daughter State, composed of millions of wheat-growers and backwoodsmen of British race. It surprises him to learn that more than a quarter of the population is of French descent, that many of them cannot speak English, that they control a province, form the majority in the biggest city in Canada, and are a perpetual complication in the national politics. Even a stranger who knows this is startled at the complete separateness of the two races. Inter-marriage is very rare. They do not meet socially; only on business, and that not often. In the same city these two communities dwell side by side, with different traditions, different languages, different ideals, without sympathy or comprehension. . . .

Montreal and Eastern Canada suffer from that kind of ill-health which afflicts men who are cases of 'double personality' —debility and spiritual paralysis. The 'progressive' British-Canadian man of commerce is comically desperate of peasants who *will not* understand that increase of imports and volume of trade and numbers of millionaires are the measures of a city's greatness; and to his eye the Roman Catholic Church, with her invaluable ally Ignorance, keeps up her incessant war against the general good of the community of which she is part. So things remain.

c. Ottawa

Ottawa came as a relief after Montreal. There is no such sense of strain and tightness in the atmosphere. The British, if not greatly in the majority, are in the ascendency; also, the city seems conscious of other than financial standards, and quietly, with dignity, aware of her own purpose. The Canadians, like the Americans, chose to have for their capital a city which did not lead in population or in wealth. This is particularly fortunate in Canada, an extremely individualistic country, whose inhabitants are only just beginning to be faintly conscious of their nationality. Here, at least, Canada is more than the Canadian. A man desiring to praise Ottawa would begin to do so without statistics of wealth and the growth of population; and this can be said of no other city in Canada except Quebec. Not that there are not immense lumber-mills and the rest in Ottawa. But the Government farm, and the Parliament buildings, are more imporant. Also, although the 'spoils' system obtains a good deal in this country, the nucleus of the Civil Service is much the same as in England; so there is an atmosphere of Civil Servants about Ottawa, an atmosphere of safeness and honour and massive buildings and well-shaded walks. After all, there is in the qualities of Civility and Service much beauty, of a kind which would adorn Canada. . . .

The streets of Ottawa are very quiet, and shaded with trees. The houses are mostly of that cool, homely, wooden kind, with verandahs, on which, or on the steps, the whole family may sit in the evening and observe the passers-by. This is possible for both the rich and the poor, who live nearer each other in Ottawa than in most cities. In general there is an air of civilization, which extends even over the country round. . . .

. . . What Ottawa leaves in the mind is a certain graciousness —dim, for it expresses a barely materialised national spirit— and the sight of kindly English-looking faces, and the rather lovely sound of the soft Canadian accent in the streets.

d. Toronto

Toronto (pronounce *T'ranto,* please) is difficult to describe. It has an individuality, but an elusive one; yet not through any queerness or difficult shade of eccentricity; a subtly normal, an indefinably obvious personality. It is a healthy, cheerful city (by modern standards) ; a clean-shaven, pink-faced, respectably dressed, fairly energetic, unintellectual, passably sociable, well-to-do, public-school-and-'varsity sort of city. One knows in one's own life certain bright and pleasant figures; people who occupy the nearer middle distance, unobstrusive but not negligible; wardens of the marches between acquaintanceship and friendship. It is always nice to meet them, and in parting one looks back at them once. They are, healthily and simply, the most fitting product of a not perfect environment; good-sorts;

normal, but not too normal; distinctly themselves, but not distinguished. They support civilisation. You can trust them in anything, if your demand be for nothing extremely intelligent or absurdly altruistic. One of these could be exhibited in any gallery in the universe, 'Perfect Specimen; Upper Middle Classes; Twentieth Century'—and we should not be ashamed. They are not vexed by impossible dreams, nor outrageously materialists, nor perplexed by overmuch prosperity, nor spoilt by reverse. Souls for whom the wind is always nor'-nor'-west, and they sail nearer success than failure, and nearer wisdom than lunacy. Neither leaders nor slaves—but no Tomlinsons! —whomsoever of your friends you miss, *them* you will certainly meet again, not unduly pardoned, the fifty-first by the Throne.

Such is Toronto. A brisk city of getting on for half a million inhabitants, the largest British city in Canada (in spite of the cheery Italian faces that pop up at you out of excavations in the street), liberally endowed with millionaires, not lacking its due share of destitution, misery, and slums. It is no mushroom city of the West, it has its history; but at the same time it has grown immensely of recent years. It is situated on the shores of a lovely lake; but you never see that, because the railways have occupied the entire lake front. So if, at evening, you try to find your way to the edge of the water, you are checked by a region of smoke, sheds, trucks, wharves, store-houses, 'depôts,' railway-lines, signals, and locomotives and trains that wander on the tracks up and down and across streets, pushing their way through the pedestrians, and tolling, as they go, in the American fashion, an immense melancholy bell, intent, apparently, on some private and incommunicable grief. Higher up are the business quarters, a few sky-scrapers in the American style without the modern American beauty, but one of which advertises itself as the highest in the British Empire; streets that seem less narrow than Montreal, but not unrespectably wide; "the buildings are generally substantial and often handsome" (the too kindly Herr Baedeker). Beyond that the residential part, with quiet streets, gardens open to the road, shady verandahs, and homes, generally of wood, that are a deal more pleasant to see than the houses in a modern English town.

Toronto is the centre and heart of the Province of Ontario; and Ontario, with a third of the whole population of Canada, directs the country for the present, conditioned by the French on one hand and the West on the other. And in this land, that is as yet hardly at all conscious of itself as a nation, Toronto and Ontario do their best in leading and realizing national sentiment. A Toronto man, like most Canadians, dislikes an Englishman; but, unlike some Canadians, he detests an American. And he has some inkling of the conditions and responsibilities of the British Empire. The tradition is in him. His father fought to keep Canada British. . . .

Toronto, soul of Canada, is wealthy, busy, commercial, Scotch, absorbent of whisky; but she is duly aware of other things. She has a most modern and efficient interest in education; and here are gathered what faint, faint beginnings or premonitions of such things as Art Canada can boast (except the French-Canadians, who, it is complained, produce disproportionately much literature, and waste their time on their own unprofitable songs). Most of those few who have begun to paint the landscape of Canada centre there, and a handful of people who know about books. In these things, as in all, this city is properly and cheerfully to the front. It can scarcely be doubted that the first Repertory Theatre in Canada will be founded in Toronto, some thirty years hence, and will very daringly perform *Candida* and *The Silver Box*. Canada is a live country, live, but not, like the States, kicking. In these trifles of Art and 'culture,' indeed, she is much handicapped by the proximity of the States. For her poets and writers are apt to be drawn thither, for the better companionship there and the higher rates of pay.

But Toronto—Toronto is the subject. One must say something—*what* must one say about Toronto? What can one? What has anybody ever said? It is impossible to give it anything but commendation. It is not squalid like Birmingham, or cramped like Canton, or scattered like Edmonton, or sham like Berlin, or hellish like New York, or tiresome like Nice. It is all right. The only depressing thing is that it will always be what it is, only larger, and that no Canadian city can ever be anything better or different. If they are good they may become Toronto.

e. Winnipeg

Winnipeg is the West. It is important and obvious that in Canada there are two or three (some say five) distinct Canadas. Even if you lump the French and English together as one community in the East, there remains the gulf of the Great Lakes. The difference between East and West is possibly no greater than that between North and South England, or Bavaria and Prussia; but in this country, yet unconscious of itself, there is so much less to hold them together. The character of the land and the people differs; their interests, as it appears to them, are not the same. Winnipeg is a new city. In the archives at Ottawa is a picture of Winnipeg in 1870—Mainstreet, with a few shacks, and the prairie either end. Now her population is a hundred thousand, and she has the biggest this, that, and the other west of Toronto. A new city; a little more American than the other Canadian cities, but not unpleasantly so. The streets are wider, and full of a bustle which keeps clear of hustle. The people have something of the free swing of Americans, without the bumptiousness; a tempered democracy, a mitigated independence of bearing. The manners of Winnipeg, of the West, impress the stranger as better than those of the East, more friendly, more hearty, more certain to achieve graciousness, if not grace. There is, even, in the architecture of Winnipeg, a sort of *gauche* pride visible. It is hideous, of course, even more hideous than Toronto or Montreal; but cheerily and windily so. There is no scheme in the city, and no beauty, but it is at least preferable to Birmingham, less dingy, less directly depressing. It has no real slums, even though there is poverty and destitution.

But there seems to be a trifle more public spirit in the West than the East. Perhaps it is that in the greater eagerness and confidence of this newer country men have a superfluity of energy and interest, even after attending to their own affairs, to give to the community. Perhaps it is that the West is so young that one has a suspicion money-making has still some element of a child's game in it—its only excuse. At any rate, whether because the state of affairs is yet unsettled, or because of the invisible subtle spirit of optimism that blows through the heavily clustering telephone-wires and past the neat little modern villas and down the solidly pretentious streets, one can't help finding a tiny hope that Winnipeg, the city of buildings and the city of human beings, may yet come to something. It is a slender hope, not to be compared to that of the true Winnipeg man, who, gazing on his city, is fired with the proud and secret ambition that it will soon be twice as big, and after that four times, and then ten times . . .

> "Wider still and wider
> Shall thy bounds be set,"

says that hymn which is the noblest expression of modern ambition. *That* hope is sure to be fulfilled. But the other timid prayer, that something different, something more worth having, may come out of Winnipeg, exists, and not quite unreasonably. That cannot be said of Toronto.

f. Prairie Cities

These cities grow in population with unimaginable velocity. From thirty to thirty thousand in fifteen years is the usual rate. Pavements are laid down, stores and bigger stores and still bigger stores spring up. Trams buzz along the streets towards the unregarded horizon that lies across the end of most roads in these flat, geometrically planned, prairie-towns. Probably a Chinese quarter appears, and the beginnings of slums. Expensive and pleasant small dwelling-houses fringe the outskirts; and rents being so high, great edifices of residential flats rival the great stores. In other streets, or even sandwiched between the finer buildings, are dingy and decaying saloons, and innumerable little booths and hovels where adventurers deal dishonestly in Real Estate, and Employment Bureaux. And there are the vast erections of the great corporations, Hudson's Bay Company, and the banks and the railways, and, sometimes almost equally impressive, the public buildings. There are the beginnings of very costly universities; and Regina has built a superb great House of Parliament, with a wide sheet of water in front of it, a noble building.

The inhabitants of these cities are proud of them, and envious of each other with a bitter rivalry. They do not love their cities as a Manchester man loves Manchester or a Münchener Munich, for they have probably lately arrived in them, and will surely pass on soon. But while they are there they love them, and with no silent love. They boost. To boost is to commend outrageously. And each cries up his own city, both from pride, it would appear, and for profit. For the fortunes of Newville are very really the fortunes of its inhabitants. From the successful speculator, owner of whole blocks, to the waiter bringing you a Martini, who has paid up a fraction of the cost of a quarter-share in a town-lot—all are the richer, as well as the prouder, if Newville grows. It is imperative to praise Edmonton in Edmonton. But it is sudden death to praise it in Calgary. The partisans of each city proclaim its superiority to all the others in swiftness of growth, future population, size of buildings, price of land—by all recognized standards of excellence. I travelled from Edmonton to Calgary in the company of a citizen of Edmonton and a citizen of Calgary. Hour after hour they disputed. Land in Calgary had risen from five dollars to three hundred; but in Edmonton from three to five hundred. Edmonton had grown from thirty persons to forty thousand in twenty years; but Calgary from twenty to thirty thousand in twelve. . . . "Where"—as a respite—"did I come from?" I had to tell them, not without shame, that my own town of Grantchester, having numbered three hundred at the time of Julius Cæsar's landing, had risen rapidly to nearly four by Doomsday Book, but was now declined to three-fifty. They seemed perplexed and angry.

g. Vancouver and Victoria

Vancouver's career has been a chequered one; it was utterly destroyed by fire nineteen years ago, and only within the last five years has emerged from insignificance. Like all Canadian cities, it is handsomely provided with electric power, and its lighting and tramway services give an exaggerated impression of its development. Its only real claim to distinction is the possession of Stanley Park, probably the most beautiful natural park in the world. Here, as in Winnipeg, the stranger is amazed by the profusion of solid banking-houses; it would almost seem as if the inhabitants must be a race of financiers, concerned purely with money and stocks and shares.

And, in point of fact, this is a land of speculation, in mining properties, lumber lands, fruit farms, and, above all, in city lots, the pick of which has doubled in value during the last two years. . . .

That there is much jealousy between the two cities [Vancouver and Victoria] goes without saying. . . . For there are many reasons why it would be convenient that the capital should be removed to the larger mainland city, with a bigger business and a brighter future, and the horrible thought rankles in the Victorian breast. For Victoria is proud of herself, and not without reason: she has beauty, and more pretensions to culture, or at any rate settled luxury of living, than any other city of the Canadian west; she has "antiquity," dating back to the gold rush of "the fifties," and all the dignity which belongs to officialism and the higher arts of Government. The pressure of British "loyalty" and "patriotism" is probably stronger to the square inch in Victoria than in any other spot in the Dominion: perhaps it is not idle to suggest that the name has contributed to that fact. The claim, however, is not distinctively political. It is upon their English ways of living, their English society, mode of speech, tone of voice, that the Victorians pride themselves. It is certainly the case that this older settlement, with its temperate atmosphere and its beautiful surroundings (there are few fairer scenes in the world than that furnished by a summer sail through the archipelago of islets that skirt the eastern shore of Vancouver), has impressed on its inhabitants gentler manners and more quiet and dignity of bearing than is elsewhere found. Probably this is due chiefly to the fact that for a generation or more Victoria has been the chosen place of residence and retirement for those British Columbians who have made their "pile," or at any rate their "modest competence," and have been tempted to withdraw from the ruder hustle of the mining and commercial centres.

XX:5 THE APPEAL OF THE WILDERNESS

The northern wilderness was the essence of prewar Canada, just as it has always been the essence of Canada. This is how Rupert Brooke reacted to northern Manitoba.

It is that feeling of fresh loneliness that impresses itself before any detail of the wild. The soul—or the personality— seems to have indefinite room to expand. There is no one else within reach, there never has been anyone; no one else is *thinking* of the lakes and hills you see before you. They have no tradition, no names even; they are only pools of water and lumps of earth, some day, perhaps to be clothed with loves and memories and the comings and goings of men, but now dumbly waiting their Wordsworth or their Acropolis to give them individuality, and a soul. In such country as this there is rarefied clean sweetness. The air is unbreathed, and the earth untrodden. All things share this childlike loveliness, the grey whispering reeds, the pure blue of the sky, the birches and thin fir-trees that make up these forests, even the brisk touch of the clear water as you dive.

That last sensation, indeed, and none of sight or hearing, has impressed itself as the token of Canada, the land. Every swimmer knows it. It is not languorous, like bathing in a warm Southern sea; nor grateful, like a river in a hot climate; nor strange, as the ocean always is; nor startling, like very cold water. But it touches the body continually with freshness, and it seems to be charged with a subtle and unexhausted energy. It is colourless, faintly stinging, hard and grey, like the rocks around, full of vitality, and sweet. It has the tint and sensation of a pale dawn before the sun is up. Such is the wild of Canada. It awaits the sun, the end for which Heaven made it, the blessing of civilisation. Some day it will be sold in large portions, and the timber given to a friend of ——'s, and cut down and made into paper, on which shall be printed the praise of prosperity; and the land itself shall be divided into town-lots and sold, and sub-divided and sold again, and boomed and resold, and boosted and distributed to fishy young men who will vend it in distant parts of the country; and then such portions as can never be built upon shall be given in exchange for great sums of money to old ladies in the quieter parts of England, but the central parts of towns shall remain in the hands of the wise. And on these shall churches, hotels, and a great many ugly sky-scrapers be built, and hovels for the poor, and houses for the rich, none beautiful, and there shall ugly objects be manufactured, rather hurriedly, and sold to the people at more than they are worth, because similar and cheaper objects made in other countries are kept out by a tariff. . . .

But at present there are only the wrinkled, grey-blue lake, sliding ever sideways, and the grey rocks, and the cliffs and hills, covered with birch-trees, and the fresh wind among the birches, and quiet, and that unseizable virginity. Dawn is always a lost pearly glow in the ashen skies, and sunset a multitude of softly-tinted mists sliding before a remotely golden West. They follow one another with an infinite loneliness. And there is a far and solitary beach of dark, golden sand, close by a deserted Indian camp, where, if you drift quietly round the corner in a canoe, you may see a bear stumbling along, or a great caribou, or a little red deer coming down to the water to drink, treading the wild edge of lake and forest with a light, secret, and melancholy grace.

XXI. The Conscription Crisis Of World War I

XXI: 1 ROBERT BORDEN INTRODUCES CONSCRIPTION

The issue of compulsory military service in World War I produced the most serious racial conflict in Canadian history. For the first three years of the war Canada was able to meet her military commitments through voluntary enlistment. In 1917, however, Prime Minster Borden returned from Europe convinced that conscription was now necessary. On June 11, 1917, he introduced the Military Service Bill, stating his reasons for taking this momentous step.

. . . During April and May we enlisted 11,790 men and during these same two months our casualties were 23,939. During the next seven months we need enforcements to the number of at least 70,000 in order to keep four divisions in the field, and to keep five divisions in the field we need 84,000 men, in both cases principally infantry. Continued offensive operations, such as those of April and May, might increase this number, and if the offensive continues it is not too much to say that we must expect this.

What is the conclusion I have drawn from all this? It is, as I have said before, that reinforcements must be obtained or the three divisions must dwindle; there is no alternative. The reinforcements now available will last for only a few months, the precise number of which, for military reasons, I am not at liberty to state. We all are proud that Canada has played a splendid and notable part in this war. The achievements of her troops have placed her in the very forefront of the nations, and the question before the House and the country today is this: Is Canada content to relax her efforts in the most critical period of a war which concerns her heritage, her status, and her liberty? . . .

. . . I desire to point out that this enactment is based upon the principle, which is as old as the principle of self-government, that while the state owes to its citizens certain duties, the citizen also owes corresponding duties to the state. To the citizen the state assures protection and security of his person and property, the enforcement of law and orderly government. To the state, each citizen owes a duty of service, and the highest duty of all is the obligation to assist in defending the rights, the institutions and the liberties of his country. . . .

XXI: 2 BOURASSA REJECTS CONSCRIPTION

> Only lukewarm in its support of the war, and already seething with dissatisfaction at attempts to limit the use of French in Ontario schools, Quebec violently opposed conscription. Even Laurier knew that he dared not try to swing Quebec in its favour. Henri Bourassa was once again the stormy spokesman for French Canada.

WHO SPOKE THE TRUTH?

For nearly three years of war, for more than seven years since *Le Devoir* was born to speak its mind, for eighteen years since I began the struggle against British Imperialism,—a foolish struggle, if you will, certainly without delusion, but also without capitulation—we never ceased saying: a blood tax is the logical, inevitable outcome of the principles laid down and actions pursued by the two parties which have in turn governed the country. The germ of conscription was contained in the "voluntary" expedition to South Africa; the regime of Imperial Conferences hatched it; the Navy Act of 1910 contributed to its growth; the emergency contribution proposed in 1913 strengthened it; the participation of Canada in the present war, decided in the name of the imperial solidarity of all British Countries, brought it to its deadly climax. . . .

CANADA HAS DONE ENOUGH

. . . All Canadians who want logically and effectively to oppose conscription ought to have the courage to say and to repeat everywhere: *"No conscription, no enlistments: Canada has done enough."* . . . we have enlisted for the European war six per cent of our population. That is the equivalent of an army of 2,400,000 for France and 2,700,000 for the United Kingdom. Now, despite its enormous army on paper England has not yet sent to France, in the two years and ten months of the war, this number of men.

. . . Another question may be fairly put in respect to our principal allies:—*How many French soldiers, or even British soldiers, would they send to America, if Canada was attacked by the United States?* . . .

THE LABOUR CRISIS—DANGER OF FAMINE

. . . What England has most need of is not soldiers, but bread, meat and potatoes.

. . . If the government at Ottawa had a real grasp of the situation, they would at once cease the enlistment and the transportation of new troops to Europe, and seek to stimulate agricultural production in Canada by all means at their command.

CONSCRIPTION OF WEALTH AND INDUSTRY

Another measure of conscription far more imperatively needed than conscription for cannon food is the conscription of capital and industry. . . . If it is just to let fall upon all classes of society the tax of blood and the heavy burden of military duties (or so-called duties), it is infinitely more equitable to distribute the charges of the war budget in proportion to the *capacity for paying*.

That millions of fathers of families, who can hardly balance their modest domestic budget, should be burdened with our taxes, while a few thousand vampires receive twenty, fifty, and as high as *nine hundred per cent*, thanks to the war and war operations, is absolutely unjust, immoral, contrary to social order and destructive of all economic equilibrium.

. . . let me remind you of a fundamental truth, and at the same time give you a piece of advice. The truth is that before being charged with the care of "saving" the Empire of France, "superior civilization" and "democracy", you are under the bounden obligation of saving Canada, its national unity, its internal peace. In the execution of what you believe to be your duty towards an Empire and humanity, you are preparing to increase the sufferings of the Canadian people, to make mothers weep, and to reduce to misery thousands of homes by depriving them of their natural sustenance. Take care that the people do not soon rise against you and against the vultures who are gorging themselves with millions torn from the vitals of the nation. The danger of to-morrow, threatening and formidable, all the world over, is not the triumph of "German Barbarism"; it is class hatred and social war. Even here the tempest is gathering more quickly than you imagine; conscription may be the first lightning in the storm. . . .

THE WAR AND THE RACE PROBLEM

French-Canadians, it cannot be too often repeated, are exclusively *Canadians*. Canada is their only country, their *unique patrie*. To no other country in the world—not to France, not to Britain—they acknowledge those duties which, at all times and in all lands, have been incumbent on the citizens of each country. Foremost among these exclusively *national* duties is military service, which entails the tax of blood.

Separated from France for one hundred and fifty years, first by the Cession, and perhaps even more by the French Revolution, the French-Canadians have preserved for the land of their origin a sincere affection. . . . But they do not consider themselves *obliged* to fight for France, any more than the French of Europe would believe themselves *bound* to fight for French Canada if "civil war" broke out here, or for Canada as a whole if the United States or Japan were to attack it. . . . If painful misunderstandings between Old and New France are to be averted, it is high time that this elementary truism should be stated.

As regards Great Britain, French-Canadians hold themselves bound—as all Canadians—by *all* the duties resulting from the Constitution (voted by the British Parliament), from the agreements made fifty years ago and over by the Imperial authorities and the Canadian government, and also from the respective positions occupied in the world by the two countries—but by *nothing more.* For a century and a half their religious and civil heads, the leaders of all parties, Liberal, Conservative, National, English and French, Protestant and Catholic, have taught them that they have no other military duty to perform than to defend the territory of Canada when it is directly attacked. That England, being sole mistress of the Empire's foreign policy, is alone bound to bear the burdens of imperial wars, has been the oft-repeated and never contradicted assertion of all those leaders. . . .

. . . The mentality of a people, its temperaments and ideas, cannot be changed in a moment; its principles of national life, its habits, its prejudices, if you will, cannot be destroyed in an hour, especially when they are of a sudden confronted with a doctrine radically opposed to that which has been, for a century and a half, presented to them as the only true one. . . .

It is idle to disguise the truth: *two millions of French-Canadians are opposed* en masse *to conscription.* . . .

Let these words be well pondered: the adoption of conscription will mark for the French-Canadians the beginning of an evolution that will soon transform the most peaceable, perhaps the most orderly, population of the two Americas into a revolutionary people. Once unleashed this revolutionary spirit will not rest; it will not only smart under military rule: it will make itself manifest in the factories, in the fields, everywhere, in all functions of our industrial, social, and political life. . . .

XXI: 3 ENGLISH CANADIAN SUPPORT FOR THE UNION GOVERNMENT

The election of 1917, really a plebiscite on the Union Government's conscription policy, was unparalleled in the bitterness of its charges and countercharges of cowardice, treason, corruption and tyranny. The great surge of English Canadian idealism that went into both the war effort and the election campaign is well illustrated in this pre-election statement by the Rev. S. D. Chown, General Superintendent of the Methodist Church of Canada (who in 1914 had volunteered for active service at age 61). Clergy of all Protestant denominations used their pulpits to urge voters to support the Union Government.

At the present time the supreme issue of winning the war so dominates the whole of Canada's present and future life, and will so affect the relation of our country to the world at large, that the old modes of political thought should be entirely superseded by loftier conceptions of patriotism, and our action as voters should be determined not by parochial, but by world-wide issues. The old bottles of party tradition must be burst with the new wine of national duty. . . .

This is a redemptive war, and its success depends entirely upon the height of sacrifice to which our people can ascend. It is under this conviction that ministers of the gospel feel in duty bound to enter the political arena. We shall fail and fail lamentably as Christian people unless we catch the martyr spirit of true Christianity and do our sacrificial duty between now and on the 17th of December. But if we do fail, I, for one, will never be sorry that I tried to bear aloft the banner of the cross amidst the fight. . . .

This war has so related our Dominion to the greatest nations on earth that we must ask regarding each ballot what effect it will have in London, Paris, Rome and Washington, on the one hand, and upon Berlin, Vienna, Sofia and Constantinople on the other. We must enquire what effect each ballot will have upon Christian civilization as opposed to undiluted barbarism: upon heaven as in contrast with hell. Surely we shall not permit ourselves to give a fiendish joy to the Turks, who, in their butchery of Armenian Christians, considered bullets too expensive, and used axes instead. . . .

The Borden Government certainly deserves criticism. Perhaps it should have punishment. But we are not dealing with it now, and if we stop to do so we would be like a man punishing a boy for some misconduct while the house about them both is burning to the ground.

To me it is as clear as the day that if we defeat conscription we cannot possibly get the last available man and fulfil our promise to Great Britain. We would then be a fit ally for the nation which has become notorious for tearing up scraps of paper. The Hun might well strike a medal to commemorate our defeat because it would be no less deadly to the national honor of Canada than the sinking of the *Lusitania* was to human life.

For these and other reasons I have been led to accept the policy of conscription or the selective draft. . . . I believe . . . that under any conditions it is the fairest, most democratic, most expeditious and least expensive method of raising an army in this country: and under present conditions it is the only possible way of fulfilling our obligations to Christian civilization. I also believe that socially considered it is the most moral and profoundly religious method of doing our national duty. . . .

If the Government be not sustained, the heart will be taken out of our soldiers. How could we face these men upon their return if we forsake them now? But I fear they would scorn to return. I fear they might forswear their country and die fighting, if need be, under another flag.

In my judgment, the elector who votes for the anti-conscription policy and the repeal of the Military Service Act, with the consequent inevitable withdrawal of Canada from the war, forges three links in a fatal chain of personal humiliation, public contempt and national decay. He alienates Canada from the rest of the Empire and from association with the respectable portion of mankind. He degrades the term Canadian from a synonym of glory to a badge of dishonour and a by-word of reproach. "Lo this man began to build and was not able to finish." If I voted against a Union Government candidate I would feel that I was opposing the most patriotic movement ever known in the Dominion of Canada. . . .

XXI:4 QUEBEC DEBATES SEPARATION

The Liberal party's crushing defeat in the 1917 election (82 Liberals to 153 Unionists) marked the lowest point in racial relations in Canada since 1759. In January, 1918, the Quebec Legislature debated J. N. Francoeur's motion suggesting the breaking of Confederation. These excerpts from his speech indicate the sense of resignation and futility most French Canadians felt about Confederation. The motion was withdrawn without a vote.

THE MOTION: "That this House is of the opinion that the Province of Quebec would be disposed to accept the breaking of the Confederation Pact of 1867 if, in the other provinces, it is believed that she is an obstacle to the union, progress and development of Canada."

. . . Have we met the wishes of the fathers of confederation? Has the province of Quebec in particular respected the undertakings implied in this partnership agreement? Has she neglected or fulfilled the duties and obligations it imposes? Without fear of contradiction we can affirm that we have never shrunk from any duty and that we have never shirked any responsibility.

We have enjoyed the liberty that was granted us while respecting that of others. We have preserved and defended our autonomy without ever infringing upon that of others. We have respected the rights of the minority here and we have demanded that the same thing be done elsewhere. As Brown wished, we have wanted everybody placed on a footing of equality.

No idea of domination entered our efforts in favor of the use of our language, the respect of our rights recognized by our constitution. No desire for conquest has animated us in our aspirations. All the struggles we have carried on had as their aim nothing but the defense of what we considered to be the expression of the constitution. Impartial history will bear witness that the French-Canadians remained Canadians before everything. . . .

To bring about . . . reunion of the races, we have gone to the extreme limit of conciliation and of concessions. Sometimes we have even made sacrifices at the expense of our acquired rights and our race pride. We have not got credit for it. . . .

They have said that in presenting this motion we were acknowledging ourselves discouraged, and even beaten, that the time was badly chosen for reminding this province of the position she occupies just now. We have been told, further, that in putting forward the problem in this way we ran the risk of still further arousing against us those who have been fighting us for years. We wished to express the sentiment of the very great majority of our people who are tired of being treated in this manner and who think that the time has come either to stop these futile struggles or to accept their logical consequences. This resolution gives notice to her detractors that if the province of Quebec is in the way in Confederation she is ready to discuss the matter and accept her responsibility. She did not want this extreme recourse, but she has never faltered at any sacrifice when her honor was at stake. . . .

A United States newspaper, in speaking some days ago of the situation in the province of Quebec, asked what was the real desire of the French-Canadians. What we want is *to live*

and let live. To live observing not only the letter of the
constitution but its spirit more particularly; to live according
to our tastes, our temperament and our mentality; to live as
free citizens, conscious of our duties and careful of our
responsibilities; to live working for the progress and development of our province, convinced that in this way we are assuring the progress and development of the country; to live
preserving our language, our faith, our traditions, our institutions and our laws; to live, in a word, as loyal Canadians
devoted to the British crown. *Let Live!* To respect among
others those things we demand that they respect among us; to
recognize the liberty they wished to enjoy in the exercise of
their acquired rights; to let them speak and teach their
language, retain their faith and their traditions, and even to
struggle with them, if it is necessary, for the defense of this
heritage which they hold as dear as we. . . . It is in this way
that we will become in real truth a Canadian nation. . . .

XXII. Postwar Ferment

XXII: 1 THE FARMERS' PLATFORM, 1918

Believing that the old parties had long been controlled by eastern businessmen hostile to agrarian interests, and concerned with the uncertain postwar economic situation, Canadian farmers massively rejected the major political parties immediately after World War I. The Farmers' Platform, portions of which follow, was originally drawn up by the Canadian Council of Agriculture and reissued in 1918 as The New National Policy. It became the doctrinal basis of the Progressive Party. Basically a demand for low tariffs, the Farmers' Platform also anticipated some of the radicalism of the C.C.F.

3. Whereas Canada is now confronted with a huge national war debt and other greatly increased financial obligations, which can be most readily and effectively reduced by the development of our natural resources, chief of which is agricultural lands;

And whereas it is desirable that an agricultural career should be made attractive to our returned soldiers and the large anticipated immigration, and owing to the fact that this can best be accomplished by the development of a national policy which will reduce to a minimum the cost of living and the cost of production; ...

And whereas Agriculture—the basic industry upon which the success of all other industries primarily depends—is unduly handicapped throughout Canada as shown by the declining rural population in both eastern and western Canada, due largely to the greatly increased cost of agricultural implements and machinery, clothing, boots and shoes, building material and practically everything the farmer has to buy, caused by the Protective Tariff, so that it is becoming impossible for farmers generally, under normal conditions, to carry on farming operations profitably;

And whereas the Protective Tariff is the most wasteful and costly method ever designed for raising national revenue, because for every dollar obtained thereby for the public treasury at least three dollars pass into the pockets of the protected interests, thereby building up a privileged class at the expense of the masses, thus making the rich richer and the poor poorer;

And whereas the Protective Tariff has been and is a chief corrupting influence in our national life because the protected interests, in order to maintain their unjust privileges, have contributed lavishly to political and campaign funds, thus encouraging both political parties to look to them for support, thereby lowering the standard of public morality;

Therefore be it resolved that the Canadian Council of Agriculture, representing the organized farmers of Canada, urges that as a means of remedying these evils and bringing about much needed social and economic reforms, our tariff laws should be amended as follows:

(a) By an immediate and substantial all-round reduction of the customs tariff.

(b) By reducing the customs duty on goods imported from Great Britain to one-half the rates charged under the general tariff, and that further gradual, uniform reductions be made in the remaining tariff on British imports that will ensure complete Free Trade between Great Britain and Canada in five years.

(c) That the Reciprocity Agreement of 1911, which still remains on the United States statute books, be accepted by the Parliament of Canada.

(d) That all foodstuffs not included in the Reciprocity Agreement be placed on the free list.

(e) That agricultural implements, farm machinery, vehicles, fertilizers, coal, lumber, cement, illuminating fuel and lubricating oils be placed on the free list, and that all raw materials and machinery used in their manufacture also be placed on the free list.

(f) That all tariff concessions granted to other countries be immediately extended to Great Britain. . . .

4. As these tariff reductions may very considerably reduce the national revenue from that source, the Canadian Council of Agriculture would recommend that, in order to provide the necessary additional revenue for carrying on the government of the country and for the bearing of the cost of the War direct taxation be imposed in the following manner:

(a) By a direct tax on unimproved land values including all natural resources.

(b) By a graduated personal income tax.

(c) By a graduated inheritance tax on large estates.

(d) By a graduated income tax on the profits of corporations. . . .

7. A land settlement scheme based on a regulating influence in the selling price of land. Owners of idle areas should be obliged to file a selling price on their lands, that price also to be regarded as an assessable value for purposes of taxation.

8. Extension of co-operative agencies in agriculture to cover the whole field of marketing, including arrangements with consumers' societies for the supplying of foodstuffs at the lowest rates and with the minimum of middleman handling.

9. Public ownership and control of railway, water and aerial transportation, telephone, telegraph and express systems, all projects in the development of natural power, and of the coalmining industry.

10. To bring about a greater measure of democracy in government, we recommend:

(a) The immediate repeal of the War-Time Elections Act.

(b) The discontinuance of the practice of conferring titles upon citizens of Canada.

(c) The reform of the Federal Senate.

(d) An immediate check upon the growth of government by Order-in-Council, and increased responsibility of individual members of Parliament in all legislation.

(e) The complete abolition of the patronage system.

(f) The publication of contributions and expenditures both before and after election campaigns.

(g) The removal of press censorship upon the restoration of Peace and the immediate restoration of the rights of free speech.

(h) The setting forth by daily newspapers and periodical publications, of the facts of their ownership and control.

(i) Proportional representation.

(j) The establishment of measures of Direct Legislation through the initiative, referendum, and recall.

(k) The opening of seats in Parliament to women on the same terms as men.

XXII:2 THE IMPACT OF THE WAR AND THE SOCIAL GOSPEL

The intellectual basis of the movements for social change in postwar Canada was a synthesis of European socialism, the "Social Gospel" movement in the United States, and the lessons of wartime economic regulation. Believing that their mission was to reform society, as opposed to individuals, (hence the term "Social Gospel"), many Canadian clergy—and ex-clergy such as J. S. Woodsworth—took the lead in demanding social reforms after the war. The following excerpt from a report accepted by the Methodist Church in 1918 shows how the war experience had

> reinforced the Church's pre-war social concern. At
> the time the report was considered the most radical
> statement ever adopted by a North American religious
> body.

The present economic system stands revealed as one of the
roots of the war. The insane pride of Germany, her passion
for world-domination found an occasion in the demand for
colonies as markets and sources of raw materials—the imperative need of competing groups of industries carried on for
profits.

The war has made more clearly manifest the moral perils
inherent in the system of production for profits. Condemnation of special individuals seems often unjust and always
futile. The system rather than the individual calls for change.

The war is the coronation of democracy. No profounder
interpretation of the issue has been made than the great phrase
of President Wilson's that the Allies are fighting to "make the
world safe for democracy." It is clearly impossible for the
champions of democracy to set limits to its recognition. The
last century democratized politics; the 20th century has found
that political democracy means little without economic
democracy. The democratic control of industry is just and
inevitable.

Under the shock and strain of this tremendous struggle,
accepted commercial and industrial methods based on individualism and competition have gone down like mud walls in
a flood. National organization, national control, extraordinary
approximations of national equality have been found essential
to efficiency. . . .

The conclusion seems irresistible. The war is a sterner
teacher than Jesus and uses far other methods, but it teaches
the same lesson. The social development which it has so
unexpectedly accelerated has the same goal as Christianity,
that common goal is a nation of comrade workers, as now at
the trenches, fights so gloriously—a nation of comrade fighters.

With the earthquake shocks of war thundering so tremendous a reaffirmation to the principles of Jesus, it would be

the most inexcusable dereliction of duty on the part of the Church not to re-state her programme in modern terms and re-define her divinely-appointed goal.

The triumph of democracy, the demand of the educated workers for human conditions of life, the deep condemnation this war has passed on the competitive struggle, the revelation of the superior efficiency of rational organization and co-operation, combine with the unfulfilled, the often forgotten, but the undying ethics of Jesus, to demand nothing less than a transference of the whole economic life from a basis of competition and profits to one of co-operation and service. . . .

We, therefore, look to our national government—and the factor is a vital one—to enlist in the service of the nation those great leaders and corporations which have shown magnificent capacity in the organizing of life and resources for the profit of shareholders. Surely the same capacity can find nobler and more deeply satisfying activity in the service of the whole people rather than in the service of any particular group. . . .

But we do not believe this separation of labor and capital can be permanent. Its transcendence, whether through co-operation or public ownership, seems to be the only constructive and radical reform.

This is the policy set forth by the great labor organizations and must not be rejected because it presupposes, as Jesus did, that the normal human spirit will respond more readily to the call to service than to the lure of private gain.

The acceptance of this report, it cannot be too clearly recognized, commits this Church, as far as this representative body can commit it, to nothing less than a complete social reconstruction. . . . We think it is clear that nothing less than the goal we have outlined will satisfy the aroused moral consciousness of the Church or retain for the Church any leadership in the testing period that is upon them. And in such an heroic task as this our citizen armies will find it possible to preserve, under the conditions of peace, the high idealism with which they have fought for democracy in France.

XXII:3 THE CAUSES OF LABOUR UNREST, 1919

Canada was swept by waves of labour unrest immediately following the war, culminating in the Winnipeg General Strike in 1919. A federal Royal Commission was appointed to discover whether the strikes were the product of real grievances or of radical agitation. The Commission's assessment and recommendations are given below.

. . . The unrest is most pronounced in western Canada. There it assumes a distinctly different character from that which prevails in eastern Canada. In several western cities labour was represented by many holding extreme radical views. Undoubtedly a portion of the labour unrest at present prevailing is to be ascribed to the upheavals in Europe and the disturbed state of the public mind generally owing to the war. This has given rise to a desire on the part of workers generally to secure a position for themselves in a comparatively short period of time, which otherwise might have been the result of evolution during a long period of years. This desire varies in degree amongst different groups of workers. One group lays down as a principle the complete possession by themselves of the machinery of production and the full product of their toil, whilst the group at the other extreme would be satisfied with merely a larger purchasing power of the wages they receive. In between these groups lie the more moderate, and we believe the majority, who would welcome co-operation and industrial peace until by a gradual process of evolution a system may be ushered in by which the workers will receive a more adequate share of what their labour produces.

. . . Though the advocacy of extreme views both by speech and by the distribution of literature may be a contributing cause to occasional outbursts, the real causes of unrest are of a more fundamental nature.

The chief causes of unrest may be enumerated as follows:

1. Unemployment and the fear of unemployment.

2. High costs of living in relation to wages and the desire of the worker for a larger share of the product of his labour.

3. Desire for shorter hours of labour.

4. Denial of the right to organize and refusal to recognize Unions.

5. Denial of collective bargaining.

6. Lack of confidence in constituted government.

7. Insufficient and poor housing.

8. Restrictions upon the freedom of speech and press.

9. Ostentatious display of wealth.

10. Lack of equal educational opportunities. . . .

We recommend that legislation be enacted to provide for:

(a) Fixing of a minimum wage, specially for women, girls, and unskilled labour.

(b) Maximum work day of 8 hours and weekly rest of not less than 24 hours.

We recommend immediate enquiry by expert boards into the following subjects, with a view to early legislation:

(a) State insurance against unemployment, sickness, invalidity and old age.

(b) Proportional representation.

We recommend that suitable action be taken by the Government to:

(a) Regulate public works to relieve unemployment.

(b) Help the building of workers' homes.

(c) Establish a bureau for promoting Industrial Councils.

(d) Restore fullest liberty of freedom of speech and press.

Other general recommendations are:

(a) Right to organize. Recognition of Unions.

(b) Payment of a living wage.

(c) Collective bargaining.

(d) Extension of equal opportunities in education.

(e) Steps towards establishment of Joint Plant and Industrial Councils.

(f) That the findings of the Commission be put into effect in all work controlled by the Government where the principles of democratic management can be applied. . . .

XXIII. The Achievement Of Independence

XXIII: 1 GAINS DURING THE WAR

The huge contributions of Britain's Dominions to the war effort were vitally important in quickening the expansion of the sphere of colonial autonomy. Selection (a), Resolution 9 of the Imperial War Conference of 1917, pointed the way to the progress of the 1920's. In his comments on Resolution 9, selection (b), Robert Borden gives his view of the evolution of the Empire.

a. Resolution 9 of the Imperial War Conference, 1917

The Imperial War Conference are of opinion that the readjustment of the constitutional relations of the component parts of the Empire is too important and intricate a subject to be dealt with during the war, and that it should form the subject of a special imperial conference to be summoned as soon as possible after the cessation of hostilities. They deem it their duty, however, to place on record their view that any such readjustment, while thoroughly preserving all existing powers of self-government and complete control of domestic affairs, should be based upon a full recognition of the dominions as autonomous nations of an imperial commonwealth, should recognize their right to an adequate voice in foreign policy and in foreign relations, and should provide effective arrangements for continuous consultation in all important matters of common imperial concern and for such necessary concerted action founded on consultation as the several governments may determine.

b. Borden on Resolution 9

. . . Foreign policy and foreign relations, with which is intimately connected the question of the common defence of the Empire, have been under the immediate control of the government of the United Kingdom, responsible to the Parliament of the United Kingdom. It would appear from the views of constitutional critics that this condition during the later phases of the growth of the overseas dominions has proceeded on a theory of trusteeship which, whatever may be said of it in the past, is certain to prove not only entirely inadequate to the needs of the Empire, but incompatible with the aspirations of the people of the dominions in the future. . . .

. . . I say this with a full understanding that it is unwise, having regard to the lessons of the past, for any of us to predict absolutely the developments of the future. But, nevertheless, the line of development which has been noticeable during the past twenty or twenty-five years seems to point unmistakeably to that conclusion. Indeed, the action of the dominions in this war has made the spirit of nationhood splendidly manifest. The fact that one million men in the dominions have taken up arms for the defence of the Empire's existence and the maintenance of its future influence is so significant a lesson that one would be unwise not to have it constantly in mind. I believe that the dominions fully realize the ideal of an imperial commonwealth of united nations, and one should not forget the importance of the Crown as a tie between the dominions and the mother country. . . .

XXIII:2 AN INDEPENDENT FOREIGN POLICY, 1923

Until the early 1920's it was still hoped that Britain and her Dominions could follow a common foreign policy in which each nation had a voice. The Chanak crisis of 1922 showed the futility of this hope. In these resolutions regarding the making of treaties, the Imperial Conference of 1923, in effect, recognized the existence of separate foreign policies within the Empire. The resolutions were necessitated by Canada's unprecedented negotiation of the Halibut Treaty with the United States earlier in the year.

. . . The Conference recommends for the acceptance of the governments of the Empire represented that the following procedure should be observed in the negotiation, signature and ratification of international agreements. . . .

1. *Negotiation*

(a) It is desirable that no treaty should be negotiated by any of the governments of the Empire without due consideration of its possible effect on other parts of the Empire, or, if circumstances so demand, on the Empire as a whole.

(b) Before negotiations are opened with the intention of concluding a treaty, steps should be taken to ensure that any of the other governments of the Empire likely to be interested are informed, so that, if any such government considers that its interests would be affected, it may have an opportunity of expressing its views, or, when its interests are intimately involved, of participating in the negotiations.

(c) In all cases where more than one of the governments of the Empire participates in the negotiations, there should be the fullest possible exchange of views between those governments before and during the negotiations. In the case of treaties negotiated at International Conferences, where there is a British Empire Delegation, on which, in accordance with the now established practice, the Dominions and India are separately represented, such representation should also be utilised to attain this object.

(d) Steps should be taken to ensure that those governments of the Empire whose representatives are not participating in the negotiations should, during their progress, be kept informed in regard to any points arising in which they may be interested. . . .

XXIII: 3 THE BALFOUR REPORT, 1926

The 1926 Imperial Conference adopted the report of a committee chaired by Lord Balfour, which defined the new relationship among the members of the British Commonwealth. This remains the classic definition of Canada's status within the Commonwealth.

The Committee are of opinion that nothing would be gained by attempting to lay down a Constitution for the British Empire. Its widely scattered parts have very different characteristics, very different histories, and are at very different stages of evolution; while, considered as a whole, it defies classification and bears no real resemblance to any other political organization which now exists or has ever yet been tried.

There is, however, one most important element in it which, from a strictly constitutional point of view, has now, as regards all vital matters, reached its full development—we refer to the group of self-governing communities composed of Great Britain and the Dominions. Their position and mutual relation may be readily defined. They are autonomous Communities within the British Empire, equal in status, in no way subordinate one to another in any aspect of their domestic or external affairs, though united by a common allegiance to the Crown, and freely associated as members of the British Commonwealth of Nations.

A foreigner endeavouring to understand the true character of the British Empire by the aid of this formula alone would be tempted to think that it was devised rather to make mutual interference impossible than to make mutual co-operation easy.

Such a criticism, however, completely ignores the historic situation. The rapid evolution of the Oversea Dominions during the last fifty years has involved many complicated adjustments of old political machinery to changing conditions. The tendency towards equality of status was both right and inevitable. Geographical and other conditions made this impossible of attainment by the way of federation. The only alternative was by the way of autonomy; and along this road it has been steadily sought. Every self-governing member of the Empire is now the master of its destiny. In fact, if not always in form, it is subject to no compulsion whatever.

But no account, however accurate, of the negative relations in which Great Britain and the Dominions stand to each other can do more than express a portion of the truth. The British Empire is not founded upon negations. It depends essentially, if not formally, on positive ideals. Free institutions are its life-blood. Free co-operation is its instrument. Peace, security, and progress are among its objects. Aspects of all these great themes have been discussed at the present Conference; excellent results have been thereby obtained. And though every Dominion is now, and must always remain, the sole judge of the nature and extent of its co-operation, no common cause will, in our opinion, be thereby imperilled.

Equality of status, so far as Britain and the Dominions are concerned, is thus the root principle governing our Inter-Imperial Relations. . . .

XXIII:4 THE STATUTE OF WESTMINSTER, 1931

The Balfour Report had also recommended the specific changes necessary to make this new status a reality. The Statute of Westminster put most of these changes into effect. With the passage of the Statute the only restriction on Canada's independence was the lack of a formula to amend the British North America Act. Such a formula could not be devised because of disagreements between the federal and provincial governments in Canada.

An Act to give effect to certain resolutions passed by Imperial Conferences held in the years 1926 and 1930

Whereas the delegates to His Majesty's Governments in the United Kingdom, the Dominion of Canada, the Commonwealth of Australia, the Dominion of New Zealand, the Union of South Africa, the Irish Free State and Newfoundland, at Imperial Conferences holden at Westminster in the years of our Lord nineteen hundred and twenty-six and nineteen hundred and thirty did concur in making the declarations and resolutions set forth in the Reports of the said Conferences:

And whereas it is meet and proper to set out by way of preamble to this Act that, inasmuch as the Crown is the symbol of the free association of the members of the British Commonwealth of Nations, and as they are united by a common allegiance to the Crown, it would be in accord with the established constitutional position of all the members of the Commonwealth in relation to one another that any alteration in the law touching the Succession to the Throne or the Royal Style and Titles shall hereafter require the assent as well of the Parliaments of all the Dominions as of the Parliament of the United Kingdom:

And whereas it is in accord with the established constitutional position that no law hereafter made by the Parliament of the United Kingdom shall extend to any of the said Dominions as part of the law of that Dominion otherwise than at the request and with the consent of that Dominion:

And whereas it is necessary for the ratifying, confirming and establishing of certain of the said declarations and resolutions of the said Conferences that a law be made and enacted in due form by authority of the Parliament of the United Kingdom:

And whereas the Dominion of Canada, the Commonwealth of Australia, the Dominion of New Zealand, the Union of South Africa, the Irish Free State and Newfoundland have severally requested and consented to the submission of a measure to the Parliament of the United Kingdom for making such provision with regard to the matters aforesaid as is hereafter in this Act contained:

Now, therefore, be it enacted by the King's Most Excellent

Majesty by and with the advice and consent of the Lords Spiritual and Temporal, and Commons, in this present Parliament assembled, and by the authority of the same, as follows:

1. In this Act the expression "Dominion" means any of the following Dominions, that is to say, the Dominion of Canada, the Commonwealth of Australia, the Dominion of New Zealand, the Union of South Africa, the Irish Free State and Newfoundland.

2. (1) The Colonial Laws Validity Act, 1865 [making void Dominion statutes that conflicted with Imperial statutes] shall not apply to any law made after the commencement of this Act by the Parliament of a Dominion.

(2) No law and no provision of any law made after the commencement of this Act by the Parliament of a Dominion shall be void or inoperative on the ground that it is repugnant to the law of England, or to the provisions of any existing or future Act of Parliament of the United Kingdom, or to any order, rule, or regulation made under any such Act, and the powers of the Parliament of a Dominion shall include the power to repeal or amend any such Act, order, rule or regulation in so far as the same is part of the law of the Dominion.

3. It is hereby declared and enacted that the Parliament of a Dominion has full power to make laws having extraterritorial operation.

4. No Act of Parliament of the United Kingdom passed after the commencement of this Act shall extend or be deemed to extend, to a Dominion as part of the law of that Dominion, unless it is expressly declared in that Act that that Dominion has requested, and consented to, the enactment thereof.

7. (1) Nothing in this Act shall be deemed to apply to the repeal, amendment or alteration of the British North America Acts, 1867 to 1930, or any order, rule or regulation made thereunder. . . .

11. Notwithstanding anything in the Interpretation Act, 1889, the expression "Colony" shall not, in any Act of the Parliament of the United Kingdom passed after the commencement of this Act, include a Dominion or any Province or State forming a part of a Dominion. . . .

XXIV. Dealing With The Depression

XXIV:1 MACKENZIE KING ON UNEMPLOYMENT RELIEF

Mackenzie King's government, like the governments of most other countries, did not really understand what had happened in 1929. The Liberals pursued a negative policy of denying there was a crisis and hence doing little to alleviate it other than calling for "confidence." King's attitude is obvious in this House of Commons speech in reply to criticisms of the government's failure to give funds for unemployment relief to the provinces. His now famous remark, "I would not give them a five-cent piece," was to haunt King in the 1930 election and for the rest of the depression.

. . . I submit that there is no evidence in Canada to-day of an emergency situation which demands anything of that kind. Every winter in this country, ever since there was a winter or a Canada, there has been unemployment and there always will be. That situation unquestionably may be aggravated by particular conditions, and when a condition becomes aggravated for any locality, human justice and feeling would demand that those localities that are immediately associated should come as neighbours and share in the relief of the situation. When a local condition becomes too great to deal with, the province in which that municipality is situated should be the body next to deal with the matter. . . . But in the absence of any representations whatever from any provincial government to the federal government for aid of this kind, or representations indicating that there is an unemployment situation which the provinces cannot cope with, we have no right to say that there is any national unemployment problem in this country.

. . . May I say this to my hon. friend, in order that he may get the real point of what I am saying? What does the suggestion amount to that is being made by those who ask us to dip into the federal treasury and take out money raised by taxation from the people of Canada as a whole to give it to certain of the provinces? It amounts to this. A Liberal government was returned to power in this country in 1921 on certain policies which we believe have made for prosperity, which we believe have made for economy, which we believe and which the country knows have made for a reduction of public debt and a reduction of taxation. We, as a Liberal government, are standing by our policies and are seeking to maintain our position. But hon. gentlemen opposite say to us: Now that you have got the country into this favourable position, we ask you to take part of the moneys that you may raise in taxes from the people of this Dominion as a whole, and give it to other administrations to spend, and to whom, if you please? To a Tory government in the province of British Columbia; to a Progressive government in the province of Alberta; to a Tory government in the province of Saskatchewan; to a Progressive government in the province of Manitoba; to a Tory government in the province of Ontario; to a Tory government in the province of New Brunswick; to a Tory government in the province of Nova Scotia. No request has come from or been made on behalf of either Quebec or Prince Edward Island, where there are Liberal governments attending to the affairs of the province. If you wish to play politics, that is the way to play it. Give to these Tory governments and to those Progressive governments at the present or all times

money raised by taxation of the people of Canada as a whole
to spend in their respective provinces and thereby save them
raising taxes for their own purposes. . . .

. . . So far as giving money from this federal treasury to
provincial governments is concerned, in relation to this question of unemployment as it exists to-day, I might be prepared
to go a certain length possibly in meeting one or two of the
western provinces that have Progressive premiers at the head
of their governments—

Some hon. Members: Oh!

Mr. Mackenzie King: —but I would not give a single cent to
any Tory government.

Mr. Bennett: Shame!

Mr. Stevens: Shame!

Mr. Mackenzie King: Do my hon. friends say "shame"?

Mr. Bennett: Yes, shame!

Mr. Mackenzie King: What is there to be ashamed of?

Mr. Stevens: You ought to be ashamed of that.

Mr. Mackenzie King: My hon. friend is getting very indignant. Something evidently has got under his skin. May I
repeat what I have said? With respect to giving moneys out
of the federal treasury to any Tory government in this country
for these alleged unemployment purposes, with these governments situated as they are to-day, with policies diametrically
opposed to those of this government, I would not give them a
five-cent piece.

. . . What is needed in Canada to-day if we are to solve any
unemployment problem to the extent that it may exist, is to
get more capital into the country to increase the investment of
capital; and we will get it as people come to have confidence
in conditions here. Hon. gentlemen opposite in their various
discussions on tariff matters have from the beginning adopted
the attitude of seeking to undermine confidence with respect
to industry, commerce and trade in this Dominion; that has
been the whole nature of their attack. We had it in the early

part of the present decade; we heard from hon. gentlemen opposite, after we came into office, nothing but one dire wail, cries of unemployed Canadians leaving this country to go to the States, of the woeful condition of affairs generally, "whispers of death" and the like; in other words, everything possible was done to cause those who had capital to invest, if they were thinking of placing it in this country, to withhold it from investment altogether. If we are prosperous it is not because of any assistance we have had from hon. gentlemen opposite; it is in spite of everything they have done to try to defeat our ends. . . .

XXIV: 2 R. B. BENNETT'S CAMPAIGN PROMISES

> Positive action was the keynote of R. B. Bennett's Conservative campaign in 1930. Mincing no words, and never hesitating to make the most sweeping pledges, Bennett blamed the Liberal government for the depression and outlined his own programme for ending unemployment—largely the traditional Conservative reliance on high tariffs. This selection of excerpts from Bennett's campaign speeches is taken from the dozens of reports that Mackenzie King deliberately read into *Hansard* to put Bennett's commitments on record.

This is a new country and there is no excuse for unemployment in Canada if a government does its duty.

I am convinced this unemployment has now ceased to be local and provincial and has become national in its importance. It has reached far beyond the narrow confines of Calgary or Alberta and is stretching into the broad confines of our Dominion. I will not permit this country with my voice or vote to ever become committed to the dole system. I will not permit those to share in any benefits that may accrue unless they are willing to work, if they are fit to work, and my duty is to provide them with work to do. . . .

I propose if elected to power, to call a session of parliament immediately after July 28 to deal with the unemployment problem, to authorize national undertakings which will give work to our workmen. Side by side, I propose to have enacted such measures as will give Canadians fair competition and equal opportunity with the nations of the world. Then the bogey of unemployment will be destroyed.

The Conservative party is going to find work for all who are willing to work, or perish in the attempt. It is going to call parliament at the earliest possible date after July 28 and take such steps as will end this tragic condition of unemployment and bring prosperity to the country as a whole. . . . Mr. King promises consideration of the problem of unemployment. I promise to end unemployment. Which plan do you like best?

. . . I say to you business men and clerks, women, housewives, and office girls, after July 28, at the first session of the new government we will pass a tariff law that will give Canadians a fair chance with their neighbours, that, or we perish in the attempt. There is no evasion, that is our promise.

Do you believe . . . In a fair deal, an even chance for Canadians? Do you believe Canadians should have a chance to work on the raw materials of this country in Canada? Do you believe Canadian industry should have the opportunity to supply the wants of Canadian consumers? If you do, vote for us. But if you believe our boys and girls should grow up to manhood and womanhood estate and then have to go to the United States to find jobs, vote for the Liberals. If you want to give work to Japan, Czechoslovakia or some other country in place of Canada, vote for the Liberals.

It will be the duty of the Conservative party to see that our tariffs can operate as well in the service of the consumer as the producer. Tariffs properly controlled will ensure our own markets to our producers, and internal competition will control prices. If any producer levies an excessive charge, I will put a stop to it.

What does the government do to-day to help you? Does it provide for you these markets? Does it provide a part of the revenue of the country to develop the foreign markets? . . . Does it say those things, so that your produce will reach out into the vast markets of the world, immediately available markets to the Orient and elsewhere? No, it does not. Oh, what an oportunity there was and what an opportunity there is at the present time for bold, constructive leadership! This opportunity the Conservative party will seize.

Listen, you agriculturists from the west and all the other parts of Canada, you have been taught to mock at tariffs and applaud free trade. Tell me, when did free trade fight for you? You say tariffs are only for the manufacturers. I will make them fight for you as well. I will use them to blast a way into the markets that have been closed to you.

. . . You have known suffering and have been patient. Let us end it. Take heart.

XXIV: 3 BIG BUSINESS IN THE DEPRESSION: THE STEVENS COMMISSION

The most comprehensive contemporary analysis of Canada's depression economy was made in 1935 by the Royal Commission on Price Spreads, chaired by H. H. Stevens, Bennett's Minister of Trade and Commerce. These excerpts from the report contain: (a) a general assessment of Canada's economic problems; (b) and (c) two examples of obvious injustice. The *Report* strongly recommended greatly increased government supervision of the economy. By the time the *Report* was published, Stevens had resigned from the government due to a clash with Bennett over one of Stevens' bitter attacks on Canadian business.

a. General Analysis

It is clear, therefore, that the Canadian economy, with a variable income from exports and certain unusually rigid costs, with extreme flexibility in some parts of its structure and great rigidity elsewhere, is in an unhappy position when rapid economic adjustments must be made. The real problem of a depression in Canada—or indeed anywhere—is how adjustment is to be made to the reduction in income, and how all groups are to share equitably in this necessary readjustment. To the extent that these economic rigidities allow some groups to resist this readjustment, the burden of it is placed unfairly on the other and unsheltered groups.

One feature of our economic rigidity should perhaps be given special mention here because it would appear to be undoubtedly a root cause of many of the evils uncovered. We refer to the growth of the corporation which has not only permitted the development of the large-scale organization of business, but largely determined the lines along which that development should proceed. In agriculture, thousands of producers must, as we have seen, sell their produce for whatever price they can get—that is, in the absence of "pooling" or other control, the price moves low enough to clear the market or move the crop. No one producer is so large that the withholding of his supply from the market will appreciably alter the price. In such a market, prices change much more rapidly than the volume of production. In large-scale corporate manufacturing, however, owing to conventional ideas of cost and prices, the tendency is for prices to change more slowly, and the volume of production more rapidly. The producer whose supply is usually an appreciable part of the total may prefer to produce less, and maintain the price rather than spoil the market by giving consumers a taste of lower prices and new ideas as to what the price should be.

The net result of this combination of flexibility and rigidity is that unregulated competition no longer guarantees efficiency and maximum production at fair prices. Competition degenerates sometimes into economic warfare where victory may go to the strong, rather than to the efficient. Forces of economic readjustment are often not self-correcting, but cumulative in their efforts. Orderly readjustments develop into disorderly crises.

It is this situation that explains the undoubted abuses and inequities that have been evidenced before us. It is on the basis of this analysis that we shall recommend proposals for deliberate social control of certain business activities and practices. . . .

The evidence before us has shown conclusively, and at times graphically, the part played by the corporate form of business in Canada's economic life.

It has shown that a few great corporations are predominant in the industries that have been investigated; also that this power, all the more dangerous because it is impersonal, can be wielded in such a way that competition within the industry is blocked, the welfare of the producer disregarded, and the interests of the investor ignored. . . .

b. Corporate Practices: Meat Packing

In 1929, sales of the packing industry in Canada totalled $186,000,000 and the cost of materials was $152,000,000. In 1932 with a decrease in physical volume of only 7 per cent, sales had fallen to $91,000,000 and the cost of materials to $66,-000,000. Thus, while sales fell by 50.9 per cent and the return to the primary producer fell by 56.8 per cent, the return to the packing company declined only 24.5 per cent. This indicates clearly that the live stock producers suffered much more severely than the packing companies. . . .

In 1929, for every dollar's worth of meat sold, 81.7 cents went to the suppliers of materials, and the value added by manufacture amounted to 18.3 cents; in 1933 however, although the consumer's dollar purchased approximately 80 per cent more meat than in 1929, out of each dollar the producer received only 76.3 cents (or 5.4 cents less than in 1929), and the packer 23.7 cents.

The manner in which these results have been achieved has a direct relation to the monopolistic character of the structure of the industry. The dominant position of the two large companies, with extensive storage facilities and control of a great proportion of the slaughtering equipment in the country, has undoubtedly secured for them some measure of control over both live stock prices and selling prices for their product. While there is no direct evidence of a combination between these companies, we are not persuaded that prices have been subject to the same fluctuations as might be expected in a more generaly competitive field. . . .

c. Garment-Makers' Wages

(1) There are extreme variations in wage rates; ranging from less than 5 cents per hour in a Quebec country home-work contract shop, to 65 cents in a Toronto union factory. These variations are of two main types; variations between factory levels and, even more important, variations between provincial levels.

(2) There are therefore extreme and unfair differences in cost, 'unfair' because they do not result from differences in efficiency of management. For example, the making of boys' pants cost 25 cents per dozen in a Quebec country home work-shop, $1.50 in a union shop; men's suits of comparable quality varied in direct labour costs from $2.26 (Quebec country factory) to $4.71 (Toronto non-union). Differences resulting from efficiency are desirable and healthy. Differences that result from exploitation cannot continue to be tolerated. Humane consideration for labour's welfare, and economic consideration for the success of business enterprise alike condemn them. They produce intolerable conditions of employment and life, and create intolerable industrial chaos. In the long run, they profit not even the exploiter.

(3) Wage rates and earnings are often exceedingly low. Quebec country home-workers probably cannot average 50 cents per day. Male piece-workers in one large Montreal factory averaged 16 cents per hour, less than the minimum of 18 cents for inexperienced females. One man of ten years' experience worked 70 hours per week in a Montreal contract shop, to earn $7 at 10 cents per hour. One man of four years' experience earned $3 per week, or 5.5 cents per hour in a Quebec country factory. In one Montreal factory, all workers, men and women together, averaged 25 cents per hour. In 1932, out of 115 men in two thoroughly good Toronto union shops, 57 earned for

the year less than $800; 88, less than $1,000; only 27 over $1,000; and only 2 over $1,600.

It is bad enough to pay such wages as these. It is adding insult to injury to hand them to the workers, as is often done, in pay envelopes which, thoughtfully provided by banks, bear such encouraging advice as:

> Think of tomorrow
> Divide your pay in two,
> Take what you need to live,
> Put the balance in safety.

• • •

(4) Hours of employment are often oppressively long. Thirteen hours a day, 60 hours a week, are not uncommon in rush periods. One man in a Toronto ladies' cloak contract shop, for nine consecutive weeks, worked over 16 hours per day; in this same shop, a woman often worked till midnight, 2 a.m. or 5 a.m. Eighteen, out of one group of 26 Toronto factories, reported frequent overtime. . . .

With a full recognition of the problems that this industry has to meet, problems which have existed for years and which have only been intensified by mass buying and depressed conditions, and, without condemning every unit in the industry, we cannot, in frankness, refrain from stating that the labour and wage conditions in this branch of Canada's industrial activity are such as to merit the most emphatic condemnation. They should not be tolerated in any state that claims to call itself civilized. . . .

XXIV: 4 BENNETT'S "NEW DEAL"

In January 1935, R. B. Bennett suddenly made a series of five radio addresses sharply condemning Canada's capitalist system and outlining the most radical and comprehensive programme of reform ever sponsored by a Canadian government. The multi-millionaire Prime Minister's astonishing change of heart has never been fully explained. The failure of his tariff programme, Franklin Roosevelt's success in the United States, the revelations of the Stevens Committee, and fear of defeat in the upcoming elections, all may have played a part. Selection (a) is taken from the radio addresses and shows the extent of Bennett's conversion (as well as his ingenious explanation of its lateness). His programme is outlined in selection (b), from the Throne Speech at the opening of Parliament. Most of the proposals became law, but were eventually disallowed by the Judicial Committee of the Privy Council because they were beyond the scope of federal power.

a. The Radio Addresses

. . . We will examine the system without prejudice of any sort. We neither hate nor love it. It is here to do you service. That is its only purpose. *If it has failed, then we must change it.* Quite properly, we have a regard for those things with which we have long been beneficially associated, but allegiance to a system does not involve our condonation of its defects. Possibly some of you will maintain that, because the system has served us well in the past, there is a presumption in favour of its continuing to do so in the future. But clearly, that is no proof that it will do so. Indeed, present conditions are surely proof enough that it will not. And, as I say, if it does not serve us, we must reform it. . . .

I do not intend to trouble you just now with the history of the capitalist system. But, in my opinion, it is important that you should carefully examine the origin of capitalism, its place in the early days, and the theory upon which it operated. It would be helpful to a clearer understanding of some of our present difficulties if you were to trace the development which carried the system from the simple practice of a simple theory to the complex practice of a theory strained and wrenched out of its original form. You would then see that for the old checks and balances which ensured the proper working of the original system, the system today has provided no counterpart within itself. You would agree that free competition and the open market place, as they were known in the old days, have lost their place in the system, and that the only substitute for them, in these modern times, is government regulation and control. You would understand that past depressions were caused by maladjustments in the operation of this system, and were corrected only after intense suffering and hardship, that these depressions were so many crises, dangerous and difficult to surmount, but that, in comparison with them, this depression is a catastrophe, and therefore demands the intervention of the Government. . . .

. . . even though from the outset, ultimate reform of the magnitude I have indicated, was clearly necessary, it would have been the height of folly to attempt to introduce reform until the first fury of the depression had been brought under some sort of control. For reform on a comprehensive scale was impossible before we had succeeded in achieving some stabilization and improvement in conditions. That was an emergency task and we therefore applied emergency measures to accomplish it. Before repairing the ship it was our job to navigate it through the storm. . . .

Selfish men, and this country is not without them,—men whose mounting bank rolls loom larger than your happiness, corporations without souls and without virtue—these, fearful that this Government might impinge on what they have grown to regard as their immemorial right of exploitation, will whisper against us. They will call us radicals. They will say that this is the first step on the road to socialism. We fear them not. We think that their ready compliance with our programme would serve their interests better than any ill-timed opposition to it. We invite their cooperation. We want the cooperation of all. . . .

The agencies of production, of manufacture, of distribution, of finance: all the parts of the capitalist system, have only one purpose and that is to work for the welfare of the people. And when any of those instruments in any way fails, it is the plain duty of a government which represents the people, to remove the cause of failure. This I do not say by way of threat. I have told you that we hope for the unanimous support of all classes, in this great and difficult task of reform, but I think it is only right to add that opposition from any class which imperils the future of this great undertaking we will not tolerate. The lives and the happiness and the welfare of too many people depend upon our success to allow the selfishness of a few individuals to endanger it. . . .

b. The Throne Speech, 1935

Better provision will be made for the security of the worker during unemployment, in sickness, and in old age.

The measures taken respecting public and private debts have done much to lighten the burden of the taxpayer and to improve the position of the farming community. My ministers are now engaged upon a survey of the national debt structure to determine what action may be practicable and advisable to effect further improvement in it. . . .

Action will be taken to ameliorate the conditions of labour, to provide a better and more assured standard of living for the worker, to secure minimum wages and a maximum working week, and to alter the incidence of taxation so that it will more directly conform to capacity to pay.

You will be invited to enact measures designed to safeguard the consumer and primary producer against unfair trading practices and to regulate, in the public interest, concentrations in production and distribution.

You will be invited also to enact measures to provide the investing public with means to protect itself against exploitation. . . .

My ministers have under preparation a plan for the re-organization of the government services so that they may be better equipped to discharge the onerous duties which devolve upon them. You will be invited to consider measures, the purpose of which will be to authorize the first stage in this plan of reorganization.

You will be invited to authorize the constitution of an economic council, the functions of which will be to advise my ministers upon all economic questions which concern the national welfare. . . .

XXIV:5 RECOMMENDATIONS OF THE ROWELL-SIROIS COMMISSION

As the fate of Bennett's reform programme illustrated, Canadians had reached an impasse in Dominion-provincial relations by the late 1930's. The provinces, with limited financial resources, could not bear the strain of providing the increased social services that had been judged to be their responsibility. In 1940, after three years of exhaustive research into the Canadian federal system, the Rowell-Sirois Royal Commission on Dominion-Provincial Relations recommended a sweeping revision of Dominion-Provincial spheres of authority. The main recommendations of the Commission's *Report* follow. Although provincial opposition prevented the implementation of the *Report* as such, wartime and post-war financial agreements based largely on the *Report's* recommendations were negotiated between the federal and provincial governments.

. . . The striking fact in the Commission's study of Canadian conditions is that many provinces, whose financial position is not the result of emergency conditions, are unable to find the money to enable them to meet the needs of their citizens. The basic problem before the Commission lies, therefore, in finding a way in which the financial position of the provinces could be improved and assured, without disastrous financial consequences to the Federal Government on whose efficient functioning all provinces are dependent. National unity and provincial autonomy must not be thought of as competitors for the citizen's allegiance for, in Canada at least, they are but two facets of the same thing—a sane federal system. National unity must be based on provincial autonomy, and provincial autonomy cannot be assured unless a strong feeling of national unity exists throughout Canada. . . .

The Commission did . . . find one onerous function of government which cannot, under modern conditions, be equitably or efficiently performed on a regional or provincial basis. This function is the maintenance of those unemployed who are employable and of their dependents. . . . So firmly is the Commission convinced of the validity of this conclusion that, even when it comes to consider the situation which will arise if its main recommendations are not implemented, it proceeds on the assumption that the relief of the unemployed who are able and willing to work will become a federal function.

Another function closely analogous to that of relief for employables is that of assistance to a primary industry (e.g., agriculture) in the form of operating cost advances. When relief is on a small scale the responsibility can be borne without difficulty by the province. But in the event of widespread disaster with which a province is unable to cope without assistance from the Dominion, or in the event that the Dominion by such means as an exclusive marketing organization has already established effective control of the industry concerned, the Commission recommends that the Dominion should assume direct administrative and financial responsibility rather than render indirect assistance by way of advances to the provinces affected.

. . . The Commission is of the opinion that if non-contributory old age pensions were to be superseded or supplemented by a contributory system the latter should, for various reasons, be under the control of the Dominion.

There is, however, an important financial burden of which provincial governments can be relieved without any sacrifice of autonomy. This is the deadweight cost of their debt service. The burden taken up by the Dominion, if it were to assume this deadweight cost, would be less than the burden of which the provinces were relieved because, as maturities occurred, the debts could be refunded more advantageously by the Dominion than by the provinces. To this extent a saving would accrue to Canadian taxpayers. The Commission has, therefore, recommended that the Dominion should assume all provincial debts (both direct debts and debts guaranteed by the provinces) and that each province should pay over to the Dominion an annual sum equal to the interest which it now receives from its investments. . . .

If the provinces are relieved, in accordance with this recommendation, of the deadweight burden of their debt, it is not unreasonable that they should surrender to the Dominion the subsidies, whatever their character, which they now receive. Prince Edward Island alone would give up subsidies more than equivalent to the deadweight cost of its debt, and, as will be seen, this apparent loss will be more than made up in other ways. The abolition of the provincial subsidies will be in itself no inconsiderable reform, for their history . . . is long and tortuous. The subsidies have been based on no clear principles and it has been impossible to say whether or not different provinces have received equal treatment. Specious reasons have often been advanced, and not infrequently accepted, in support of readjustments in order to avoid the full implications of genuine reasons, and negotiations between the Dominion and the provinces have lacked the candour which is desirable in a democracy.

Up to this point the Commission's proposals, enormously beneficial as they would be to the provinces, would be very onerous to the Dominion. The Commission had, therefore, to consider how to provide the Dominion with sources of revenue which would enable it to carry its new burdens. . . .

There could be no question of increasing the legal taxing powers of the Dominion since these are already unlimited. But the provinces, in return for the benefits which they would receive, and for further payments which the Commission finds it necessary to recommend, should be prepared to renounce some of the taxes which they employ (or are entitled to employ) at present. The Dominion, for its part, should be able and willing to refrain from competing with the provinces in respect of sources of revenue left to them and should leave the provinces free to collect these revenues in whatever way appears to them most efficient even if the method of indirect taxation should be involved. . . .

The first of the taxes which the Commission recommends that the provinces should renounce is the tax on personal incomes. Not all provinces impose this tax. Those which get most revenue from it are often taxing incomes which other provinces think that they should have a share in taxing, because they are in part at least earned in them although they are received in those provinces in which investors live, or in which large corporations have their head offices. Nor is this all. The general equity of the whole Canadian tax system—and the Commission has been instructed to concern itself with equity as well as with efficiency in taxation—requires that the tax on personal incomes, which is one of the very few taxes capable of any desired graduation, should be used to supplement other taxes and should be uniform throughout Canada.

The second form of taxation which the Commission recommends that the provinces should forgo includes those taxes imposed on corporations which individuals or partnerships, carrying on the same business as the corporation, would not be required to pay, and taxes on those businesses which only corporations engage in. They include, therefore, the tax on the net income of corporations and a multitude of taxes devised to raise revenue from particular classes of corporations which a province cannot conveniently subject to a tax on net income. They do not include bona fide licence fees, the power to impose which would remain with the province. These provincial corporation taxes are peculiarly vexatious to those who pay them and particularly detrimental to the expansion of the national income. The cost of tax compliance is high. The tax is often payable by a corporation which has no net income. The tax is very likely to be a tax on costs rather than on profits. These taxes are also a frequent source of interprovincial jealousy. Great benefits may be expected if they are swept away and the equivalent revenue raised by federal taxes chiefly on corporate net income. . . .

The third tax which the Commission recommends that the provinces should forgo consists of various forms of succession duty. These differ from the income taxes in that they have not hitherto been used by the Dominion: but they are taxes to which the Dominion might at any time be compelled to resort. The use made of them by the provinces has given rise to bitter complaint because the provinces have not made equitable arrangements with one another so as to tax each item in an estate in one province only. The differences in rates between provinces, and the dangers of double taxation, seriously distort investment in Canada. The potential competition between provinces desirous of attracting wealthy residents has made it impossible to use these delicate instruments of taxation as a means for giving effect to social policies. Many provinces feel aggrieved because estates which have been built up by investment throughout the whole of Canada are taxed, not for national purposes, but for the benefit of strategically situated provinces.

If the Commission's recommendations stopped at this point, they would, instead of being enormously beneficial to the provinces, leave some of them in a parlous financial position. After the provinces had, on the one hand, been relieved of the cost of unemployment relief and of the deadweight burden of their debt, and had, on the other hand, given up their right to impose personal income taxes, corporation taxes and succession duties, they would find themselves with far less variable expenditures than in the past and with less variable revenues. It is, therefore, possible to form an idea of the size of the probable surplus or deficit of each province. There is a purpose in making this calculation for, if a province were left with a prospective annual deficit, it would not be able to provide for the reasonable needs of its citizens unless it were able, without causing hardship, to increase the revenue which it derived from the sources remaining at its disposal, or to reduce its expenditures while still providing services equivalent to those provided by other provinces.

At this point there must be a refinement in the calculations. What is significant for the purposes of the Commission is the size of the surplus or deficit which would exist in a province if it were to provide the normal Canadian standard of services and impose taxation of normal severity. It is not the services which each province is at present providing, but the average Canadian standard of services, that a province must be put in a position to finance. It is not the revenue which its taxes yield at their present level which matters, but the revenue which it would derive from them if its people were as heavily taxed as Canadians in general. Just as in the case of debt it is necessary to take account of the fact that some provinces are more accustomed than others to provide services for their people through municipalities or other agencies instead of directly. The Commission has, therefore, attempted to compute, province by province, what the cost would be if the province and its municipalities taken together were to provide services on the Canadian standard. Adjustments have been made for the cost of the developmental services appropriate to the province, and for the weight of taxation in the province. The result has been that the Commission has been able to make a recommendation as to the amount, if any, which each individual province should receive from the Dominion annually to enable it to provide normal Canadian services with no more than normal Canadian taxation. . . . the Commission recommends that each province found to be in need of such a payment should receive it by way of an annual National Adjustment Grant from the Dominion. This grant as originally fixed would be irreducible. The Commission recommends, however, that National Adjustment Grants should be re-appraised every five years. For special emergencies, which might arise in respect of any province (and which exist in one province today), special provision should be made, as it would be undesirable either to fix an annual grant in perpetuity on the basis of conditions that are transitory, or to fail to provide for serious emergencies. The Commission believes that these provisions will permit of the necessary elasticity in the financial relations between the provinces and the Dominion which has been lacking in the old subsidy system. . . .

The recommendations which have been described would, if implemented, safeguard the autonomy of every province by ensuring to it the revenue necessary to provide services in accordance with the Canadian standard. Every provincial government (including those whose position will be so good as to make adjustment grants unnecessary) would be placed in a better financial position than it is in today. And the financial position of every province would be immeasurably more secure than it is today. The Commission looks on this as its primary achievement. It is convinced that this fundamental problem must be faced and it has not been able to discover any alternative way in which it could be solved. The recommendations which the Commission has made must be judged as a whole. They cannot with fairness either to the provinces or to the Dominion be considered in isolation for any one of them taken alone might produce grotesque results.

XXV. New Parties

XXV:1 THE REGINA MANIFESTO OF THE C.C.F.

Depression conditions in Canada produced an inevitable shift away from the traditional political parties, especially in the West and Quebec. The first new party was the Co-operative Commonwealth Federation, an alliance between farmer organizations, a few labour unions and a number of socialist intellectuals, under the leadership of J. S. Woodsworth. At its second conference in Regina in 1933, the C.C.F. issued its socialist programme in what came to be called the Regina Manifesto.

The C.C.F. is a federation of organizations whose purpose is the establishment in Canada of a Co-operative Commonwealth in which the principle regulating production, distribution and exchange will be the supplying of human needs and not the making of profits.

We aim to replace the present capitalist system, with its inherent injustice and inhumanity, by a social order from which the domination and exploitation of one class by another will be eliminated, in which economic planning will supersede unregulated private enterprise and competition, and in which genuine democratic self-government, based upon economic equality will be possible. The present order is marked by glaring inequalities of wealth and opportunity, by chaotic waste and instability; and in an age of plenty it condemns the great mass of the people to poverty and insecurity. Power has become more and more concentrated into the hands of a small irresponsible minority of financiers and industrialists and to their predatory interests the majority are habitually sacrificed. When private profit is the main stimulus to economic effort, our society oscillates between periods of feverish prosperity in which the main benefits go to speculators and profiteers, and of catastrophic depression, in which the common man's normal state of insecurity and hardship is accentuated. We believe that these evils can be removed only in a planned and socialized economy in which our natural resources and the principal means of production and distribution are owned, controlled and operated by the people. . . .

. . . It is a democratic movement, a federation of farmer, labor and socialist organizations, financed by its own members and seeking to achieve its ends solely by constitutional methods. It appeals for support to all who believe that the time has come for a far-reaching reconstruction of our economic and political institutions and who are willing to work together for the carrying out of the following policies:

1 PLANNING

The establishment of a planned, socialized economic order, in order to make possible the most efficient development of the national resources and the most equitable distribution of the national income.

The first step in this direction will be setting up of a National Planning Commission consisting of a small body of economists, engineers and statisticians assisted by an appropriate technical staff.

The task of the Commission will be to plan for the production, distribution and exchange of all goods and services necessary to the efficient functioning of the economy; to coordinate the activities of the socialized industries; to provide for a satisfactory balance between the producing and consuming power; and to carry on continuous research into all branches of the national economy in order to acquire the detailed information necessary to efficient planning. . . .

2 SOCIALIZATION OF FINANCE

Socialization of all financial machinery—banking, currency, credit, and insurance, to make possible the effective control of currency, credit and prices, and the supplying of new productive equipment for socially desirable purposes.

. . . Control of finance is the first step in the control of the whole economy. The chartered banks must be socialized and removed from the control of private profit-seeking interests; and the national banking system thus established must have at its head a Central Bank to control the flow of credit and the general price level, and to regulate foreign exchange operations. A National Investment Board must also be set up, working in co-operation with the socialized banking system to mobilize and direct the unused surpluses of production for socially desired purposes as determined by the Planning Commission.

Insurance Companies, which provide one of the main channels for the investment of individual savings and which, under their present competitive organization, charge needlessly high premiums for the social services that they render, must also be socialized.

3 SOCIAL OWNERSHIP

Socialization (Dominion, Provincial or Municipal) of transportation, communications, electric power and all other industries and services essential to social planning, and their operation under the general direction of the Planning Commission by competent managements freed from day to day political interference.

. . . Transportation, communications and electric power must come first in a list of industries to be socialized. Others, such as mining, pulp and paper and the distribution of milk, bread, coal and gasoline, in which exploitation, waste, or financial malpractices are particularly prominent must next be brought under social ownership and operation.

In restoring to the community its natural resources and in taking over industrial enterprises from private into public control we do not propose any policy of outright confiscation. ... We recognize the need for compensation in the case of individuals and institutions which must receive adequate maintenance during the transitional period before the planned economy becomes fully operative. But a C.C.F. government will not play the role of rescuing bankrupt private concerns for the benefit of promoters and of stock and bond holders. It will not pile up a deadweight burden of unremunerative debt which represents claims upon the public treasury of a functionless owner class. ...

4 AGRICULTURE

Security of tenure for the farmer upon his farm on conditions to be laid down by individual provinces; insurance against unavoidable crop failure; removal of the tariff burden from the operations of agriculture; encouragement of producers' and consumers' co-operatives; the restoration and maintenance of an equitable relationship between prices of agricultural products and those of other commodities and services; and improving the efficiency of export trade in farm products. ...

5 EXTERNAL TRADE

The regulation in accordance with the National plan of external trade through import and export boards. ...

6 CO-OPERATIVE INSTITUTIONS

The encouragement by the public authority of both producers' and consumers' co-operative institutions. ...

7 LABOR CODE

A National Labor Code to secure for the worker maximum income and leisure, insurance covering illness, accident, old age, and unemployment, freedom of association and effective participation in the management of his industry or profession.

. . . A labor code must be developed which will include state regulation of all wages, equal reward and equal opportunity of advancement for equal services, irrespective of sex; measures to guarantee the right to work or the right to maintenance through stabilization of employment and through unemployment insurance; social insurance to protect workers and their families against the hazards of sickness, death, industrial accident and old age; limitation of hours of work and protection of health and safety in industry. Both wages and insurance benefits should be varied in accordance with family needs.

In addition workers must be guaranteed the undisputed right to freedom of association, and should be encouraged and assisted by the state to organize themselves in trade unions. By means of collective agreements and participation in works councils, the workers can achieve fair working rules and share in the control of industry and profession; and their organizations will be indispensable elements in a system of genuine industrial democracy. . . .

8 SOCIALIZED HEALTH SERVICES
Publicly organized health, hospital and medical services.

With the advance of medical science the maintenance of a healthy population has become a function for which every civilized community should undertake responsibility. Health services should be made at least as freely available as are educational services today. But under a system which is still mainly one of private enterprise the costs of proper medical care, such as the wealthier members of society can easily afford, are at present prohibitive for great masses of the people. . . .

9 B.N.A. ACT
The amendment of the Canadian Constitution, without infringing upon racial or religious minority rights or upon legitimate provincial claims to autonomy, so as to give the

Dominion Government adequate powers to deal effectively with urgent economic problems which are essentially national in scope; the abolition of the Canadian Senate. . . .

The Canadian Senate, which was originally created to protect provincial rights, but has failed even in this function, has developed into a bulwark of capitalist interests, as is illustrated by the large number of company directorships held by its aged members. In its peculiar composition of a fixed number of members appointed for life it is one of the most reactionary assemblies in the civilized world. It is a standing obstacle to all progressive legislation, and the only permanently satisfactory method of dealing with the constitutional difficulties it creates is to abolish it.

10 EXTERNAL RELATIONS

A Foreign Policy designed to obtain international economic co-operation and to promote disarmament and world peace. . . .

11 TAXATION AND PUBLIC FINANCE

A new taxation policy designed not only to raise public revenues but also to lessen the glaring inequalities of income and to provide funds for social services and the socialization of industry; the cessation of the debt creating system of Public Finance. . . .

At the present time capitalist governments in Canada raise a large proportion of their revenues from such levies as customs duties and sales taxes, the main burden of which falls upon the masses. In place of such taxes upon articles of general consumption, we propose a drastic extension of income, corporation and inheritance taxes, steeply graduated according to ability to pay. Full publicity must be given to income tax payments and our tax collection system must be brought up to the English standard of efficiency. . . .

12 FREEDOM

Freedom of speech and assembly for all; repeal of Section 98 of the Criminal Code; amendment of the Immigration Act to prevent the present inhuman policy of deportation; equal treatment before the law of all residents of Canada irrespective of race, nationality or religious or political beliefs. . . .

14   AN EMERGENCY PROGRAMME

The assumption by the Dominion Government of direct responsibility for dealing with the present critical unemployment situation and for tendering suitable work or adequate maintenance; the adoption of measures to relieve the extremity of the crisis such as a programme of public spending on housing, and other enterprises that will increase the real wealth of Canada, to be financed by the issue of credit based on the national wealth. . . .

Emergency measures, however, are of only temporary value, for the present depression is a sign of the mortal sickness of the whole capitalist system, and this sickness cannot be cured by the application of salves. These leave untouched the cancer which is eating at the heart of our society, namely, the economic system in which our natural resources and our principal means of production and distribution are owned, controlled and operated for the private profit of a small proportion of our population.

No C.C.F. Government will rest content until it has eradicated capitalism and put into operation the full programme of socialized planning which will lead to the establishment in Canada of the Co-operative Commonwealth.

XXV:2 SOCIAL CREDIT'S REMEDY FOR THE DEPRESSION

The theories of Social Credit first came to Canada through the writings of Major Douglas, an English engineer. In Alberta the teacher-evangelist William Aberhart swept the 1935 provincial elections with his promise of $25.00 a month for everyone under Social Credit. Once in power the Aberhart government found its economic programme beyond the constitutional powers of the province. Thus, although Social Credit governments have been formed in British Columbia and Alberta, the monetary theories outlined below have never been put into practice. The "Socred" governments in Canada have adopted a generally conservative approach to policy. The following selection is a portion of Aberhart's *Social Credit Manual*.

OUR BASIC PREMISE

It is the duty of the State through its Government to organize its economic structure in such a way that no bona fide citizen, man, woman, or child, shall be allowed to suffer for lack of the bare necessities of food, clothing, and shelter, in the midst of plenty or abundance. . . .

SOCIAL CREDIT AS A REMEDY

The Social Credit Proposals Go Right to the Source of the Trouble.

To understand the Social Credit philosophy it is necessary for the individual to get the language or terms used in Social Credit:

1. CULTURAL HERITAGE This is the inheritance that falls to the right of the individual citizen living within the bounds of the province. The pioneering work of our forefathers and the inventive genius of scientists and others have enabled mankind to harness the solar energy and produce machinery that will do the work that was formerly done by mankind. The great wealth of our natural resources has, by this means, been brought to the very door of the individual consumer. Social Credit claims that each of these consumers has a right to a share in the production from the natural resources of the province. At the present time this great wealth is being selfishly manipulated and controlled by one or more men known as the "Fifty Big Shots of Canada." Social Credit claims that this cultural heritage is the property of the individuals who are bona fide citizens of our province, and should never be allowed to go entirely to the control of any small group of men. We call this heritage cultural because it gives the individual an opportunity to develop his individuality.

2. BASIC DIVIDENDS   The cultural heritage is made operative by the regular issuance of dividends from month to month sufficient to secure for the individual citizen the bare necessities of food, clothing and shelter. Social Credit claims that this is the least that could be offered to any citizen. It is wholly unreasonable to expect any person or group of persons in a province as wealthy as Alberta to exist without the bare necessities of food, clothing and shelter. To enable each citizen to secure these bare necessities, each of them will receive a pass-book in which at the beginning of each month will be entered the basic dividend for that month, say $25.00. This is supposed to provide for the bare necessities of food, clothing and shelter for every bona fide citizen, whether he works or does not work, and he shall not be required to pay it back or work it out. The only stipulation will be that the recipient must co-operate in every way possible. Those who work will be given their salaries, wages, or commissions over and above the basic dividends. This would at once remove all relief and dole from our land and recover the morale of our people. Our bona fide consumers will at once have purchasing power amounting to $10,000,000 dividends, and probably in addition $20,000,000 salary, wages, and commission.

Basic dividend credit will be used by means of non-negotiable certificates issued in blank to each consumer.

3. NON-NEGOTIABLE CERTIFICATES   These are blank forms issued to each bona fide citizen to enable him to fill in the amount and signature, also the name of the recipient to whom he is transferring the credit. As it is non-negotiable, the person receiving the certificate must of necessity deposit it in the bank or Provincial Credit House. When this is done the issuer is debited in his account and the recipient is credited in his account. The recipient, therefore, is able to issue another non-negotiable certificate of his own to pay his debts, and thus the circulation of the credit is possible. It is very evident to anyone who follows this thus far that this issuance of free dividends in order to prevent the province from

continuously getting into debt, must be recovered in some scientific manner without introducing a huge tax scheme. . . .

Question—Where will all the credit come from to pay the basic dividends?

Answer—The credit issued will be a charge against the Natural Resources of the Province much in the same way as the present Government Bonds are.

Question—Will not the issuance of these Basic Dividends rapidly sink the province into an enormous debt?

Answer—The scientific system of recovery through the cycle of credit will have to be introduced at the same time that the Basic Dividends are issued. This must not be a gigantic scheme of taxation. It has been called to the attention of the public that there is an enormous spread in price between the producer's cost and the consumer's price. It is the intention under the Social Credit system to reduce this spread, increasing the producer's cost so that he may have a fair turn-over if it is not at present adequate, or reducing it if it is too high. The same procedure will be followed all the way through in the marketing or processing of the goods. On account of the increased turn-over that will be produced by the augmented purchasing power through dividends, salaries, commissions and so forth, it is felt that the producer and distributor will be able to carry on their business with a closer margin of profit or commission on turn-over. Thus the province will be able to collect a levy that will provide basic dividends to distribute to the various citizens. . . .

XXV: 3 THE ORIGINAL PLATFORM OF THE *UNION NATIONALE*

In Quebec social reform and French Canadian nationalism were combined in an alliance between the Conservative party and a radical Liberal group to form the *Union Nationale*. The leader was Maurice Duplessis. The new party adopted the programme of the Liberal group, *L'Action Liberale Nationale,* which was an attempt to apply recent Catholic social teaching to the newly industrialized Quebec economy. Although elected in 1936 as a reform party, the *Union Nationale* quickly lost everything but its nationalist tone and its desire for power. The Quebec it left behind after twenty years of power is revealed in documents XXX:1 and 2 on pages 336-342. The platform on which it was initially elected is outlined below.

The present crisis is due in large part to the unequal economic distribution, the greed of high finance and the abuses of all kinds which have slipped into democratic government. There is no point in hoping that a balance will occur of itself without the assistance of a well-defined plan of action. The necessity of political evolution accompanied by economic evolution is obvious. In the United States the Democrats, now rejuvenated, are presently working towards this double transformation. In Canada and in the province of Quebec we are still working on theories. Our elected representatives have not yet taken a stand on reforms of the political, economic and social order which our best informed minds are advocating. . . .

We believe that a political evolution is necessary in our country and in our province so as to assure that the doctrines worked out by our economists will be brought into operation. . . .

L'Action libérale nationale thus offers the following overall plan which, even if it is not perfect, will work toward this double political and economic evolution, the sole means of assuring a better distribution of wealth and the resultant ending of unemployment and Depression.

I. AGRARIAN REFORMS

1. The preparation and implementation of a vast plan of colonization.

2. The rejuvenation of our farms through winning local and foreign markets, as well as through electrification of the countryside, and for these purposes, an increase in subsidies. . . .

IV. ECONOMIC REFORMS

1. To break, by every means possible, the hold which the great financial institutions, the electricity trust and the paper industry trust have on the province and the municipalities.

2. To lower the electricity rates: the acquisition by the Province, according to its needs, of all water rights not yet granted as well as those granted but not yet exploited; moreover, the immediate investigation, by an independent commission especially appointed, with all the necessary powers, to determine whether it is in the Province's interest to acquire gradually, at a cost which would permit a substantial reduction of the present rates and which at the same time would pay off the purchase price, the companies producing or distributing electric power in the Province;

3. To combat the coal, gasoline and bread combines, by creating state competition if necessary.

4. To combat the Milk Trust by consolidating into a closed association all milk producers of the Province.

5. A total investigation into the structure and the financial methods of Public Utility Companies and a clean-up of their capitalization.

6. An increased and strict application of the Combines Law. . . .

VI. POLITICAL AND ADMINISTRATIVE REFORMS

1. Thrift and honesty in the public administration.

2. The prevention of ministers from being stock-holders or interested parties in any way in a company which obtains government contracts.

3. The prevention of ministers from being directors of a bank, trust company, a public utility, an insurance company, or a railway company.

4. The transformation of the Legislative Council into an Economic Council. . . .

VII. ELECTORAL REFORMS

2. Obligatory voting (this measure subject to plebiscite).

3. A by-election within three months following the date of vacancy.

4. Identity cards in cities of more than 10,000 population.

5. A decrease in election expenses.

6. The control of election subscriptions made by limited companies.

7. The limitation of election subscriptions made by individuals.

8. Cases of false identity to be punishable by one year in prison at least, and the same measure against all those who have employed, paid, or assisted any person guilty of this infraction.

VIII. FISCAL REFORMS

1. A temporary law granting the right of re-purchase to any person dispossessed of property by sheriff's sale on mortgage loans, . . .

2. A readjustment of the rate of interest on mortgages.

3. A decrease in interest charged by banks for the purpose of aiding industry and commerce.

4. The conversion of the provincial debt at the best rate possible.

5. A readjustment of federal subsidies for the purpose of increasing the share of the provinces.

6. A redistribution of taxation, federal, provincial and municipal, so that commercial corporations and certain classes of individuals which often enjoy unfair exemptions, may make their fair contribution to the public purse. . . .

XXVI. A Wider World

XXVI: 1 CANADA AND COLLECTIVE SECURITY

Canada's first major appearance on the world diplomatic stage was as a full-fledged member of the League of Nations. As the following selections show, however, Canada played a largely negative role, for she was only slightly less isolationist between the wars than the United States. Selection (a) is an early protest by the Canadian delegation against Article X of the League's Covenant, which bound the members to mutual assistance in the face of aggression. The isolationist spirit is even more evident in selection (b), an excerpt from the Canadian delegate's expression of disapproval at the binding provisions of the 1924 Geneva Protocol.

a. Objections to Article X, 1921

This article is open, in my judgment, to the very gravest objections, both generally, and from the point of view of countries in the condition and stage of development of Canada in particular.

Of the gravity of the obligations by it imposed upon the parties to the convention, there can be no question. It makes of the League, as *The Times* expresses it, 'a mutual guarantee society of unlimited liability'. . . .

. . . Even if . . . it is right that a guarantee such as proposed should be given, it does not follow that it should be given by all the states. It may be right that one class of states should give it, and entirely wrong to exact it of another. Many reasons for such a distinction exist, and all of them justify Canada's being classed with those states upon which this onerous obligation should not be imposed. Canada has no say in, and no responsibility for, any settlement that may be made by the powers of general interests, after hearing those of particular interests directly concerned therein, as to territory to be allotted to, or determined for, revived or newly created states, out of that formerly held by the vanquished powers. There is, therefore, in the fact of that settlement itself, to be found no reason why she should guarantee its being executed and continuously respected. . . .

If it is true that the formation of a general association of nations 'under specific covenants for the purpose of affording mutual guarantee of political independence and territorial integrity to great and small states alike' is one of the 'fourteen points' generally regarded as the basis on which peace terms are to be settled. But to give effect to this point, it is not essential that *all* the nations of the League should be guarantors. Surely it can be fully carried out in the spirit, and without derogation to its letter, by guarantee being given by those whose super-eminent power enables them to do it, and whose interests in obtaining it furnish adequate consideration for giving it. . . .

b. Objections to the Geneva Protocol, 1924

. . . We have already demonstrated that in times of serious crisis we have a full appreciation of our international responsibilities. Canada, in complete independence, entered the great war, out of sentiment, not out of interest or necessity, and today she is raising in taxes for the payment of interest on her war debt and war pensions a sum exceeding her whole annual revenues before the war. Nearly five hundred thousand men, out of a population of eight millions, crossed the Atlantic and sixty thousand of them did not return.

When the war was over, we signed at Versailles the Covenant of the League of Nations. We will be loyal to that covenant. We are not forgetful, however, of the conditions under which we signed it. Canada was then far from thinking that she would have the whole burden of representing North America when appeals would come to our continent for assistance in maintaining peace in Europe.

The falling away of the United States has increased, in our eyes, the risks assumed, and the history of Europe in the past five years has not been such as to lessen that apprehension.

The heavy sacrifices to which we agreed for the re-establishment of peace in Europe led us to reflect on what the future might hold in store.

May I be permitted to add that in this association of mutual insurance against fire the risks assumed by the different states are not equal? We live in a fire-proof house, far from inflammable materials. A vast ocean separates us from Europe. . . .

XXVI:2 SANCTIONS AGAINST ITALY, 1935

> The most interesting incident in Canada's early participation in international affairs came in 1935, during the Italian-Abyssinian crisis. The Canadian delegate at the League, Dr. W. A. Riddell, proposed adding those materials to the sanctions list that would have made the embargoes against Italy truly effective. Selection (a) is Riddell's proposal; selection (b) is his government's reaction.

a. Dr. W. A. Riddell

Mr. Riddell (Canada) reminded the committee that in Proposal IV, concerning the embargo on certain exports to Italy, they were entrusted with the task of making suitable proposals to governments on this subject. He imagined they were all agreed that the list of key products was not complete inasmuch as such important products as petroleum and its derivatives, coal, iron, and steel were not on the list. The committee had been successful in obtaining acceptances regarding the embargo as far as it went, and he thought all the states members of the League were to be congratulated on that. He now ventured to propose that the substances he had named should be added to the list in principle, and that measures with regard to them should come into effect whenever the committee found that an embargo could be made effective. The inclusion of iron and steel in this way, he hoped, would also give satisfaction to the Spanish delegate. He accordingly suggested the following proposal:

> In execution of the mission entrusted to it under the last paragraph of Proposal IV, the Committee of Eighteen submits to governments the following proposal:
>
> It is expedient to adopt the principle of the extension of the measures of embargo provided for in the said proposal to the following products: petroleum and derivatives; coal, iron, cast iron, and steel.
>
> As soon as it appears that the acceptance of this principle is sufficiently general to ensure the efficacy of the measures thus contemplated, the Committee of Eighteen will propose to governments a date for bringing them into operation.

b. Ernest Lapointe

Upon being asked for an explanation of reports as to Canadian initiative in the extension of the oil embargo, Mr. Lapointe gave the following explanation:

The suggestion which has appeared in the press from time to time that the Canadian government has taken the initiative in the extension of the embargo upon exportation of key commodities to Italy, and particularly in the placing of a ban upon shipments of coal, oil, iron, and steel, is due to a misunderstanding. The Canadian government has not and does not propose to take the initiative in any such action; and the opinion which was expressed by the Canadian member of the committee—and which has led to the reference to the proposal as a Canadian proposal—represented only his own personal opinion, and his views as a member of the committee—and not the views of the Canadian government.

XXVI: 3 CANADA AND APPEASEMENT

The extent of Canada's support for the British policy of conciliation with Hitler and Mussolini in the late 1930's is shown by these two statements of Mackenzie King. Selection (a) is a letter to a British cabinet minister approving of the general policy of appeasement. Selection (b) is King's cablegram of congratulations to Neville Chamberlain, the British Prime Minister, immediately after the Munich agreement with Hitler.

a. King to M. Macdonald, April, 1938

I hope you will tell Mr. Chamberlain that I cannot begin to express the admiration I feel for the manner in which he has performed a task more difficult, I believe, than any with which any prime minister of Great Britain has ever before been faced. I approve wholeheartedly the course he has adopted, particularly his determination to get into touch with Italy and Germany, to seek to restore goodwill between these countries and the United Kingdom, instead of permitting ill will to develop to the point of another world war, and his exposure of the unreality, and worse, of the situation at Geneva. The one mistake that I see in British policy—and I believe it to be a very great one—is that Great Britain has been far too slow in taking the steps which Mr. Chamberlain himself has found it necessary to take within the past few weeks.

b. King to Neville Chamberlain, September 29, 1938

The heart of Canada is rejoicing tonight at the success which has crowned your unremitting efforts for peace. May I convey to you the congratulations of the Canadian people, and with them an expression of the gratitude that is felt from one end of the Dominion to the other? My colleagues in the government join with me in unbounded admiration for the service you have rendered mankind. Your achievements in the past month alone will assure you an illustrious and abiding place among the great conciliators which the United Kingdom, the British Commonwealth, and the whole world will continue to honour.

On the very brink of chaos with passions flaming and armies marching, the voice of reason has found a way out of the conflict which no people in their hearts desire but none seemed able to avert. A turning point in the world's history will be reached if, as we hope, tonight's agreement means a halt in the mad race of arms and a new start in building the partnership of all peoples. May you have health and strength to carry your work to completion.

XXVI:4 CANADA GOES TO WAR

Although the Canadian government had rejected the old theory that Canada was bound to participate in Britain's wars, and although there had been talk of Canadian neutrality in the event of a European war, there was never any serious question of Canada not entering World War II. On September 8, 1939, Mackenzie King gave his explanation to the House of Commons. It was a long way from the "fire-proof house."

. . . I noticed in the press last evening that one of the German papers which is supposed to be an organ of the administration had quoted Hitler as saying that if England wished to fight she must remember that if she entered this fight the prize of victory would be the British Empire. Well, that includes Canada. As my honourable friend has said, there is no portion of the globe which any nation would be likely to covet more than this Dominion of Canada. There is no other portion of the earth's surface that contains such wealth as lies buried here. Nowhere are there such stretches of territory capable of feeding for generations to come—not hundreds of thousands, but millions of people. No, Mr.

Speaker, the ambition of this dictator is not Poland. . . . Where
is he creeping to? Into those communities of the north, some
of which today say they are going to remain neutral. I tell
them if they remain neutral in this struggle, and Britain and
France go down, there is not one of them that will bear for
long the name that it bears at the present time; not one of
them. And if this conqueror by his methods of force, violence,
and terror, and other ruthless iniquities is able to crush the
peoples of Europe, what is going to become of the doctrine
of isolation of this North American continent? If Britain goes
down, if France goes down, the whole business of isolation
will prove to have been a mere myth. There will in time be
no freedom on this continent; there will in time be no liberty.
Life will not be worth living. It is for all of us on this
continent to do our part to save its privileged position by
helping others. . . .

XXVII. Conscription Again

XXVII:1 KING'S DILEMMA

> Mackenzie King's stand against conscription in 1939 was crystal clear. But by 1942 he was forced to ask the nation to release him from his promise never to introduce conscription. The plebiscite was defeated by a three to one majority in Quebec, but passed by a four to one majority in the rest of Canada. Knowing conscription would split the country, King continued to avoid the issue with his theme, "not necessarily conscription, but conscription if necessary."

a. The Pledge, 1939

I wish now to repeat the undertaking I gave in parliament on March 30 last. The present government believe that conscription of men for overseas service will not be a necessary or an effective step. No such measure will be introduced by the present administration. . . .

b. The Plebiscite, 1942

Are you in favour of releasing the Government from any obligation arising out of any past commitments restricting the methods of raising men for military service?

XXVII:2 J. L. RALSTON'S RESIGNATION, 1944

Canadians first became aware of a cabinet crisis over
conscription on November 2, 1944, when King announced the resignation of J. L. Ralston as Minister
of National Defence and his replacement by General
A. G. L. McNaughton. The issue between King and
Ralston is explained in Ralston's letter of resignation
(a) and King's reply (b).

a. Ralston to King

Dear Mr. Prime Minister:

When I returned on October 18 from a visit to the Canadian troops in Italy, in northwestern Europe and the United
Kingdom, I felt compelled to recommend as a result of my
own observations and inquiries in the battle theatres, and on
the information and advice received from my officers, that due
to infantry casualties being much greater than had been
forecasted on the best information available, it had become
necessary to secure substantial numbers of additional trained
infantry personnel in order to make reasonable provision for
the reinforcement of our troops overseas.

Since it appeared clear to me that enough volunteer
personnel could not be made available to meet the need, I
considered that I had no alternative but to recommend that
N.R.M.A. personnel [men conscripted for home duty only]
be sent overseas as reinforcements. I felt that this was necessary to fulfill our pledges to our fighting men.

The whole question was discussed at very considerable
length both at meetings of the cabinet and of the war committee of the cabinet. My recommendation was not accepted.

Alternatives were suggested such as reducing our commitments or breaking up units or formations. I felt I could not
concur in this when these trained N.R.M.A. men were available; and that at this crucial period Canada's duty was to
support our men in the line, and not to relax but to go on
with the task to help shorten the war and speed the victory.

It was suggested that, if a further appeal were made to

trained N.R.M.A. personnel by ministers of the crown and others, such personnel might volunteer for general service in sufficient numbers to meet the need. This suggestion involved delays which I considered would be serious if the appeal was not successful. Consequently I wished to be assured that it was government policy that if, after the appeal, the need for reinforcements overseas still existed and volunteers were not available, N.R.M.A. personnel would be sent. This was the course which I and some other colleagues had understood would follow from your speech in 1942. It was in effect what I, as minister, have repeatedly said in the house since then.

No such assurance was forthcoming. On the contrary it has developed in the discussions that the government as a whole (certain colleagues excepted) do not consider that your speech committed the government to this course.

I consider myself bound by what I have said in the house. Our differences are fundamental on the vital matter of reinforcing our troops, and consequently and as requested by you, I at once tender my resignation as Minister of National Defence.

In the stand I have taken I have considered that my first thought should be my duty to our fighting men in our overseas army.

I wish every success to the distinguished citizen who I understand will take up the duties of this department, and at the same time I want to express to you my very sincere appreciation of the opportunity I have had of serving in Canada's war activities.

Yours very sincerely,

J. L. Ralston.

b. King's Reply

Dear Colonel Ralston:

. . . In your letter you also say "In the stand I have taken I have considered that my first thought should be my duty to our fighting men in our overseas army". I need scarcely say that I have always had the same thought and conception of duty towards all of our fighting men. It is for this reason that I have striven as I have to see that Canada's effort in the present war should be the maximum of which our country is capable. That is why I feel so strongly that at the present time no course of action should be taken if it can possibly be avoided, which, while not certain of accomplishing its purpose, would divide the country and thereby prejudice much that has been so magnificently accomplished throughout more than five years of war—and this on the eve of certain victory.

I have made it clear that I am prepared to follow the course outlined in my speeches in parliament in 1942, if that course should ever be necessary, but I do not believe that it has become necessary.

There has not been a time since the war began that it has not been recognized that resort to conscription for service overseas would occasion the most serious controversy that could arise in Canada. I can think of no course of action fraught with greater danger to our war effort—to say nothing of the unity and strength of Canada to-day and for generations to come—than a general election at this late stage of war on the conscription issue. I believe that such an issue would almost certainly arise were the House of Commons to be asked to endorse an order in council extending the terms of service of N.R.M.A. personnel to include service overseas. Until it is apparent that conscription for overseas service is necessary to the full support of Canada's forces overseas, and that its application would prove effective, the government would not be justified in taking the risk of widespread national dissension.

As to any request by me for your resignation, you will recall that on several occasions you stated that if the recommendation contained in the report of the chief of staff was formally made to the cabinet and not accepted, you would feel compelled to resign, in view of what you had said in parliament. Subsequently you stated that you saw clearly that the cabinet were not disposed to accept your recommendation. In view of your possible resignation on these grounds, I felt it necessary to ascertain the views of General McNaughton. This I did, and ascertained that General McNaughton was not satisfied that compulsory service was necessary to provide full support for the army overseas. In reply to my further inquiries, General McNaughton indicated to me that, with the co-operation of the cabinet, he believed it would be possible to obtain the necessary reinforcements by voluntary means, and that in this belief he would be prepared to assume the responsibility of Minister of National Defence should you resign. In these circumstances, I expressed the opinion that there should not be further delay in reaching a decision. . . .

Yours very sincerely,

W. L. Mackenzie King.

XXVII: 3 KING EXPLAINS THE INTRODUCTION OF CONSCRIPTION

On November 23 Mackenzie King suddenly announced an order-in-council introducing limited conscription. On November 27 he explained his reasons to the House of Commons. King's reference to "anarchy" (after quoting Macdonald on the need for Confederation to avoid anarchy in Canada) may have been a veiled reference to his belief that the country was facing military revolt if conscription was not introduced. How accurate that belief was has been a matter of debate.

. . . Well, having been fortunate enough to secure General McNaughton as Minister of Defence, the government then started to see what could be done in the way of a public appeal. General McNaughton himself began the appeal. . . .

. . . I believe with all my heart that a public appeal would have succeeded if we had received the support of honourable leaders opposite, if we had received the support of their following, if we had received the support of their press. Does anyone doubt that for one moment? I say we would have had the necessary men through voluntary enlistment but for the organized opposition that was taken to voluntary enlistment. From this time on, those who have been responsible for this organized opposition will have on their heads the responsibility for what may follow in the present and over the years.

It was in these circumstances that the cabinet met parliament and that I asked my colleagues to meet me the evening after we had concluded the first day's sitting. I had a special reason for that. It was that General McNaughton himself, in conference with his staff, had come to the conclusion that it might be taking too great a chance not to act immediately. That presentation was made to the government, and with it I made a passionate appeal to every one of my colleagues—I think I may so describe it—not to press for any extreme position; to be as united as they possibly could, yielding up the extreme position, whether it was for all-out conscription under Bill 80 or whether it was for no conscription, realizing that there and then we were face to face with a situation which meant that if we could not agree and could not meet parliament the next day in as united a position as was possible, the only result would be that I would have to announce, on behalf of the government, that we were not in a position longer to carry on because the division in the cabinet was so complete as between those supporting the one point of view and those supporting the other. . . .

. . . I say that unless this House of Commons can unite in reasonable measure to support an administration that can carry on at this stage of war we shall have to face the possibility of anarchy in Canada while our men are fighting overseas, giving their lives that we may maintain our free institutions and that we may have peace and concord through the years to come. Hon. gentlemen may belittle those words, but they are words, no matter to what party the one who uses them belongs, which are entitled to the greatest consideration that can be given. . . .

XXVII:4 FRENCH CANADIANS ON CONSCRIPTION

French Canada's attitude towards conscription in 1944 was, naturally, similar to its position in World War I. This time, however, a Liberal government was introducing conscription after making every effort to avoid it. The two most effective speeches during the debate were made by Louis St. Laurent and Hugues Lapointe. St. Laurent gave his reasons for supporting King (a); Lapointe, recently back from active duty, gave his reasons for opposing the pending vote of confidence (b). Nevertheless, as Lapointe's speech shows, Quebec was deserting King only reluctantly, and, fortunately for national unity, only temporarily.

a. Louis St. Laurent

... I fully realize the possible and probable reactions among a great many in my province to my conduct in accepting to go on when any measure whatsoever of compulsion is added to the voluntary system for service overseas as the policy of the government. But I came here to do a war job, and because it was felt by the Prime Minister, rightly or wrongly, that I could be of some help, I feel I must still go on, whatever may be the increase in the difficulties of the task, so long as it is made apparent to me that these difficulties arise out of facts which have a bearing on the security of the men who are doing so much more for us than anything we can do for them. ...

... Some members of this house wish to register again their opposition to the legal extension of the locality of service of these N.R.M.A. men. I refer, of course, to the subamendment of the hon. member for Mercier. But a majority is apt to be recorded against that subamendment, and if such should be the case I appeal to them to accept that democratic decision in a democratic way. I am sure they can do so without accepting the concept of democracy which is sometimes asserted, the concept that it is both a legal right, and a proper exercise of that right, for the majority to assert its will at all times and in all occasions regardless of the feelings and views of the minority and of the reasons for such feelings and views. That is not my concept of the kind of democracy suited to free men; the kind of democracy for which the free nations are waging this war. It is not the kind of democracy which was envisaged by the fathers of confederation; or not the kind of democracy which will bring to full fruition the constitution that unites in one nation the various elements which make up our Canadian people.

The will of the majority must be respected and it must prevail. But I trust that, here in Canada, the majority will always, as it is doing in this case, assert that will only after giving due consideration to the feelings and views of the minority and to the reasons for such feelings and views, and then only to the extent to which the majority is sincerely convinced that the general interests of the whole body politic require that it be thus asserted. . . .

Believing as I do that the majority in this house, after giving its best consideration to the facts which have been brought to light in this long and earnest debate, is sincerely convinced that the passing of this order in council P.C. 8891 was necessary to the proper conduct of the affairs of the Canadian body politic as a whole, and believing as I do that whenever the majority, after full consultation and mature deliberation, reaches a conclusion of that kind, it is proper the minority should accept it and loyally assist in carrying it out, I appeal to all the members of this house, whatever may have been their individual views—whether to do more or to do less than the order in council provides—to unite and to assert to the men overseas that this nation, from one ocean to the other, stands pledged to a victory that will be decisive and that will endure. . . .

b. **Hugues Lapointe**

. . . I have always been taught that politics was not a game of diplomacy, but that it was the most serious task to which any man could devote his talent and ability, and that to represent one's fellow citizens in the House of Commons was possibly the greatest honour and privilege to be vested in any man. I was also taught that pledges and promises once given had to be kept. . . . personally I cannot go back on the word which I solemnly gave to the people whom I represent in this house, especially when I am not convinced that this order in council was necessary for the winning of the war and the security of Canada. Furthermore, as regards this point, I will not permit any man to doubt my sincerity or impute any political motives to my action. It is purely a question to be settled as between myself and my own conscience. It may be considered as a selfish attitude to take, but I would rather withdraw from public life than have it be said by any man who had placed his faith in me that I had failed to keep the word I had given. . . .

Another reason why I cannot agree on the change of policy is the consequences which I fear will result from that change. In my mind, what is even more important than the fact that possibly 15,000 Canadians will be sent to serve overseas, against their will, in spite of the pledges made by the government, is the fact that for a long time the people of Canada will have lost some of the faith they usually have in their public men. In my opinion the value of our parliamentary institutions is based upon the good faith which can exist between electors and the men they have chosen to represent them. I fear very much that as a result of this changed policy Canadians in all provinces will no longer have in our public men that confidence which I believe is so necessary in democratic institutions.

Irrespective of the complexity of the problem now facing us, the fact remains that one responsible party which, for many years, shaped the opinion of the majority of the people in this country, has brought into force an act which is absolutely contradictory to all its pledges and undertakings. It is not the judgment which the electors may pass now, at a time when the country is going through a period of mob hysteria, that is important; it is the judgment they will pass after the war is over, when they can analyze the facts in their true light, in an atmosphere of peace. I, for one, do not want to share in any way the responsibility for a policy whose enactment by this government may in future undermine faith and confidence in public men. Certainly I do not want to criticize the Prime Minister unduly. I realize as well as any one, and better than some people, the situation in which has has been placed, . . .

. . . I believe I truly express the sentiments of the people whom I have the honour to represent here when I tell the Prime Minister that there is no one else whom they want to see as the head of the government of Canada, but on the other hand they cannot forget the breaking of a pledge which to them was sacred. I hope, Mr. Speaker, that the task to which the Prime Minister has devoted his whole life, and the national unity which he succeeded in realizing in Canada, will not come to an end because of the present issue. I trust that, once the turmoil of this battle is ended, Canadians will realize at last that they should not be separated from one another, that they should not hate one another because of a mere political issue. . . .

XXVIII. The New Diplomatic Role

XXVIII:1 LOUIS ST. LAURENT PROPOSES AN ATLANTIC ALLIANCE, 1948

World War II profoundly changed Canada's international outlook. The extent of the change is shown in these excerpts from a famous speech by External Affairs Minister St. Laurent to the House of Commons on April 29, 1948, which contain one of the first suggestions of what was to become the North Atlantic Treaty Organization.

It is now, I believe, an accepted fact that practically everything of importance that happens in the international sphere is of interest to Canada—often of direct and immediate interest. For us there is no escape, even if we wish to seek one, in isolation or indifference. Recent events have brought home to all of us the increasing threat to our democratic national existence of the rising tide of totalitarian communism. . . .

On repeated occasions the government has indicated that collective security through the operations of an effective international organization was a primary objective in the foreign policy of this country. This continues to be our policy. We are fully aware, however, of the inadequacy of the United Nations at the present moment to provide the nations of the world with the security which they require. . . .

I referred to one possible line of development when I spoke seven months ago at the General Assembly. I stated then that it was not necessary to contemplate the break-up of the United Nations or the secession from it of the Soviet group in order to build up a stronger security system within the organization. Without sacrificing the universality of the United Nations, it is possible for the free nations of the world to form their own closer association for collective self-defence under article 51 of the charter of the United Nations. Such an association could be created within the United Nations by those free states which are willing to accept more specific and onerous obligations than those contained in the charter in return for greater national security than the United Nations can now give its members.

It may be that the free states, or some of them, will soon find it necessary to consult together on how best to establish such a collective security league. It might grow out of the plans for "western union" now maturing in Europe. Its purpose, like that of "western union," would not be merely negative; it would create a dynamic counter-attraction to communism—the dynamic counter-attraction of a free, prosperous and progressive society as opposed to the totalitarian and reactionary society of the communist world. The formation of such a defensive group of free states would not be a counsel of despair but a message of hope. It would not mean that we regarded a third world war as inevitable; but that the free democracies had decided that to prevent such a war they would organize so as to confront the forces of communist expansionism with an overwhelming preponderance of moral, economic and military force and with sufficient degree of unity to ensure that this preponderance of force is so used that the free nations cannot be defeated one by one. No measure less than this will do. We must at all costs avoid the fatal repetition of the history of the pre-war years when the nazi aggressor picked off its victims one by one. Such a process does not end at the Atlantic. . . .

Our foreign policy today must, therefore, I suggest, be based on a recognition of the fact that totalitarian communist aggression, endangers the freedom and peace of every democratic country, including Canada. On this basis and pending the strengthening of the United Nations, we should be willing to associate ourselves with other free states in any appropriate collective security arrangements which may be worked out under articles 51 or 52 of the charter.

In the circumstances of the present the organization of collective defence in this way is the most effective guarantee of peace. The pursuit of this course, steadfastly, unprovocatively, and constructively is our best hope for disproving the gloomy predictions of inevitable war.

The burden of maintaining peace, however, will not be easy. We must constantly remember that the union of the free world which is now "painfully struggling to be born" will possess overwhelming strength only if it is based on moral as well as material force; if its citizens are bound together not merely by a hatred of communism but by their love of free democracy and their determination to make it work for the promotion of welfare and the preservation of peace.

XXVIII:2 CANADA IN THE UNITED NATIONS: THE SUEZ CRISIS, 1956

As a middle power with considerable international prestige after World War II, Canada played an active and important role in the United Nations. Undoubtedly the high point of Canada's efforts for world peace was her work in establishing a peace-keeping force during the Suez Crisis of 1956—an achievement for which Lester B. Pearson was awarded the Nobel Peace Prize in 1957. In this excerpt from his Report to the House of Commons, Mr. Pearson describes Canada's role in the crisis.

. . . On Saturday, November 3 . . . The Assembly was to meet at eight o'clock that evening. On that occasion I did produce a Canadian resolution for the setting up of a United

Nations Emergency Force for this particular situation. . . .

It was a very short resolution, and it asked the Secretary-General merely to submit, within forty-eight hours, something we had been unable to do anything about for ten years, namely, a plan for setting up an emergency international United Nations police force with the consent of the governments concerned. . . .

We obtained 57 votes as sponsors for the resolution. There were 19 abstentions. Nobody voted against us. The United Kingdom and France did not find it possible to vote for that resolution at that time but they have indicated, both privately and publicly, their great appreciation of the initiative which resulted in its being adopted and they have also stated their support for it since then. . . .

Then on November 4 we started to work. Canada had something to do with this work because we were the sponsors of the resolution and had a certain obligation to help the Secretary-General carry it out. We started to work on organizing a United Nations police force or at least to form the basis of the organization and report back in forty-eight hours.

As it happened, the Secretary-General [Mr. Hammarskjöld], who has played a magnificent part throughout these difficult days, was able to make a first report within twenty-four hours. Offers of contributions to the force began to come in within that twenty-four-hour period.

That Sunday night when we were working on the establishment of the force, the United Kingdom and French ground forces landed at Port Said. The situation at the United Nations immediately began to deteriorate. Things became very tense. The Security Council was called into emergency session and refused to consider a Soviet proposal for Soviet and United States intervention because the matter was before the United Nations Assembly. Then in the midst of rumors of Russian intervention, rumors that there would be a determined demand by the Arab and Asian members of the Assembly to brand the United Kingdom and France formally as aggressors under the Charter and to invoke sanctions against them, the Assembly met on Tuesday morning, November 6. It had before it the Secretary-General's final report on the organization of the United Nations force. At that time he was able to report progress with regard to the composition of the force. He was able to lay down certain principles and functions for that force but not to go into detail, for two reasons. He did not have enough time, in the first place; and in the second, if we had attempted to do it in detail, we would still be arguing about what those functions should be. There was, however, one important detail, namely, that the force should exclude contingents from the permanent members of the Security Council. . . .

A draft resolution was drawn up supporting this report and authorizing the Secretary-General to go ahead on that basis, to discuss participation with other governments. It set up also an Advisory Committee of seven members of the Assembly [Brazil, Canada, Ceylon, Colombia, India, Norway, Pakistan] to help him in this task. Canada is one of the members of that committee. This resolution was passed by 64 to 0, with 10 abstentions. . . . [the resolution] approved an *aide-mémoire* which gave the Secretary-General further authority to organize the United Nations police force. By a very important paragraph . . . he was told to get ahead with the clearing of the Suez Canal. . . .

The function of this force which is now in being is to secure and supervise the cessation of hostilities and carry out its task in accordance with directions received from the United Nations. The force—and it is interesting to recall that the resolution authorizing this force was passed not much more than three weeks ago—is now in being in Egypt, where it will be stationed, or any place else where the United Nations considers it necessary to be stationed. The most important function is, of course, the policing of the zone between opposing forces in Egypt in order to prevent the recurrence, if possible, of the fighting. At the present time the headquarters of the force is along the Suez, but it may of course be moved.

It is not a fighting force in the sense that it is a force operating under, say, Chapter VII of the United Nations Charter, which deals with enforcement procedures. It is not a United Nations fighting force in the sense that the force in Korea was; it is operating under a different chapter of the Charter dealing with conciliation procedures. . . .

. . . May this force succeed in its task. If it does, we may have started something of immense value for the future. We may have taken a step to put force behind the law and behind the collective will of the international community.

XXVIII: 3 LESTER B. PEARSON ON CANADIAN FOREIGN POLICY IN THE 1950's

Canada saw herself in the 1950's as an independent power, but acting as a mediator between the two countries with which she had special historical and political ties—Great Britain and the United States. This excerpt from a 1957 address by Lester Pearson analyzes the subtle interplay of our national interest and our special commitments in pursuing this policy.

. . . Canadian policy, however, at the United Nations and elsewhere has to be determined primarily by Canadian considerations and Canadian interests. This requires that Canada should not automatically follow any other government, however close and friendly. But at the same time, we should not pursue this Canadian policy in any narrow, selfish way, but with a full realization that the greatest Canadian national interest is prejudiced when there is division within the Commonwealth or between London and Washington and Paris. It is not easy for a middle power, such as Canada, with a special relationship of friendship and interest with countries like the United Kingdom and the United States, to know when to give up a national position in the interests of harmony in the group, or when to stand firm. It requires a nice, but difficult, balancing of advantages and disadvantages.

Canadian policy, for instance, must be national in formulation and execution, but it should never be isolationist or exclusive. It must, of course, protect Canadian interests, but the greatest Canadian interest, in this thermonuclear age, is peace. And we know that there can be no guarantee of peace through national policy, or no refuge from danger in national isolation.

There may be times—I hope they will be few—when, as a free and self-reliant nation, we will have to go our own way irrespective of what our closest friends do. But that must be only after we have done everything possible to avoid such a course. That is my concept of Canadian nationalism in foreign policy. It does not include being sensitive about charges of colonialism when we are in full accord with Downing Street, as we so very often are; or about allegations of being a satellite when we are in agreement with American decisions.

I return, once again, to that essential purpose of Canadian policy: the promotion, by every means within its power, of accord between London and Washington. To anyone subjected to the day-by-day problems of Canada's international relations, as I am, it seems almost impossible to overemphasize the importance of this. It means a fuller understanding of each other's point of view across the Atlantic. It means, perhaps, if not less reliance on Magna Carta and Shakespeare and our common heritage, at least far more reliance on the cold, hard facts of self-interest and mutual security. The United States and the United Kingdom need each other; need to count on each other; need each other's support in a dangerous world, more than they need anything else. And Canada needs them both.

XXIX. The End Of The Liberal Régime

XXIX: 1 THE PIPELINE DEBATE, 1956

Since 1935, the Liberal party under Mackenzie King and Louis St. Laurent had enjoyed an unprecedented ascendency in Canadian politics. By the mid 1950's, however, the government was becoming "old and tired" in office. More ominously for Liberal fortunes, it had become impatient with the parliamentary process. In 1956, the House of Commons suffered the most ignoble debate in its history when the government attempted to force C. D. Howe's Trans-Canada Pipe Lines Bill (to lend eighty million dollars to an American controlled company) through Parliament by using closure (limiting debate) at every stage of the process. The lowest of the many low points in the debate was the chaos in the House on June 1 when the Speaker, under strong pressure from the cabinet, reversed a ruling of the day before that would have allowed the Opposition to prolong the debate. Opposition protests at this obvious injustice were drowned out by Liberal singing.

Mr. Speaker: . . . What I intended to submit to the house is that in neglecting to submit at once to the house yesterday the report of the chairman of the committee on an appeal from his ruling by the hon. member for Winnipeg North Centre (Mr. Knowles) I made a serious mistake and the house should not suffer any prejudice or detriment on my account, and that the house, which is master of its own proceedings, should be placed in exactly the same position as it was when I resumed the chair yesterday . . .Those who are in favour of this course of action will please say yea.

Some hon. Members: Yea.

Mr. Drew: But, Mr. Speaker—

Mr. Speaker: Those opposed will please say nay.

Some hon. Members: Nay.

Mr. Speaker: In my opinion the yeas have it; call in the members.

Mr. Drew: Mr. Speaker—

Mr. Fleming: Mr. Speaker—

Mr. Fulton: Mr. Speaker—

Mr. Knowles: Mr. Speaker—

Some hon. Members: Hail, hail, the gang's all here.

Mr. Drew: Mr. Speaker, do I understand that you will do nothing—

Mr. Coldwell: Mr. Speaker—

Some hon. Members: Oh, oh.

Mr. Diefenbaker: Has the Prime Minister no control over his followers?

Mr. Fleming: This is organized disorder on the part of all Liberals in the house.

Mr. Coldwell: Mr. Speaker—

Some hon. Members: Sit down.

Mr. Coldwell: Mr. Speaker, are you not going to call order?

Mr. Speaker: There is nothing before the house at the moment.

Mr. Knowles: There is no house.

Mr. Coldwell: Mr. Speaker, this is a demonstration on the part of all Liberals in the house which shows a great disrespect for authority. I protest against this. Parliament has ceased to function.

Mr. Diefenbaker: Where is the Prime Minister? Is he silent in the face of this demonstration?

Mr. Rowe: Is he afraid to dissolve parliament? Why not do it yourself?—you are doing everything else yourself.

Mr. Martin: You have delayed things for three weeks. You led it, too. Don't say a word.

Mr. Fleming: Mr. Speaker, it should be placed on the record that when an hon. member rose on a question of privilege you sat down and refused to hear him and the Liberals instigated such an outburst of disorder that no one could be heard. That ought to be on the record. This is the lowest moment in Canadian parliamentary history; the lowest moment. There has never been anything like it.

Mr. Pearson: I thought that was last night.

Mr. Bell: This is black Friday, boy.

Mr. Lesage: You brought it on; you did it yourself.

Mr. Fleming: How absurd can you get?

Mr. Martin: The minority is not running this parliament.

Mr. Rowe: The majority isn't running it either; nobody is running it. The majority cannot run it, let alone the minority.

Mr. Hodgson: Hitlerism.

Some hon. Members:
There will always be a pipe line,
The pipe line shall be free;
The gas shall flow from west to east in each locality.
There'll always be a pipe line,
The pipe line shall be free—

Mr. Fleming: Not parliament.

Some hon. Members:
—for Fulton means no more to you than Fulton means
    to me.
There'll always be a pipe line, the pipe line shall be free—

Mr. Fleming: Free to American investors.

Some hon. Members:
I've been working on the pipe line all the day through,
I've been working on the pipe line just to make the Tories
    blue.
Can't you hear the Tories moaning, getting up so early in
    the morn';

Hear the C.C.F.'ers groaning, for the pipe line's getting
warm.

Mr. Rowe: He laughs best who laughs last; go to the country
and find out.

An hon. Member: You laughed yourself.

Mr. Rowe: No, I am ashamed of you; that is why I cannot
laugh.

XXIX:2 JOHN DIEFENBAKER ON THE RIGHTS OF PARLIAMENT, 1957

The complacent government never realized the
damage done by the pipeline debate. In the 1957
election campaign John Diefenbaker attracted thousands of normally Liberal voters with his strong stand
for the rights of Parliament. The passage below is
from his opening speech in the 1957 campaign. The
issue of the rights of Parliament along with his own
personal appeal (see document XXIX:3 on page 332)
were the most crucial of several factors in making John
Diefenbaker the first Conservative Prime Minister
in twenty-two years.

. . . I would be remiss, even at this late hour, if I did not
return to rediscuss something that affects the freedom of Canadians everywhere. I mean that institution that is one of the
three pillars of democracy—those pillars being the Canadian
People, the Canadian Provinces and the Canadian Parliament.
I speak now of Parliament—I speak with my colleagues here
from the House of Commons. Parliament—the place that I
love; Parliament that represents in its essence the preservation
of our freedom. What things have been done to Parliament
in recent years? In the British tradition of democracy, the
Cabinet is constitutionally responsible to the elected representatives in Parliament. Such government, such responsibility (and I make this appeal to those who in the past have
supported the Liberal Party) —such government is, in every
sense, of and by and for the people.

There was a time when I used to go to the Galleries of the House of Commons as a young man. I saw Meighen, and Borden, and King, and Lapointe. Parliament—what does it mean in the Liberal tradition? There was a time when that Party was militant, true to its faith in the cause of Freedom. I remember Mr. Lapointe using these words, and I underline them now:

> "The first duty of Parliament is to remain a Parliament, not to become a subservient and ornamental body."

It is subservient today with its majority, but it isn't ornamental. Yes—it is the will of Parliament, not that of a government, that is the will of the nation. The sovereignty of the people is delegated to Parliament, not to the Executive. When I say "Parliament", it means the minority as well as the majority in Parliament. Those were the views that are no longer held by those who profess Liberalism. The Prime Minister and members of his Cabinet have repeatedly looked at themselves and spoken of themselves as the sole interpreter of the will of the nation. Parliament—how many of you have sat in the Gallery of the House of Commons? If you have been there, you will have seen that great institution treated with shocking contempt, sorely wounded, robbed of its rights, its independence gone, usurped by a few Ministers who treat the rest of the Cabinet as juniors, and members of all Parties as though they were not entitled to be there.

I have seen the progressive restriction of the supremacy of Parliament in the last ten years. I have seen Parliament bludgeoned, and I say that is no pipe-dream. Bludgeoned by a majority. I have seen the hands of the Cabinet directing members and disciplining them into an abject servility. My friends, there is an issue that transcends all others—the preservation of freedom, its maintenance, the restoration of Parliament, and above everything else in that connection, an imperative and immediate necessity of a return to the Two-Party system in this country if freedom is to be preserved and political democracy maintained. . . .

XXIX: 3 THE DIEFENBAKER APPEAL, 1958

> After a year of vigorous Conservative minority
> government, the electorate gave John Diefenbaker the
> biggest majority in Canadian history in 1958—208
> out of 265 seats. Mr. Diefenbaker's charismatic
> presentation of his "vision" of what Canada could
> become in the next decade had an unprecedented
> impact on the Canadian imagination. After the years
> of Liberal "managerial" politics the new Conservative
> leader seemed to be the authentic voice of Canadian
> nationalism. These passages from Mr. Diefenbaker's
> opening campaign speech in Winnipeg (although
> they are meant to be heard rather than read) present
> the heart of the "vision."

. . . Ladies and gentlemen, we started in the last few months,
since June the 10th, to carry out our promises, and I can tell
you this, that as long as I am Prime Minister of this country,
the welfare of the average Canadian will not be forgotten.

We intend to launch for the future, we have laid the foundations now, the long-range objectives of this party. We ask from
you a mandate; a new and a stronger mandate, to pursue the
planning and to carry to fruition our new national development programme for Canada. For years we raised that in the
House of Commons, and those in authority ridiculed it. Day
before yesterday, Mr. Pearson came out in favour of a national
development policy. Why didn't they do it when they were
in power?

This national development policy will create a new sense of
national purpose and national destiny. One Canada. One
Canada, wherein Canadians will have preserved to them the
control of their own economic and political destiny. Sir John
A. Macdonald gave his life to this party. He opened the West.
He saw Canada from East to West. I see a new Canada—a
Canada of the North. What are these new principles? What
are our objectives? What do we propose? We propose to
assist the provinces, with their co-operation, in the financing
and construction of job-creating projects necessary for the new

development, where such projects are beyond the resources of the provinces. We will assist the provinces with their co-operation in the conservation of the renewable natural resources. We will aid in projects which are self-liquidating. We will aid in projects which, while not self-liquidating will lead to the development of the national resources for the opening of Canada's northland. We will open that northland for development by improving transportation and communication and by the development of power, by the building of access roads. We will make an inventory of our hydro-electric potential.

Ladies and gentlemen, we now intend to bring in legislation to encourage progressively increasing processing of our domestic raw materials in Canada, rather than shipping them out in raw material form. We will ensure that Canada's national resources are used to benefit Canadians and that Canadians have an opportunity to participate in Canada's development. We have not discouraged foreign investment, but we will encourage the partnership of the foreign investors with the Canadian people. . . .

Canadians, realize your opportunities! This is only the beginning. The future programme for the next five to seven years under a Progressive Conservative Government is one that is calculated to give young Canadians, motivated by a desire to serve, a lift in the heart, faith in Canada's future, faith in her destiny. We will extend aid to economically sound railway projects, such as the Pine Point Railroad to Great Slave Lake. That was promised day before yesterday in the Liberal platform. Why didn't they do it then?

Yes, we will press for hydro-electric development of the Columbia River, which now awaits completion of an agreement with the United States. I mentioned the South Saskatchewan. These are the plans.

This is the message I give to you my fellow Canadians, not one of defeatism. Jobs! Jobs for hundreds of thousands of Canadian people. A new vision! A new hope! A new soul for Canada. . . .

As far as the Arctic is concerned, how many of you here knew the pioneers in Western Canada. I saw the early days here. Here in Winnipeg in 1903, when the vast movement was taking place into the Western plains, they had imagination. There is a new imagination now. The Arctic. We intend to carry out the legislative programme of Arctic research, to develop Arctic routes, to develop those vast hidden resources the last few years have revealed. Plans to improve the St. Lawrence and the Hudson Bay route. Plans to increase self-government in the Yukon and Northwest Territories. We can see one or two provinces there.

Taxation adjustments to place Canadians on a more equal footing with foreign investors. Encourage foreign investors to make equity stock available to Canadians for purchase, to appoint Canadians to executive positions, to deny the present plan of certain American companies that do not give to Canadian plants their fair share of the export business. Those are some of the things we want to do. . . .

It is for those things that I ask a mandate, not giving you tonight the whole picture at all, by any means but giving you something of the vision as I see it. The reason that I appeal to the Canadian people, a mandate for a clear majority. You set a pace for Manitoba last time. Give us a few more, this.

We need a clear majority to carry out this long-range plan, this great design, this blueprint for the Canada which her resources make possible.

I want to see Canadians given a transcending sense of national purpose, such as Macdonald gave in his day. To safeguard our independence, restore our unity, a policy that will scrupulously respect the rights of the provinces, and at the same time build for the achievement of that one Canada, is the major reason why 35 of our 113 members in the House of Commons are sufficiently young to belong to the Young Progressive Conservatives. They caught that vision. I am not here to condemn others. I am here for the purpose, as a Canadian, to give you a picture of the kind of Canada the long-range plans that we have in mind will bring about. . . .

This party has become the party of national destiny. I hope it will be the party of vision and courage. The party of one Canada, with equal opportunities to all. The only party that can give to youth an Elizabethan sense of grand design—that's my challenge.

The faith to venture with enthusiasm to the frontiers of a nation; that faith, that assurance that will be provided with a government strong enough to implement plans for development.

To the young men and women of this nation I say, Canada is within your hands. Adventure. Adventure to the nation's utmost bounds, to strive, to seek, to find, and not to yield. The policies that will be placed before the people of Canada in this campaign will be ones that will ensure that today and this century will belong to Canada. The destination is one Canada. To that end I dedicate this party. . . .

XXX. Towards A
New Quebec

XXX: 1 THE CHURCH ATTACKS POLITICAL IMMORALITY

Throughout the 1950's in Quebec, opposition slowly developed to the arch-conservative, highly corrupt *Union Nationale* government of Maurice Duplessis. Perhaps the most significant condemnation of the *Union Nationale* came just after the 1956 election in a sensational article by Fathers Gérard Dion and Louis O'Neill, of the faculty of Laval University, entitled *L'Immoralité politique dans la province de Québec.* This outspoken indictment—obviously of the *Union Nationale*—was not repudiated by any member of the Church hierarchy. The implication was that after many years of tacit support for the *Union Nationale,* the Church was now ready to support reform.

. . . The unfurling of silliness and immorality which has just been witnessed in Quebec can leave no intelligent Catholic unmoved. Never, perhaps, has the religious crisis which exists here at home been so clearly evident.

Never however, have we been given a clearer evidence of the work of dechristianization which is going on among the masses of the people.

Right-thinking people will undoubtedly be amazed by such assertions. Those to whom morality is limited practically to

336

the problems of shorts, sun-dresses or the padlock law, will find our ideas very daring. But a Christian morality which respects the order of virtues, calls for charity, truth and justice as fundamental to social life, and which still can be scandalized in the presence of lies, perversion of consciences, and systematic corruption of the right, cannot be unmoved in the face of facts which have become quite evident. . . .

A Christian country in which lying has been systematized, is a country in which the religious sense will inevitably be attacked, for Christian faith is essentially a cult of truth. Modern methods of diffusing ideas permit the building up of huge collective lies and the repetition without limit, through newspapers, radio and television of misleading slogans, to such an extent that the man in the street can no longer hold back and willingly agrees, "that it becomes true." . . .

Systematic lying and use of the myth are already fraudulent manoeuvres. Such proceedings as vote buying, corruption of the electoral law, threats of reprisals against those who do not support the "right party," false oaths, substitution of persons, the corruption of election officers, also seem to be becoming normal elements in our social life at election time. Some urban sections saw examples of violence which would make the most fervent anarchists jealous.

Those who now employ or tolerate these proceedings can lay no claim to their invention. We must admit that our Catholic province has for a considerable length of time known what is meant by electoral frauds. But their use is more and more generous at each election. No party has the monopoly. Who will measure the after-effects of a social state where such an immorality is commonly admitted?

Here again, that which should cause us the greatest anxiety, is the fact that so few people seem to be scandalized by it all. Similar methods, utilized in Communist countries, arouse the indignation of our good people and raise the zeal of our Catholic journalists. In the province of Quebec, they quickly receive popular absolution. People even boast and laugh about it as though they were innocent pranks. . . .

Use of religion Here we are faced with one of the customary manoeuvres of our election technicians. The procedure has simply become more refined and ignoble. They go at it without scruples, denouncing pseudo-enemies of religion everywhere and succeeding in setting in motion the defensive mechanism of believers whose good will greatly excels their critical sense.

The anti-Communist slogan seems to have been employed with considerable success. A low type of literature has penetrated into the presbyteries and convents. One rector changed his conviction after reading *l'Unité Nationale,* of Mr. Adrien Arcand! Nuns read or heard strange stories about people who, until then, they thought were Catholics. There was talk about the faith being in danger, of enemies on the prowl, of the example of countries in which a handful of Communists succeeded in assuming power, etc. On close examination, it was just trumpery to amaze primitives. And yet the trick went over marvellously!

Money carries no odor There were, unfortunately, some cases in which the voting motive appears to have been less spiritual. There is reason to believe that the laity are not the only ones who are influenced by gifts in money or goods. Gifts to pious or welfare associations, contributions to parish associations know how to get through to some ecclesiastical souls. Faced with some facts, one is inclined to ponder the saying of Canon Tellier de Poncheville on the "clerical causes of anticlericalism." . . .

Clever advice from parish priests Some priests took part personally in the campaign. In a parish of a Quebec suburb a rector carried his kindness so far as to preach in his pulpit in favor of his candidate and he even solicited votes from door to door. Another case: in the same county, a rector advised his parishioners to vote for the candidate whose party would be in power: "Without that, we get nothing," he said. Another: "Vote for whoever you like, but when we have a good government, we keep it." A final case: "Before going to vote, don't forget to look at our nice new school."

Is it too late to re-act? The conclusion appears to us to be obvious: an election period like that through which we have just passed becomes an instrument of demoralization and dechristianization. That which makes a country Christian is not first and foremost, the number of churches, the pious declarations of politicians, the apparent temporal or political influence of the Church or the "good relations" between Church and State. It is primarily the respect for the truth, the cult of justice, integrity of consciences, the respect for liberty. The existing electoral proceedings are a frontal attack on all these values. . . .

XXX:2 *THE IMPERTINENCES OF BROTHER ANONYMOUS*

In 1960 an anonymous young teaching Brother (later revealed to be Jean-Paul Desbiens, Brother Pierre-Jérôme) published a satirical, biting, and above all an honest attack on Quebec society. *Les Insolences du Frère Untel,* portions of which appear below, begins with a discussion of *joual,* the nickname given to the corrupted French used by many people in Quebec. The book goes on to expose the inanities of Quebec's education system and religious life. The publication of *Frère Untel* had an incalculable impact on the province. It was at once a symbol of the end of the old Quebec and the birth of the new concern for human values and the French Canadian nation that was to produce Quebec's "quiet revolution."

I work with the axe, though I don't like to. By temperament I am rather delicate, and nostalgic about the past. I enjoy Oka cheese and coffee laced with brandy. But in the land of Quebec this is no time for delicacy. . . . If a man is asleep in a house on fire, the neighbours don't wake him up with Mozart's *Eine Kleine Nachtmusik.* They yell at him, and if he still sleeps soundly, they kick him out of bed. . . .

Joual, this absence of language, is a symptom of our nonexistence as French Canadians. No one can ever study language enough, for it is the home of all meanings. Our inability to assert ourselves, our refusal to accept the future, our obsession with the past, are all reflected in joual, our real language. Witness the abundance of negative turns of speech in our talk. Instead of saying that a woman is beautiful, we say she's not bad-looking; instead of saying that a pupil is intelligent, we say he's not stupid; instead of saying that we feel well, we say we're not too bad. . . .

Now we approach the heart of the problem, which is a problem of civilization. Our pupils speak joual because they think joual, and they think joual because they live joual, like everybody around here. Living joual means rock'n roll, hot dogs, parties, running around in cars. . . .

. . . We live joual because our souls are impoverished, and so we speak it. I am convinced there is no substantial difference between the degradation of our language and the slackness of our attitude to the fundamental liberties which a *Maclean's* survey revealed in October, 1959. When our youth has surrendered those liberties, as they seem to have done in practice if not in theory—the word liberty is still respectable —they easily give up grammar. The apostles of democracy, like the apostles of good speech, appear like gentle madmen. Our people keep their admiration for machines and technique. They are impressed by nothing but money and luxury; the graces of syntax do not interest them. I flatter myself that I speak correct French—not elegant, but correct. My pupils nonetheless speak joual; I make no impression on them. Indeed I fancy that they sometimes do not understand me. To be understood, I often must have recourse to one or another joual expression. We speak two different languages, my class and I, and I am the only one who speaks both. What can we do? The whole French Canadian society is foundering. Our merchants show off their English company names, the billboards along our roads are all in English. We are a servile race; our loins were broken two hundred years ago, and it shows. . . .

The failure of our system of teaching is the reflection of a failure, or at any rate a paralysis, of thought itself. Nobody in French Canada dares think—at least nobody dares think out loud. The lack of any serious discussion in the Province brands us in the most unforgivable way. As talking to oneself is the beginning of madness, it's clear that to spend one's time thinking, necessarily alone, is to come close to madness. French Canada's tragedy is a tragedy of communication.

What we practice here is purity through sterilization, orthodoxy through silence, security through dull repetition. We imagine there is only one way to go straight, and that is never to set out; one way never to make mistakes and that is never to experiment; one way not to get lost and that is to stay asleep. We have invented a sure way to fight caterpillars—to cut down the trees. . . .

The pervading fear in which we live sterilizes all our efforts. If we write, all our propositions must be justifiable before possible inquisitors; if we act, all our actions must be measured by the traditional standard, that is, they must be repetitions of previous actions. We choose the safest way, to say nothing, to do nothing, to stand still. *Je me souviens!* (Quebec's motto) . . . .

Nothing that is oppressive is Christian. Christianity is essentially a liberating force. One of these days French Canadians will discover that liberation. It is not Christianity that crushes us, but the triple spirit of evil. Of the three lusts which all men know, the one that scourges mankind most harshly is the third, the one of which nothing is said, the one never denounced from the pulpit, the spirit of domination. Do you know any preachers who denounce the snares of authority? Any professors who tell you to read St. Bernard's *Considera-tion?* Oh no, they always hammer on the same nail, as if our national vice was rebellion, as if we were not long since a dumb people, unable to express ourselves except by swearing and getting drunk. . . .

St. Thomas Aquinas associates the gift of wisdom with the beatitude of the peacemakers. Wisdom is the active desire to partake of the spiritual. The sweetest fruit that wisdom can perceive from far away, is the fruit of liberty. It would move heaven and earth to make it grow, this fruit of liberty. Let's be done with this fear. It's now or never, the Province of Quebec is on the eve of a decisive move. . . .

XXX:3 THE PARENT COMMISSION REPORTS ON EDUCATIONAL REFORM, 1963

Under Jean Lesage the Liberal party took office in Quebec in 1960 as the party of reform. Unlike the *Union Nationale* after 1936, the new government actually put reform into practice. One of its first actions was to appoint a Royal Commission—the Parent Commission—to examine education in Quebec. These excerpts from the first report of the Commission indicate both the failures of the old system and the ideals that were to be the basis of the new. The Commission's major recommendation, a Ministry of Education, was implemented in March, 1964, with the passage of the hotly debated Bill 60.

Like every other country throughout the world, the Province of Quebec must examine the educational problems confronting it in the light of objectives which originate in its own economic and social development and from modern trends in education generally. While taking full account of the special problems arising from its own traditions and history, the Province must seek with clarity of vision and practical good sense to endow its educational system with a structure suited to its present needs. . . .

The determination to make available to all pupils instruction in any field or at any level encounters one particularly serious obstacle in the French Roman Catholic schools of Québec. The historical account of its development has shown how public and private education evolved along parallel lines, with only the latter leading to classical college and university.

By tradition, the public school child was directed toward manual work, subordinate jobs in business and the service industries and toward the skilled trades. Seldom did he even consider—and the system did not encourage him—continuing his studies in the classical college and the university. By contrast, the child whose social background naturally suggested the liberal professions began in, or early transferred to, private institutions. In very recent years attempts have been made to co-ordinate the public system with classical and university studies, but passage from one to the other still remains difficult. Such a transfer may involve the loss of one or two years. This lack of continuity compromises a student's chances of admission to the university and of success in his studies. Then again, the educational institutions which have recently seen rapid development—normal, vocational and domestic science schools—are under the direction of different and wholly unrelated agencies. Hence their graduates encounter the same barriers at the threshold of the university. This is especially regrettable for the normal school graduate who, despite his grade A diploma, equivalent to a bachelor's degree in pedagogy, finds he cannot follow many university courses, even those which could help him as a teacher.

Education for all therefore presumes that a student will not encounter too many dead-ends as he moves vertically from the public schools to advanced studies. It likewise presumes that on the horizontal level he can pass without difficulty from one institution to an equivalent grade in any other, and that, without any loss of self-esteem, he may drop a classical or scientific secondary course to take up a vocational course at the same level. A re-arrangement of the educational structures, a better sequence of levels of study, a more rational distribution of programmes and institutions will eliminate losses of time which are injurious to students and wasteful to the country's general economy. This necessary co-ordination cannot be promptly achieved unless it is encouraged, and, if need be, imposed by a single authority with jurisdiction over the whole educational system. . . .

Private initiative certainly is unable effectively to carry out such ambitious objectives or suffice for so many tasks—construction, geographic allocation, co-ordination, recruitment of personnel, finance. . . .

A master plan is needed, an orientation united to serve the common good, a general economy for the whole system which will avoid duplication, focus effort and establish budgetary priorities aimed at a better or more extensive use of present resources. This task of organization and finance properly belongs to the political authorities responsible for the common good. In a democratic society, the government represents all those interested in education: families, religious groups, educational institutions, professional associations. Its policy regarding education is of deep consequence, for all the great economic and social problems it confronts—full employment, health, social security. An analysis of the responsibilities at present assumed by the government of Québec and a search for the means whereby they may be exercised more effectively in future lead us to recommend a major reform in the educational system. . . .

One of the reasons most frequently alleged for excluding the State from direct exercise of its responsibilities in this domain is the determination to protect the schools from the pressure of politics. . . . Why is it so dangerous and improper for educational policy to be discussed openly before the electorate and the Legislative Assembly? A better-informed public opinion would look askance upon it being treated as a mere political football. In quite a different spirit, the political parties should inform the voters of their programmes in education, and governments should give an accounting to the public of how they have exercised their mandate in a field so vital to the general welfare. To place education at the very forefront of political issues will invest it with the importance it should have. Another traditional objection to bringing education into the market place of political life is the danger of secularization. It is forgotten that in a truly democratic society, the school can never be secularized so long as the majority is not in favour of doing so, and that any juridical barriers against secularization will eventually disappear if such be the will of the majority.

Three serious defects in school administration prevent the government from exercising its educational functions effectively. The first springs from the fragmentation of the school system. Different authorities govern the private institutions, the schools operated by the Ministry of Youth and the public schools; the Roman Catholic and the Protestant sectors of the public system are autonomous; a wall divides the colleges and universities from the primary, secondary and normal schools. A second obstacle is the division of government authority itself between several ministries, each managing its own schools and determining its curricula without co-ordination or over-all planning. The third difficulty arises from the way in which the personnel of the government's educational services is recruited, especially in the Department of Education. The selection is almost invariably restricted to those sectors under the Department's immediate control and is in competition with school commissions able to offer higher salaries than those permitted under civil service regulations. . . . Thus it would seem that the State, if it is henceforth to meet more effectively the responsibilities which belong to it, must simplify the present structural pattern. At this stage, only a strong and forthright authority can put the house in order. Minor adjustments will not do. To effect this essential renovation, it is the duty of the State to look ahead with clarity and breadth, to act promptly and with competence. . . .

XXX:4 RENE LEVESQUE ON THE STATE AND THE QUEBEC ECONOMY

Above all else, Quebec's "quiet revolution" meant coming to terms with twentieth century industrialization and technology. With such steps as the nationalization of electric power in 1963, the Liberal government showed its determination to take the leading role in making French Canadians *"Maîtres Chez Nous."* In a 1963 interview, the Honourable René Levesque, Minister of Natural Resources and the most controversial figure in the government due to his outspoken nationalism, discussed the revolution and the role the state should play in shaping Quebec's economy. Portions of the interview are presented here.

Do you think people tend to exaggerate when they talk about the 'new atmosphere' that has been typical of Quebec for the past several years?

This is no exaggeration, and indeed we have not yet finished measuring the significance of the recent changes in Quebec. They were at first imperceptible, but are now affecting nearly every aspect of our life, not least the outlook and psychology of the French Canadian. For a quarter of a century a sort of revolution has been going on here. It is our version of the world phenomenon referred to as the 'speeding-up of history': the second world war, the rapid industrialization and even more rapid urbanization of society, the massive introduction of technology, the advance in comfort and leisure for the greatest number—which, by contrast (and the gap is still growing), shows up only too clearly the misery of certain groups which the mainstream of change has by-passed: the marginal-land farmers, the pool of unskilled labourers in the cities, etc.

To all these factors we must add the advent and the spread of new information media, especially television; and the soaring of tourism. These have turned our society upside-down and led it to ask itself questions.

What is the result? A nation awake, in full swing, fed up with being seen as a museum, as 'the quaint old province of Quebec'; a nation bent on advancing, rising; no longer just content to endure. Involved in this is the something we call nationalism; it is, at bottom, merely the very normal desire for a dignity that comes from having control over oneself and one's destiny. I do not see how we can do without nationalism in this sense; and I pity those who, in the name of an artificial and misguided concern for the individual and for human values (which they feel we would be unable to respect, unless properly hemmed in), superciliously isolate themselves from the errors as well as the collective achievements of French Canada. . . .

Which are the priority tasks you would assign to this nation today?

Our great weakness (individual and collective), and the source of nearly all the others, is economic. That, in my opinion, is the No. 1 problem. . . .

To develop an ever greater number of ever better-equipped minds is not enough. There must be careers for these minds; and there must be spring-boards for these careers. Besides, here too there is a 'chain reaction' between education and the economy. Hence the essential need to free our economy without delay. Otherwise, we would be letting short-sighted conservatism lay the groundwork for a shattering explosion of built-up collective pressure. Education's priority is already widely recognized; but the associated and equally urgent need for economic development and control is far less widely understood. . . .

Were I to have any general ideas on the role of the State in Quebec at the present time, this is how I would sum them up.

It is especially necessary for us to use the economic power of the State as we are one of Canada's 'have-not' minorities. The private sector of our economy is too weak to provide us with the 'rocket launchers' that can blast us off the ramp of our debilitating poverty. Our principal 'capitalist' for the moment —and for as far into the future as we can see—must therefore be the State. It must be more than a participant in the economic development and emancipation of Quebec; it must be a creative agent. Otherwise, we can do no more than we have been doing so far, i.e., wait meekly for the capital and the initiative of others. The others, of course, will come for their own sake, not for ours. It is we alone, through our State, who can become masters in our own house. That, on top of many other motives, is the essential reason for insisting that the State and all its key men must unceasingly be more competent, more effective, and more incorruptible.

It is precisely because of, rather than in spite of, the weakness of the private sector of our economy that the State, with its powerful role and the means at its disposal, may run the risk of getting out of bounds. Traditional patronage is an incipient form of something that could end up as absolute and widespread dependence upon public authority. We could, almost without being aware of it, plunge into the dangerous paradise of the 'Big Brother' State. That is why it is important to analyse carefully the State's activities in the economic field, so as to be sure that any extension of public authority is either necessary or truly useful to the people as a whole. As the European countries, especially Italy, have done, we must learn to make use of the formula of 'mixed enterprise'. . . .

It is infinitely more important to make Quebec progressive, free, and strong, than to devote the best of our energies to propagating the doubtful advantages of biculturalism. Moreover, if French culture is to spread, if the French language is to be respected, that will depend above all on the vigour, on the economic and political importance, of Quebec. These must become and must remain our first concern, by far our most decisive and constant preoccupation.

XXXI. The Search For National Unity

XXX:1 MARCEL CHAPUT: *WHY I AM A SEPARATIST*

An integral part of Quebec's new self-awareness was a revived French Canadian nationalism. This time, however, the new nationalists were determined to make Quebec something more than a French Catholic enclave in English-speaking Canada. Unfortunately many English Canadians only noticed the new spirit in Quebec with the publicity given to Dr. Marcel Chaput's 1961 book *Pourquoi Je Suis Séparatiste* and to his new party the *Rassemblement pour l'Indépendence Nationale*. The two selections below represent two sides of the separatist case. Selection (a) is a reasonably accurate account of the contradictions of French Canadian life in Canada in 1960. Selection (b) is Chaput's list of reasons why independence would benefit Quebec. Although it was rejected by the majority of French Canadians, the separatist movement persisted in the mid-1960's as a small but potentially explosive force in Canadian politics.

a. The Contradictions of French Canadian Life

. . . As far as the French-Canadian is concerned, life in Canada is a tissue of daily contradictions which surely constitute the most highly developed form of brainwashing ever invented. Under such conditions, very few people would have been able to hold out.

You think I am exaggerating, that the Canadian psychological climate has nothing terribly evil about it? Let us examine some of these contradictions, against which any national of a normal state is protected, but with which, on the contrary, every French-Canadian must struggle daily.

- He is a Canadian, but he is also a French-Canadian.
- His country is the whole of Canada, but he is accepted only in Quebec.
- He is told that he belongs to the great French civilization, but simultaneously he hears someone speak of "those damned Frenchmen."
- He is forced to be bilingual; the others are unilingual.
- He hears nothing but praise at school and elsewhere for the beauty of the French language; he is obliged to learn English.
- He is told that Canada is a country which united two cultures; he has difficulty getting service in west Montreal if he uses French.
- He thinks he speaks an international language; people snarl out "Speak White" in his face.
- He enters the French university only to study from American text-books.
- He is told all about national unity, but he is ordered: "Stay in your province."
- He hears people insist that Canada is an independent country; every day he sees another country's queen on his coinage and on his stamps.
- He is told that his province is the most wealthy; it is always in his province that there is the most unemployment.
- He is told that he is eligible for any position, but he is hampered by the extra obligation of bilingualism.
- He is roused to Canadian patriotism, but all he hears played is God Save the Queen.
- He sees the fleur-de-lis waving from all the flagpoles on the twenty-fourth of June; a week later he sees the Red Ensign waving over his town-hall.

• He is incited to rid himself of his inferiority complex; then he hears someone assert that he is not mature enough to govern himself.

• He is urged toward self-respect, and as his emblem he is given a sheep.

And so on down to the last death rattle. Yet people are at a loss to explain why the corner merchant doesn't make it a point of pride to advertise in French, why our young men lack the power to think big, why the pupil who tops his class suddenly loses his enthusiasm.

Anyone who would want a nation to disappear would not act differently. . . .

b. The Benefits of Independence

Historically, Quebec's independence would allow the French-Canadians to enjoy liberty. History intended that there should be a free French people on American soil. By claiming independence for Quebec, we are merely leading our people back to its historic destiny. After being conquered by armed might, dominated by a foreign nation, after having fought the hard battle for survival, French Canada, by leaving Confederation, will be doing nothing more than leaving behind it one further stage in its long march toward full sovereignty.

Politically, Quebec's independence is desirable because it would take the French-Canadians out of their position of numerical helplessness. In politics as in everything else, for the French-Canadians as for all people, numerical balance is essential to the smooth running of affairs. Starting with our Independence Day, Quebec will negotiate on equal terms with other countries, including the rest of Canada. Once it has become the recognized master of its destiny, a sovereign Quebec can then approve any unions, sign any treaties, practise any amount of friendly relations, set up any plans for helping underdeveloped countries or Canadian provinces, that are dictated by its own responsibilities and interests.

Independence is politically desirable because it is always good for people to be free, and because no nation has ever become great by leaving the political control of its destiny in the hands of another.

Economically, political independence is desirable for Quebec because, without control over political power, economic independence remains a sweet day-dream. . . .

Culturally, independence would be the nation's salvation. Do you realize what life would be like in a unilingual country? Morning to night you would hear the same language, the national language.

It would mean the end of the absurd and deadly situation, economically and culturally, for the majority of French-Canadians, the situation of working in English after having gone to French schools.

It would mean the end of this noxious co-existence of two languages and two systems of thought which makes French-Canadian bilingualism into the *doubtful art of speaking two languages at once.* . . .

Socially, Quebec's independence cannot be other than desirable, since everything would contribute to making life in Quebec a coherent whole. If politics support the economy, and if both economics and politics favour culture, then social conditions cannot help but be improved. Once they are masters in their own home, the French-Canadians can develop their institutions and orient them according to the French-Canadian way of thinking. Once French has become a paying proposition, once the stupidity of everyday bilingualism has been eliminated, the French-Canadians will no longer form a mass on the lower levels of industry, commerce, army and government. They will be found in all positions. . . .

Psychologically, above all, independence would be desirable for Quebec. I say "above all" because the problem of the French-Canadian has become a psychological one. He is no longer kept down by force of arms, it is not the barbed-wire of a concentration camp that forces him into solitude. It is something far more serious. His very will-power has been affected. He could be free but refuses to believe it. He could be himself, but he continually seeks reasons to flee his own nature.

For men as for peoples, independence is above all a state of mind. But the state of mind of a man or a people is always conditioned by the surroundings which fashioned it. If you spend your time exhorting your compatriots to the purchase of home-grown products, to renewed interests in French culture, to careful speech, to civic pride, you will be treating symptoms. Give the people back their liberty and half the symptoms will disappear. . . .

XXXI: 2 QUEBEC'S APPROACH TO FEDERALISM: THE TREMBLAY *REPORT*

What did Quebec really want? The most comprehensive statement of Quebec's case was made in 1956 in the *Report of the Royal Commission of Inquiry on Constitutional Problems*. The Commission had been established by the provincial government in 1953 under the chairmanship of Mr. Justice Thomas Tremblay. The *Report* carefully assessed Quebec's past and present role in the Canadian federal system and made recommendations as to its future role. Since 1956 the Tremblay Commission's conclusions have formed the basic programme of moderate French Canadian nationalism. The passages quoted below state Quebec's reasons for rejecting political centralization and outline the approach to federalism that would satisfy Quebec's aspirations.

We pose the fundamental and even crucial question—can a system of legislative centralization give justice to the French-Canadians and promote their interests as such, that is to say, not merely as individuals but also as members of a national group whose culture has a right to live, to expand and to spread throughout this country? . . .

Let us examine the facts in all their clarity. French-Canadian Catholics constitute an immense majority of the population of Quebec, but Anglo-Canadian Protestants control the governments, not only of the nine other provinces, but of the Canadian federation itself. These latter years have witnessed fiscal and economic centralization, and, to a lesser degree, centralization of social policy. Now, of all the federal measures adopted in these three fields within the past dozen years, how many have drawn their inspiration from the French-Canadian group's philosophy of life, and how many have concerned themselves with safeguarding and promoting the national values which are peculiar to this group?

We would like it well understood that there is no question here of attributing to the federal government sentiments of hostility with respect to the French-Canadian nationality. The question, rather, is to know whether, when the central government makes laws, it can do otherwise than draw its inspiration from the Anglo-Protestant majority's mentality, requirements and philosophy of life. Can it really do otherwise or, in a democratic system, seek its inspiration elsewhere? But, then, how can it adapt its legislation to a different mentality, a different culture and different institutions? From whatever angle we look at it, legislative centralization can mean nothing but levelling and standardization and thus enfeeblement and ruin for the national values special to the French-Canadian group. . . .

In conclusion, it seems to us that the supporters of centralization purposely exaggerate the difficulties both of autonomy and of co-ordinating policies in Canada. Their main argument in favour of a new federalism rests on a purely theoretical basis and is developed in terms of a constantly evolving theory which is still hotly debated and contested. Such a situation does not recommend, either objectively or within the limits of political prudence, that changes which put fundamental liberties at stake should be accepted.

Since there must be an interventionist policy in the economic domain, a solution for the problems it presents should be sought in the same spirit as presided over the confederative compact, and according to the rules of a democratic federalism. In practice, that means the central government should assume only such control powers as do not produce repercussions on institutional structures, or on the qualitative aspects of a civilization. If the realities of modern life require general controls which exceed this measure—a situation which was not foreseen in 1867—it is through the co-ordination of policies and not through their unification that it must first be sought to exercise them. Moreover, to respect the rules of any democratic federalism, every purely technical control which can be exercised locally should be left with the provinces which, in turn, by virtue of the same principle, should tend to regionalize it within their own territory.

In matters of economic policy, for example, permanent co-operating organisms which would work in a truly federative manner, would fill a serious void in Canada and would give results by which the interested governments would be the first to benefit. In times of economic difficulties, this co-operation should be even closer. . . . there is nothing to prevent the governments, on the approach of a depression, from meeting and from drawing up joint plans and co-ordinating the projects which each of them declares itself ready to carry out. The experience of 1929, like that of 1954-55, shows that, even after a tragic beginning like a stock-market crash, the start of a depression is a matter of months, during which it is possible for the interested governments to prepare themselves to intervene and even to co-ordinate their efforts.

As for social policy, it seems to us that, in a federation composed of elements which are heterogeneous, from the cultural and religious point of view, it should not depend on the central authority. The Fathers of Confederation understood this perfectly well and it is, perhaps, on this point that the centralization policy of recent years has sabotaged their work most cruelly. All the difficulties brought forward against provincial action in this field are susceptible of solution, provided they are handled with a reasonable amount of good will, good faith and co-operative spirit, the three qualities which are indispensable for the proper functioning of any federative system. In short, instead of resorting to centralization to settle all difficulties, it would be much better to seek a solution within the framework and in the spirit of federalism.

And so we return to the fundamental option. . . . At the crossroads where it is now situated, the Province of Quebec still maintains its original choice; it wants neither unitarism nor separatism, but it declares itself still faithfully attached to federalism. It refuses, however, to be satisfied with a surface federalism, which is only for show, like a theatre decoration, even if it is presented to it under the seductive name of the "new Canadian federalism." Instinctively, because its vital interests are at stake, it knows how to distinguish between a policy of imperialist inspiration which tends to reduce it to the status of a Crown colony, and of a colony subsidized, dominated and controlled by the mother country, which in the present instance would be the central government, and a truly federalist policy which respects its liberty and dignity and appeals to its co-operation in accomplishing tasks of joint interest. And when it thus makes a claim for the sincere practice of federalism, it does so in the belief that it is thereby rendering service to the whole of Canada, because it has long known—nor is it the only one to have so discovered—that vigorous provincial institutions are indispensable to the political stability and maintenance of democracy in Canada.

XXXI: 3 THE ENGLISH CANADIAN RESPONSE: EUGENE FORSEY

English Canadian opinions about Quebec's demands ranged from complete sympathy to outright hostility. This speech of Eugene Forsey's, delivered in 1961 at the first Congress on Canadian Affairs, held in Quebec City, is perhaps representative of the moderate, thoughtful English Canadian response to the problem of national unity. The excerpts presented below combine a basic willingness to resolve French Canadian grievances with a determination to maintain national unity within the basic constitutional framework of 1867.

I don't think the Canadian experiment *has* been a failure. It hasn't been a perfect success: what human effort, what human institution, is, or can be? But I think it's been doing better and better. I think the ferment of ideas in Quebec is already making it easier for English-speaking Canadians and French-speaking Canadians to understand and appreciate each other. I think narrowness and bigotry in English-speaking Canada are declining, markedly. They have certainly not disappeared; but I am sure they are declining. I think there is more and more appreciation of the French Canadian culture, more and more realization that, by not knowing French, English-speaking Canadians are missing a lot, missing the tremendously rich, lively, varied, exciting, valuable intellectual, literary and artistic life that is going on in French Canada. I think there is much more desire to learn French. I think there is much more willingness to find out what French Canadians feel are their rights, how they feel those rights are being infringed or violated, and to do something about it. Official bilingualism in the central Government and its agencies, however inadequate, has, I think, gone beyond what it was even when I was growing up: there are, to take a small but not insignificant example, bilingual calendars on the Table of the House of Commons, something which not so many years ago, Sir George Foster (if my memory serves), dismissed as preposterous. (Don't laugh! The point is not that there are now French calendars where there weren't before; the point is the change of attitude. Sir George Foster was a highly civilized, cultivated man, by no means a boor or a bigot. But it just didn't occur to him that French Canadian members of the House of Commons were entitled to have French calendars on the Table. Now it just doesn't occur to anybody that they shouldn't.) There is simultaneous translation. There is, I am sure, far more, and far prompter, publication of the French text of official documents. There is a French Canadian Governor-General. There are other things. I don't think this is enough. I'd like to see more. But there *has* been progress, and I think more is coming, though it may be delayed by all this talk of separatism and a "bi-national state". I think, for example, that the day is not distant when French will be recognized in the legislatures and courts of Ontario and New Brunswick. . . .

I am in favour of equal rights for Canadians of French and English speech throughout Canada, within the limits of the practicable. I am not in favour of insisting that every postal clerk in Vancouver shall speak French, or every postal clerk in Chicoutimi English. They don't need to: there are not enough French-speaking people in Vancouver or English-speaking people in Chicoutimi. I don't think it is feasible to try to make everybody in Canada bilingual, though I should like to see as many people as possible become so; but, in general, people won't learn a second language unless they have to. Most English-speaking Canadians have little need, or even opportunity, to speak French; and I think the majority of French-speaking Canadians haven't much need or opportunity to speak English, though of course, because the majority of people on this continent speak English, the economic pressure on, or inducement to, French Canadians to speak English, and their opportunities for doing so, are greater than the other way round.

I am also in favour of giving French Canadians their proportionate share of jobs at all levels in the national armed forces and the national civil service, provided that competent French Canadians can be found. . . .

I think we English Canadians need to sit down and think hard and work hard at making Canada one nation in the sense that the Fathers intended. Most of us are deplorably ignorant of French Canada. (Some of you are perhaps equally ignorant of English-speaking Canada; but that's primarily a matter for you to deal with). We need to ask ourselves constantly how we'd feel if we were a relatively small English-speaking island in an ocean of French-speaking people, and what rights we'd feel we had, and what we'd expect the majority to do about it.

But I think we've made progress, and I'm frightened that

all this talk of separatism and hemi-demi-semi-separatism may undo much of what has been accomplished. There is, I am afraid, a serious risk that English-speaking Canadians, hearing it, will say, "Oh! well, if that's what they want, let them go. Let them have their separate state. Perhaps the whole attempt to build a Canadian nation has been a mistake and a failure. Perhaps we may as well give up, and join the United States." I assure you this is a perfectly serious possibility. I am sure it would be bad for us; and I think it might be very much worse for you. You would run the risk either of being isolated on this continent, economically at the mercy of the American Colossus grown more colossal still, or of being absorbed. assimilated like your Franco-American brethren.

I remain an unrepentant believer in the Canadian nation the Fathers of Confederation thought they were founding. I think they wrought well. The noble constitutional fabric they reared stands unshaken. Its design was sound. Its foundations were laid on rock as enduring as the Laurentian Shield. Its walls were solidly built, of good Canadian stone. It may need restoration where the Judicial Committee of the Privy Council has defaced it. It may need a repair here, an alteration there. But it does not need a wrecking crew or a bombing squad. It needs builders; builders who will carry on the work that Cartier and Macdonald began, and that generations of their successors have continued.

XXXI:4 THE ROYAL COMMISSION ON BILINGUALISM AND BICULTURALISM ASSESSES THE CRISIS

The dialogue between Canada's two "nations" continued through the early 1960's. In 1963 the federal government established a Royal Commission to report on the state of bilingualism and biculturalism in Canada and to recommend steps that would equalize the partnership between Canada's two founding races. In February, 1965, after its initial tour of the country, the Commission issued a *Preliminary Report* describ-

ing the situation as it stood then, two years before
Canada's Centennial. Excerpts from the Commission's
summary of the problem follow.

All that we have seen and heard has led us to the conviction that Canada is in the most critical period of its history
since Confederation. We believe that there is a crisis, in the
sense that Canada has come to a time when decisions must
be taken and developments must occur leading either to its
break-up, or to a new set of conditions for its future existence.
We do not know whether the crisis will be short or long. We
are convinced that it is here. The signs of danger are many
and serious.

The ways in which important public and private institutions now operate strongly dissatisfy a very significant part
of the Canadian population, while the other part remains
largely indifferent to this situation, or does not even know
of its existence.

A strong impression we drew from our contacts with
thousands of French-speaking Canadians of all walks of life
and of all regions of the country was the extent to which, for
most of them, questions of language and culture do not
occur in the abstract. They are rooted in the experiences of
daily life, in jobs, in meetings, in correspondence with public
and private corporations, in the armed forces. They are insep-
arably connected with the social, economic and political
institutions which frame the existence of a people and which
should satisfy their many needs and aspirations. The opinions
we heard were often the result of ordinary individual and
collective experiences; hence our conviction that they can
hardly be changed by simple appeals to abstract ideas like
"national unity". It seemed to us that the dissatisfaction and
the sense of revolt came from aspects of reality rather than
from doctrines that had been preached.

At the same time we were confronted constantly by English-
speaking Canadians, including many expressing sentiments
of goodwill, who seemed to have no realization of the daily
experiences that cause the discontent among so many of their

French-speaking fellow citizens. Nor do most understand the underlying trend toward the increasing autonomy of Quebec and the strengthening of the belief among her people that she is now building herself into a distinct form of nationhood with full control of all her social and economic institutions. What is grasped is frequently rejected. Thus there exists a deep gulf, with unawareness on one side, and strongly rooted feeling on the other.

We are convinced that it is still possible to rectify the situation. But a major operation will perhaps be unavoidable. The whole social body appears to be affected. The crisis has reached a point where there is a danger that the will of people to go on may begin to fail. . . .

The chief protagonists, whether they are entirely conscious of it or not, are French-speaking Quebec and English-speaking Canada. And it seems to us to be no longer the traditional conflict between a majority and a minority. It is rather a conflict between two majorities: that which is a majority in all Canada, and that which is a majority in the entity of Quebec.

That is to say, French-speaking Quebec acted for a long time as though at least it had accepted the idea of being merely a privileged "ethnic minority." Today, the kind of opinion we met so often in the province regards Quebec practically as an autonomous society, and expects her to be recognized as such.

This attitude goes back to a fundamental expectation for French Canada, that is, to be an equal partner with English-speaking Canada. If this idea is found to be impossible, because such equality is not believed in or is not acceptable, we believe the sense of deception will bring decisive consequences. An important element in French-speaking Quebc is already tempted to go it alone. . . .

On the other hand we are not blind, nor do we think any Canadian should be, to hopeful aspects in the situation. In spite of present differences in outlook Canadians of different origins have much in common. They share many facets of a great common European tradition; and they maintain many connections across the Atlantic. They have lived together for

200 years. Geography and conditions of life in the northern half of North America have a common influence on them. They join in a common love for their land as such. Abroad, English-speaking and French-speaking Canadians have often found that they have more in common with each other than with citizens of other countries. All Canadians are members of a modern, technologically advanced society, with all that this implies in problems and in opportunities. The advances taking place in Quebec, while they may increase the sense of competition between French and English-speaking Canadians, may also give them more to talk about together than ever in the past.

We think that there are grounds for hope in the signs we discovered of evolving attitudes among English-speaking Canadians. The number of those who understand the issues seems to be increasing; the number who wants to understand appears to be growing still more rapidly. In Quebec the very vigour of developments may reduce the frustrations felt by many people, and at the same time, lead them to put less blame on the English-speaking majority in Canada, and to accept more responsibility for themselves. During the year we have noted in New Brunswick in particular, but also in other parts of Canada, positive signs of better understanding of the aspirations and needs of the French-speaking minorities. In our opinion, there is substantially more comprehension in English Canada of the need for adjustments than there was a few years ago.

It is hardly possible to travel across Canada from coast to coast, and to talk to literally thousands of Canadians of different origins and background, as we have done, without being struck by the enormous potentialities of this country and its people. It seemed to us again and again that current problems between the peoples of Canada are impeding great advances. A solution to the dilemma posed by duality would, we are sure, release immense energy and creative power. Vitality could then come from the very differences and tensions among Canadians. The extra power released could be turned to making Canadian life as a whole better for all its citizens: to economic and social improvements; to increasing opportunities for the individual as a human being whatever his language; to enhancing Canada's contribution to all humanity. Then the potentialities of the two cultures, English and French-speaking, with the enriching contributions from those of other origins, each working in its own way for common purposes, could be enormous. . . .

But it appears to us that there are some vital prerequisites to a positive outcome of the present state of crisis. There must be important changes in attitudes.

In particular we suggest that all Canadians examine closely the concept of democracy itself. Too often, it has been reduced to the simple game of majority versus minority. Some English-speaking citizens before the Commission invoked the "law of the majority" as though they were brandishing a threatening weapon; some French-speaking people, who had complained bitterly of the consequences of this "law," expressed the desire to make use of it to their own advantage in a more or less independent Quebec. . . .

From evidence so far accumulated, it appears to us that English-speaking Canadians as a whole must come to recognize the existence of a vigorous French-speaking society within Canada, and to find out more about the aspirations, frustrations and achievements of French-speaking Canadians, in Quebec and outside it. They must come to understand what it means to be a member of a minority, or of a smaller partner people, and to be ready to give that minority assurances which are unnecessary for a majority. More than a century ago, Sir John A. Macdonald wrote to an English-speaking friend: "Treat them as a nation and they will act as a free people generally do—generously. Call them a faction and they become factious." They have to face the fact that, if Canada is to continue to exist, there must be a true partnership, and that the partnership must be worked out as between equals. They must be prepared to discuss in a forthright, open-minded way the practical implications of such a partnership. To some extent, they must be prepared to pay by way of new conditions for the future of Canada as one country, and to realize that their partner of tomorrow will be quite different from their partner of yesterday.

On the same evidence, it seems to us that French-speaking Canadians for their part must be ready to respond positively if there are to be truly significant developments toward a better partnership. It would be necessary for French-speaking Quebecers to restrain their present tendency to concentrate so intensely on their own affairs, and to look so largely inward. Problems affecting all Canada are their problems too. They would need to beware of the kind of thinking that puts "la nation" above all other considerations and values. They too, like the English-speaking, should forget the conquest and any psychological effects they think it left. They would have to avoid blaming English-speaking Canadians for shortcomings which are their own; and at times, to remember that English-speaking Canadians have their feelings too. They, as well as the English-speaking, must remember that, if a partnership works, each party must give as well as get. . . .

More than most other countries, Canada is a creation of human will. It has been called a "geographical absurdity", an "appendange of the United States", a "4,000-mile main street" with many bare stretches. Nevertheless this country has existed for a long time, because its people have never stopped willing that there be a Canada.

Each age is fascinated by the difficulties it must face; hence most generations go through periods of doubt. Present day Canada is no exception. But is it more difficult to maintain the entity of Canada today, to make necessary changes, than it was to create it yesterday?

Canada will continue to exist, will grow and progress, will surmount the present crisis, if Canadians have the will—a will like that of the men who built the country. . . .

XXXII. Canada: Sovereign Power Or Satellite?

XXXII:1 THE CULTURAL PROBLEM: THE MASSEY *REPORT*, 1951

In the post-war era many Canadians began to wonder whether Canada had given up to the United States the national independence she had so recently won from Britain. American influence was so pervasive in Canada that her official independence sometimes seemed to be a form without content. In 1949, the Royal Commission on National Development in the Arts, Letters, and Sciences was established under the chairmanship of the Right Honourable Vincent Massey to study the means by which a distinctively Canadian culture could be encouraged. As these excerpts show, the Massey Commission's *Report* found American cultural influence the greatest obstacle to the growth of an indigenous culture in Canada. Although many of the Commission's recommendations have been implemented—such as the Canada Council—the problem of American cultural influence will probably always remain.

Canadians, with their customary optimism, may think that the fate of their civilization is in their own hands. So it is. But this young nation, struggling to be itself, must shape its course with an eye to three conditions so familiar that their significance can too easily be ignored. Canada has a small and scattered population in a vast area; this population is clustered along the rim of another country many times more populous and of far greater economic strength; a majority of Canadians share their mother tongue with that neighbour, which leads to peculiarly close and intimate relations. One or two of these conditions will be found in many modern countries. But Canada alone possesses all three. What is their effect, good or bad, on what we call Canadianism? . . .

. . . On this continent, as we have observed, our population stretches in a narrow and not even continuous ribbon along our frontier—fourteen millions along a five thousand mile front. In meeting influences from across the border as pervasive as they are friendly, we have not even the advantages of what soldiers call defence in depth.

From these influences, pervasive and friendly as they are, much that is valuable has come to us, . . . gifts of money spent in Canada, grants offered to Canadians for study abroad, the free enjoyment of all the facilities of many institutions which we cannot afford, and the importation of many valuable things which we could not easily produce for ourselves. We have gained much. In this preliminary stock-taking of Canadian cultural life it may be fair to inquire whether we have gained a little too much. . . .

Finally, we benefit from vast importations of what might be familiarly called the American cultural output. We import newspapers, periodicals, books, maps and endless educational equipment. We also import artistic talent, either personally in the travelling artist or company, or on the screen, in recordings and over the air. Every Sunday, tens of thousands tacitly acknowledge their cultural indebtedness as they turn off the radio at the close of the Sunday symphony from New York and settle down to the latest American Book of the Month.

Granted that most of these American donations are good in themselves, it does not follow that they have always been good for Canadians. We have not much right to be proud of our record as patrons of the arts. Is it possible that, beside the munificence of a Carnegie or a Rockefeller, Canadian contributions look so small that it seems hardly worth while making them? Or have we learned, wrongly, from our neighbour an unnecessary dependence on the contributions of the rich? A similar unworthy reliance on others appears in another field. Canada sends a number of students abroad, many of them on fellowships provided by other countries; Canada offers very few of her own fellowships to non-Canadians, none at all until very recently. Perhaps we have been tempted by a too easy benevolence, but this leaves us in an undignified position, unworthy of our real power and prestige.

Canada has, moreover, paid a heavy price for this easy dependence on charity and especially on American charity. First, many of our best students, on completing their studies at American institutions, accept positions there and do not return. The United States wisely relaxes its rigid immigration laws for all members of "learned professions" and profits accordingly. Our neighbours, able to take their choice of the foreign students attracted to their universities by far-seeing generosity, naturally choose many Canadians, partly because they are there in such numbers, partly because they fit in more readily with American ways than do others. . . .

In this general picture of American influence on our cultural life it is perhaps permissible to mention that it extends to an extraordinary degree into an area beyond the limits of our inquiry, but closely related to it. Teachers from English-speaking Canada who wish to improve their talents or raise their professional status almost automatically make their pilgrimage to Teachers' College at Columbia University or to one of half a dozen similar institutions. They return to occupy senior positions in elementary and high schools and to staff our normal schools and colleges of education. How many Canadians realize that over a large part of Canada the schools are accepting tacit direction from New York that they would not think of taking from Ottawa? . . . But for American hospitality we might, in Canada, have been led to develop educational ideas and practices more in keeping with our own way of life.

It may be added that we should also have been forced to produce our own educational materials—books, maps, pictures and so forth. As it is, the dependence of English-speaking Canada on the United States for these publications is excessive. . . .

In our universities the situation is very much more serious. The comparative smallness of the Canadian university population, and the accessibility of American publishing houses with their huge markets has resulted in an almost universal dependence on the American product. It is interesting that a vigorous complaint of American text books should come from a scientist:

> "Where personalities and priorities are in question, American writings are very much biased in favour of the American. This is not to suggest that the facts will be distorted, but by mentioning the American names and industries and omitting mention of any others, a very unbalanced picture can be given. To subject Canadian students year in and year out to these influences is not particularly good for the growth of a wholesome Canadianism." . . .

Although in French-speaking Canada the difference in language offers some measure of protection, elsewhere in Canada the uncritical use of American training institutions, and therefore of American educational philosophy and what are referred to as teaching aids, has certainly tended to make our educational systems less Canadian, less suited to our traditions, less appreciative of the resources of our two cultures. It has also meant—and this is a matter with which we have a direct concern—that a large number of our leading teachers who are not only teachers but community leaders have received the final and often the most influential part of their training in the United States. This training may be excellent in itself, but it is surely permissible to wish that men and women who are going to exercise such a powerful influence on Canadian life should meet and work in some institution which, however international its staff may be, could put Canadian interests and problems in the first place. . . .

Every intelligent Canadian acknowledges his debt to the United States for excellent films, radio programmes and periodicals. But the price may be excessive. Of films and radio we shall speak in more detail later, but it may be noted in passing that our national radio which carries the Sunday symphony from New York also carries the soap-opera. In the periodical press we receive indeed many admirable American journals but also a flood of others much less admirable which, as we have been clearly told, is threatening to submerge completely our national product. . . .

The Canadian Periodical Press Association tells the same tale. Although during the last generation our periodicals have maintained and greatly strengthened their position, the competition they face has been almost overwhelming. Canadian magazines with much difficulty have achieved a circulation of nearly forty-two millions a year as against an American circulation in Canada of over eighty-six millions. "Canada . . . is the only country of any size in the world," one of their members has observed, "whose people read more foreign periodicals than they do periodicals published in their own land, local newspapers excluded." . . .

The American invasion by film, radio and periodical is formidable. Much of what comes to us is good and of this we shall be speaking presently. It has, however, been represented to us that many of the radio programmes have in fact no particular application to Canada or to Canadian conditions and that some of them, including certain children's programmes of the "crime" and "horror" type, are positively harmful. News commentaries too, and even live broadcasts from American sources, are designed for American ears and are almost certain to have an American slant and emphasis by reason of what they include or omit, as well as because of the opinions expressed. We think it permissible to record these comments on American radio since we observe that in the United States many radio programmes and American broadcasting in general have recently been severely criticized. It will, we think, be readily agreed that we in Canada should take measures to avoid in our radio, and in our television, at least those aspects of American broadcasting which have provoked in the United States the most out-spoken and the sharpest opposition.

American influences on Canadian life to say the least are impressive. There should be no thought of interfering with the liberty of all Canadians to enjoy them. Cultural exchanges are excellent in themselves. They widen the choice of the consumer and provide stimulating competition for the producer. It cannot be denied, however, that a vast and disproportionate amount of material coming from a single alien source may stifle rather than stimulate our own creative effort; and, passively accepted without any standard of comparison, this may weaken critical faculties. We are now spending millions to maintain a national independence which would be nothing but an empty shell without a vigorous and distinctive cultural life. We have seen that we have its elements in our traditions and in our history; we have made important progress, often aided by American generosity. We must not be blind, however, to the very present danger of permanent dependence.

XXXII:2 THE ECONOMIC PROBLEM

By the middle 1950's, as American control of Canadian industry approached the fifty per cent level, there were many doubts as to whether Canadians still held the reins of their own economy. Selection (a), excerpts from the 1957 *Report of the Royal Commission on Canada's Economic Prospects,* presents a balanced assessment of the problem and a number of suggestions for increased Canadian influence in the use and development of her resources. Almost a decade later, however, there had been no significant reduction in the growth of American control. In 1966 Walter Gordon, chairman of the 1957 Commission and Minister of Finance from 1963 to 1965, attempted to rekindle Canadian economic nationalism with the programme outlined in his book, *A Choice for Canada.*

Mr. Gordon's view of the problem is presented in selection (b), an excerpt from his book. Perhaps the most widespread Canadian attitude in the mid-1960's towards the problem of economic relations with the United States is represented by selection (c), an excerpt from a December 31, 1965, editorial in the Toronto *Globe and Mail*. It was entitled "Facing the Sovereign Facts."

a. The Gordon Commission Examines American Investment, 1957

The benefits of foreign investment that we have mentioned are very real and tangible. It is more difficult to state in similarly precise terms what the dangers are in the present situation and what conflicts might occur between the interests of Canadians and the interests of the foreign owners of wholly-owned subsidiaries of foreign companies operating in Canada. In the course of the Commission's hearings, concern was expressed over the extent to which our productive resources are controlled by non-residents, mostly Americans. Many Canadians are worried about such a large degree of economic decision-making being in the hands of non-residents or in the hands of Canadian companies controlled by non-residents. This concern has arisen because of the concentration of foreign ownership in certain industries, because of the fact that most of it is centred in one country, the United States, and because most of it is in the form of equities which, in the ordinary course of events, are never likely to be repatriated. Some people think it is foolish to worry too much about the possible dangers of foreign investment in this country. However, the contrary opinions on this subject which we have mentioned do in fact exist and if a period of political or economic instability should occur, they might develop into demands for restrictive or discriminatory action of an extreme kind, the consequences of which would be unfortunate for all concerned.

At the root of Canadian concern about foreign investment is undoubtedly a basic, traditional sense of insecurity vis-a-vis our friendly, albeit our much larger and more powerful neighbour, the United States. There is concern that as the position of American capital in the dynamic resource and manufacturing sectors becomes ever more dominant, our economy will inevitably become more and more integrated with that of the United States. Behind this is the fear that continuing integration might lead to economic domination by the United States and eventually to the loss of our political independence. This fear of domination by the United States affects to some extent the political climate of life in Canada today. Therefore it is a factor which has some bearing upon "the probable economic development of Canada and the problems to which such development appears likely to give rise".

Undoubtedly there could be circumstances where the best interests of Canada might not be exactly the same as the best interests of the shareholders of a foreign parent company with subsidiaries in Canada and also perhaps throughout the world. [Five possible conflicts of interest are then listed.] . . .

It would be unfair to overstress these unfavourable operating patterns. There are so many real advantages to Canada arising from the activities of foreign-controlled companies in this country that conflicts or potential conflicts between the interests of Canada and those of the foreign owners seem somewhat small and unimportant by comparison. Moreover, these conflicts of interests would be more the exception than the rule. Nevertheless there can be occasions when the activities of foreign-controlled companies in Canada may not be conducted entirely from the standpoint of the best interests of our economy. . . .

In attempting to suggest reasonable and realistic objectives respecting foreign investment and the operations of Canadian subsidiaries of foreign companies, the Commission is aware that it is treading on somewhat treacherous and uncertain ground. It is important that Canada should not discourage foreign capital by unfair discriminatory action and that the free movement of interest and dividends to foreign investors should not be interfered with by currency restrictions.

Measures such as these would damage our national reputation for good faith and fairness in dealing with foreign investors who have placed their capital in Canada and could well result in a slowing down in the rate of foreign investment in the future and thus in the rate of our economic activity and expansion. At the same time we should not be unmindful of the reasons which have led to such substantial foreign investment being made in Canada including the expectations of investors that their investments here will appreciate in value very considerably in the years to come. We are in a reasonably strong position, therefore, to state the objectives and wishes of Canadians in this matter without fear that by so doing we shall precipitate a flight of capital from Canada or a drying up of further inflows—providing we are fair and reasonable about the way we go about it.

In the light of these various considerations, we believe the main objectives of Canadians in this matter should be: first, to see a larger share of foreign capital invested in the form of bonds and mortgages, which do not involve control of large sectors of the economy; secondly, to see that the part of foreign investment which is invested in the resource and manufacturing industries is associated in some degree with Canadian capital and Canadian interest; and, thirdly, to ensure that control of the Canadian banks and other financial institutions is retained in Canada. We shall propose more detailed objectives respecting the operations of foreign concerns which do business in Canada through the medium of Canadian subsidiary companies, unincorporated branches, Western Hemisphere Trade Corporations, etc. Our purpose in doing so is to ensure that such concerns are aware of and susceptible to Canadian influences and opinions when they make decisions respecting their policies and activities in Canada. We believe Canadians should have more tangible assurance than they now have that the people who are responsible for the management of such foreign-owned concerns will, whenever reasonably possible, make decisions that are in the best interests of Canada; that such concerns in effect become more "Canadian" in outlook. We do not suggest by this the development of a narrow nationalistic outlook; nor that the concerns in question should be restricted in their access to their parent companies and to all the benefits and advantages they obtain as a result. The following specific suggestions respecting desirable objectives for the operations of such foreign-owned concerns would not have these effects; we believe they would be of benefit to all concerned:

(1) wherever possible, such concerns should employ Canadians in senior management and technical positions, should retain Canadian engineering and other professional and service personnel, and should do their purchasing of supplies, materials and equipment in this country;

(2) they should publish their financial statements and make full disclosure of the results of their Canadian operations;

(3) they should include on their boards of directors a number of independent Canadians and they should sell an appreciable interest in their equity stock to Canadians. . . .

. . . Despite the tremendous contributions which foreign capital—and the management and technological skills and the access to markets that has come with it—has made and will continue to make to the development of our country, we do not believe Canadians will cease to be concerned about this matter unless something is done to make Canadian voices more strongly and effectively heard in some vitally important sectors of our economy in which non-residents exercise a large measure of control. In our view there are definite limits as to what should be done about this matter, and compulsion and discrimination should certainly not be countenanced. But to do nothing would be to acquiesce in seeing an increasing measure of control of the Canadian economy pass into the hands of non-residents and to run the risk that at some time in the future a disregard for Canadian aspirations will create demands for action of an extreme nature. . . .

b. Walter Gordon's Economic Nationalism, 1966

I believe it can be taken for granted that the great majority of Canadians want their country to remain as free and independent as possible. But the pulls and pressures in the other direction are enormous. I was aware of this long before I entered politics. The reports of the Royal Commission on Canada's Economic Prospects, which were published nearly ten years ago, dealt with the subject in some detail. But I had not fully appreciated the depth and strength of these pressures until I became Minister of Finance in April of 1963. During the two-and-one half years I held that office, the influence that financial and business interests in the United States had on Canadian policy and opinion was continually brought home to me. On occasion, this influence was reinforced by representations from the State Department and the American Administration as a whole. It was pressed by those who direct American businesses in Canada, by their professional advisers, by Canadian financiers whose interests were identified directly or indirectly with American investment in Canada, by influential members of the Canadian civil service, by some representatives of the university community, and by some sections of the press.

The effects of these pressures on the leaders and spokesmen of all the political parties in Canada are immense—and too often they are effective. I do not suggest that there is anything unnatural or unsavoury about these pressures or the influence they have on Canadian public policy. American citizens and American corporations have enormous investments in Canada and, understandably, they resent any measures that would interfere with or restrict the growth of such investments, or place obstacles in the way of making new ones. I do say, however, that Canadians should not take their independence for granted; they should not underestimate the great difficulties in the way of maintaining it; and they should insist that all public policy be aimed at protecting and preserving the independence of Canada and not eroding it. . . .

c. *The Globe and Mail:* "Facing the Sovereign Facts"

. . . It is probable that we have already advanced too far along the road to economic union with the United States for turning back to be possible. They need our resources, we want their standard of living. We are already dependent upon them in defense. Geography weds us, language weds us, culture weds us. To turn back now would be to drop Canadians far down the scale of prosperity, to retard our development drastically, to invite the mass emigration of Canadians who refused to accept such deprivations, and perhaps to drive the United States into taking by force—economic rather than military—certain of our resources.

It is not reasonable to suggest turning back. But it is dishonest to refuse to admit where advancing will land us. More, it is dangerous.

In the next few years Canada is almost certain to lose economic and, to a certain extent, political control over large areas of our national being. If we do not admit this, we will not define the extent of the loss, and we will not be in a position to determine what must not be lost.

There are certain Canadian values which few of us would like to see abandoned. By and large we prefer our system of justice to the U.S. system of justice, our police (with reservations) to their police, our method of government (again with reservations) to their method of government. Our Sammies seldom run so fast, our racial discrimination is less obvious, our witch-hunts are less respected, we tend to see greys where they see blacks and whites.

It is in such things as these, good and bad, that we are different from Americans, and probably prefer to remain different. But if we continue our present heedless march all differences will vanish. The barricades to protect essential Canadianism will not have fallen; they will simply never have been erected.

XXXII:3 FOREIGN POLICY: *PEACEMAKER OR POWDER-MONKEY*, JAMES M. MINIFIE

The generally accepted view of Canada's role in world affairs in the 1950's is presented in document XXVIII:3 on page 325. By the end of the decade, however, Canada's increasingly close military ties with the United States began to cause doubts about Canada's capacity to pursue an independent foreign policy. In his book, *Peacemaker or Powder-Monkey*, published in 1960, James M. Minifie argued that Canadian independence had been given away to the United States and could only be regained by the dissolution of all of the defensive arrangements between the two countries. Minifie won few converts to his doctrine of Canadian neutralism but he did help to create a certain uneasiness about Canada's foreign policy which continued to grow through the early 1960's.

. . . The bridge has not been crossed, but the time is near. For Canada and the United States must decide—and in the event, this decision falls on Canada—whether the defence of Canada and the North American continent is forwarded by so close an alliance with the United States that an American general commands Canadian forces in peacetime, through a legal, functioning, military command, without need of further consultation, and with steadily increasing lateral controls.

The conviction is growing in many quarters that the subordination or appearance of subordination consequent on this top-heavy integration—this horse-rabbit pie with one horse and one rabbit—deprives Canada of one of the strongest weapons in its armoury, its leadership of the middle powers in the councils of the world at a critical time when the small and middle powers are sweeping into the United Nations in such numbers as to snow under the older, conservative powers in a blizzard of new ballots. . . .

Howard C. Green, the Secretary of State for External Affairs, has pointed out that Canada is peculiarly fitted to provide that leadership because its credentials are sound. Nobody fears

Canada, since it is without territorial ambitions. Nobody harbours resentment against Canada, because it has never held sovereign control over an alien people. Nobody suspects Canada of coveting national resources—it has plenty of its own.

And he might have added that Canada has the additional advantage of coming before the world in living proof that independence can be obtained by negotiation, without recourse to force or violent revolution, and that unity can be woven from the most diverse strands without an implacably bitter civil war. He might have added also that in dealings with the Latin American world, Canada has the supreme and unique advantage of roots in Latin as well as Anglo-Saxon culture, and a Latin tongue as one of its official languages. Finally, Canada has had experience on the world stage and its contribution to peace in the critical days of Suez established Canadian diplomacy as an important weapon in the armoury of national defence.

These superb advantages, which are potentially of inestimable and lasting strength, are cancelled out by the fact that Canada is still walking with the Devil. It is caught in a too-close alliance which gives it the appearance of subordination to the United States. Indeed, the subordination is real to some degree, but even the suspicion of satellitism makes leadership unacceptable. . . .

The vivid and memorable act which would set the stage for restoration of Canadian independence would be a Declaration of Neutrality.

It would involve dissolving the smothering alliance of NORAD (the North American Air Defence command), withdrawing from a NATO already wrecked by President de Gaulle, and annulling the Permanent Joint Board on Defence, Canada-United States. It would not involve withdrawing from the Commonwealth; on the contrary it would strengthen the Commonwealth bond by severing the military fetter with a non-Commonwealth nation. Still less would it involve leaving the United Nations. Here again, it would enable fuller participation in the United Nations, bolder initiatives without the "arm-twisting" which currently goes on whenever Canada shows signs of departing from the American line. . . .

Canada must make up its mind whether to part company with its beguiling, star-spangled Devil, or resign itself to increasing subservience leading ultimately to absorption. This is the basic choice which is vital for the defence of Canada as a unit, and decisive for the defence of the continent as a whole. Shall Canada's role be that of powder-monkey or peacemaker? Powder-monkey to the protagonists of CBR, that happy set of initials which means Chemical, Bacteriological and Radiological Warfare, or prophet of that positive neutralism which the new nations of the world may well prefer to the more-death-for-a-dime philosophy of CBR? . . .

XXXII:4 THE WORKING RELATIONSHIP: THE HEENEY-MERCHANT REPORT, 1965

> Commissioned by the American and Canadian governments, and prepared by former Ambassadors to Washington and Ottawa, this report (*Canada and the United States, Principles For Partnership*) summarizes the Canadian predicament in its relations with the United States, and recommends a set of guidelines for future Canadian-American relations. The report was widely criticized in Canada at the time of its release (June, 1965), particularly for its recommendation that difference should be expressed and resolved in private. Two portions of the report are given here.

The current concern in Canada—determined as ever upon its independent North American future— has its roots in history, in its struggle to achieve its own destiny, and in the disparity of size and power. The present preoccupations of Canadians, however, relate primarily to social and economic developments of more recent date—the massive influence of American cultural expression upon Canadian life, the extent of American ownership of Canadian industry and resources, and the prevailing attractions south of the border for Canadian scientists, engineers and professional men and women. Such present phenomena must be seen by Americans as well as Canadians within the context of history and national aspirations. If in their dealings, public and private, there is to be the mutual confidence that both desire and need, there must be conscious effort on both sides to appreciate the historical as well as the current factors which tend to divide them.

The mutual involvement of the two countries and peoples has also complicated, on both sides, the problems arising from the disparity in power. In most—though not all—of their bilateral affairs the capacity of the United States to benefit or harm Canadian interests is greater than that of Canada to affect the prosperity and security of the United States. Canadians are more conscious than Americans of this element in their dealings with the United States. On the other hand, the United States, preoccupied with the responsibilities of world power, may sometimes be inhibited in its bilateral dealings by considerations which do not operate directly on Canadian attitudes. Here restraint is required of both sides.

Canadians sometimes feel that, because they are so close, so "American," there is a disposition on the part of the United States to expect more of Canada than of other allies—as in setting other countries a good example—reflecting a tendency to apply to Canada a kind of "double standard" of international conduct. The result is sometimes to tempt Canadians into demonstrating their independence by adopting positions divergent from those of the United States. In a quite different sense, Americans are inclined sometimes to suspect the application of a "double standard" on the part of Canada when, for example, in an international negotiation, the United States is urged to be "reasonable," to make unilateral concessions to break a logjam which has been created by the intransigence of others. For Canadians cannot but be disturbingly aware that, despite their underlying confidence in the basic motives of the United States, Canada could be involved inevitably in the consequences of United States' decisions in circumstances over which Canadians had little influence or control. Such tendencies, on each side, arising from mutual involvement, inequality and the facts of international life, should be recognized but not exaggerated. . . .

SOME GUIDING PRINCIPLES   From the foregoing analysis we conclude that it is feasible to formulate certain guiding principles. These we set out in the following paragraphs.

The need is clear for our two governments to confirm the practice of intimate, timely and continuing consultation on all matters of common concern, at the appropriate level, employing such machinery and procedures as are most effective for this purpose.

As partners in NATO, and sharing responsibility for the air defence of this continent, Canada and the United States have similar policies and share important common obligations. In the conduct and development of their unique bilateral relationship, however, the two countries must have regard for the wider responsibilities and interests of each in the world and their obligations under various treaties and other arrangements to which each is party.

This principle has a particular bearing upon our affairs in relation to the heavy responsibilities borne by the United States, generally as the leader of the free world and specifically under its network of mutual defence treaties around the globe. It is important and reasonable that Canadian authorities should have careful regard for the United States Government's position in this world context and, in the absence of special Canadian interests or obligations, avoid so far as possible, public disagreement especially upon critical issues. This is not to say that the Canadian Government should automatically and uniformly concur in foreign policy decisions taken by the United States Government. Different estimates of efficacy and appropriateness or degree of risk generate honest differences of opinion among the closest allies. The Canadian Government cannot renounce its right to independent judgment and decision in the "vast external realm". On its part, Canada has special relations and obligations, some of which the United States does not share but of which it should take account, in particular with Great Britain and the other states of the Commonwealth, with France, and with certain other nations.

It is in the abiding interest of both countries that, wherever possible, divergent views between the two governments should be expressed and if possible resolved in private, through diplomatic channels. Only a firm mutual resolve and the necessary practical arrangements to keep the totality of the relationship in good and friendly working order can enable our countries to avoid needless frictions and minimize the consequences of disagreement.

It is hardly necessary to add that, in these remarks concerning public statements by government spokesmen, we intend of course no reference to all those whose freedom to criticize official policies at home and abroad is clear and equally cherished in both countries.

There should be a conscious effort by the authorities on both sides to accept and extend a common approach to additional areas of the two economies where it can be demonstrated that joint undertakings are to the national advantage of each as well as to the common advantage of both.

There is another important principle. This is that the United States should be continuously alert, throughout the entire process of policy-formulation and decision-making, to the potential impact on Canada of United States' actions, especially in the economic area. By this we intend particularly commercial policy—tariffs and quantitative restrictions—and fiscal and monetary affairs. While the necessity for such constant alertness derives primarily from the economic inequality of the two countries, coupled with their close interconnection, it derives also from the different characteristics of the two economies. Decisions taken in this area by the United States can have a disproportionately heavy incidence upon Canada. This vulnerability to United States economic policies is increased by the persistent Canadian deficit on trading account with the United States and the fact that Canada is far more dependent on exports—16 per cent of GNP as compared with 4 per cent for the United States. Obviously the United States cannot renounce concern for the protection of its own economic interests, but it should maintain a conscious awareness of Canadian interests to ensure that they are not violated or prejudiced through inadvertence or ignorance.

Since Canadian actions and decisions can also seriously harm the United States, there should be a sense of reciprocal obligation on Canadian authorities to give consideration in advance to the potential impact on United States' interests of decisions and actions contemplated in the economic and financial fields.

In conclusion, we find the evidence overwhelmingly in favour of a specific regime of consultation between the two governments. We are also convinced that there are large opportunities for mutual advantage in the extension of the partnership of our two countries. Not only is the relationship unique but Canadian-American mutual involvement and interdependence grow daily more evident. For our part, we are satisfied that the process can be as mutually rewarding as it is inevitable.

DOCUMENTARY SOURCES

I 1 Shortt, A. and Doughty, A. G., eds., *Documents Relating to the Constitutional History of Canada, 1759-1791* (2 parts, King's Printer, Ottawa, 1918), pp. 163-165.

   2 (a) *Ibid.*, p. 231 (Murray to the Lords of Trade, October 29, 1764).
     (b) Kennedy, W. P. M., ed., *Statutes, Treaties and Documents of the Canadian Constitution, 1713-1929* (rev. ed., Oxford University Press, Toronto, 1930), pp. 112-116.

   3 Shortt and Doughty, *Documents*, pp. 512, 515.

   4 Kennedy, *Statutes, Treaties and Documents*, pp. 137-140.

II 1 (a) Shortt and Doughty, *Documents*, pp. 742-743.
     (b) *Ibid.*, pp. 773-774 (Petition of Sir John Johnston and Loyalists, April 11, 1785).

   2 Kennedy, *Statutes, Treaties and Documents*, pp. 194-203.

III 1 Christie, Robert, *A History of the Late Province of Lower Canada* (6 vols. Quebec, 1848-1855), v. 6, pp. 314-323.

   2 Doughty, A. G. and McArthur, D. A., eds., *Documents Relating to the Constitutional History of Canada, 1791-1818* (King's Printer, Ottawa, 1914), pp. 393-397.

   3 Kennedy, *Statutes, Treaties and Documents*, pp. 270-289.

   4 (a) *Ibid.*, pp. 342-343.
     (b) Christie, *Lower Canada*, v. 4, pp. 253-254.

IV 1 (a) Doughty and McArthur, *Documents*, pp. 207-208 (Simcoe to Portland, October 30, 1795).
     (b) Cruikshank, E. A., ed., *The Correspondence of Lieutenant Governor John Graves Simcoe* (5 vols., Ontario Historical Society, Toronto, 1923-1931), v. 5, p. 247 (Simcoe to the Archbishop of Canterbury, December 30, 1790).

   2 (a) Doughty, A. G. and Story, Norah, eds., *Documents Relating to the Constitutional History of Canada, 1819-1928* (King's Printer, Ottawa, 1935), p. 283.
     (b) *Ibid.*, p. 378.

   3 Kennedy, *Statutes, Treaties and Documents*, pp. 295-306.

   4 Head, F. B., *A Narrative*, (London, 1839), pp. 464-465.

   5 *Ibid.*, pp. 310-313 (Head to Glenelg, September 10, 1837).

   6 Fairley, Margaret, ed., *The Selected Writings of William Lyon Mackenzie* (Oxford University Press, Toronto, 1960), pp. 222-225.

V 1 Lucas, (Sir) C. P., ed., *Lord Durham's Report on the Affairs of British North America* (3 vols., Oxford, 1912), vol. 2, *passim*.

VI 1 Kennedy, *Statutes, Treaties and Documents*, pp. 382-383.

   2 Chisholm, J. A., ed., *The Speeches and Public Letters of Joseph Howe* (2 vols., Halifax, 1909), v. 1, pp. 221-222, 226, 229-232, 253-254, 262-265.

   3 (a) Kennedy, *Statutes, Treaties and Documents*, p. 482 (Bagot to Stanley, September 26, 1842).
     (b) *Ibid.*, p. 500 (Elgin to Grey, July 13, 1847).

VII 1 Mackenzie, Alexander, *Voyages from Montreal* (Radisson Society edition, Toronto, 1927), pp. 30-35, 37, 51-52.

2 (a) Innis, H. A. and Lower, A. R. M., eds., *Select Documents in Canadian Economic History* (University of Toronto Press, Toronto, 1933), pp. 275-276.
(b) McTaggart, John, *Three Years in Canada* (London, 1829), v. 1, pp. 241-243, 246.

3 Innis and Lower, *Select Documents*, pp. 100-103.

4 *Ibid.*, pp. 303-304.

5 Kohl, J. G., *Travels in Canada* (London, 1861), v. 2, pp. 344-349, 355-357.

VIII 1 Toronto *Globe*, December 30, 1852 (Address to the Reformers of Lobo).

2 Tassé, Joseph, ed., *Discours de Sir George Cartier* (Montreal, 1893), pp. 148-151 (Speech to the Legislative Assembly, June 9, 1858).

3 Public Archives of Canada, *Brown Chamberlin Papers*, Macdonald to Chamberlin, January 21, 1856.

4 Toronto *Leader*, July 20, 1858.

IX 1 Skelton, O. D., *The Life and Times of Sir Alexander Tilloch Galt* (Oxford University Press, Toronto, 1920), pp. 239-242 (Federation memorial, October 23, 1858).

2 Young, J., *Public Men and Public Life in Canada* (2 vols., Toronto, 1902), v. 1, pp. 371-375.

3 Public Archives of Canada, *George Brown Papers*, George Brown to Anne Brown, September 13, 1864.

4 Pope, (Sir) Joseph, ed., *Confederation: being a series of hitherto unpublished documents bearing on the British North America Act* (Toronto, 1895), pp. 71-73.

5 (a) London *Times*, June 6, 1862. Quoted in Skelton, *Galt*, p. 346.
(b) Herbert, (Sir) R., ed., *H. H. Molyneux (Earl of Carnarvon): Speeches on Canadian Affairs* (London, 1902), p. 128.

X 1 (a) *Parliamentary Debates on the Subject of the Confederation of the British North American Provinces* (Quebec, 1865), pp. 6, 9.
(b) *Ibid.*, pp. 60-61.

2 *Ibid.*, pp. 86-115.

3 *Ibid.*, pp. 29-45.

XI 1 *Ibid.*, pp. 599-600.

2 (a) Chisholm, *Joseph Howe*, v. 2, p. 473.
(b) *Ibid.*, pp. 508-510, 513.

3 *Confederation Debates*, pp. 483-544.

XII 1 Ollivier, Maurice, ed., *British North America Acts and Selected Statutes* (Queen's Printer, Ottawa, 1962), pp. 63-99.

XIII 1 (a) Creighton, Donald, *John A. Macdonald: The Old Chieftain* (Macmillan, Toronto, 1955), p. 141.
(b) Pope, Joseph, *Memoirs of the Right Honourable Sir John Alexander Macdonald* (2 vols., Ottawa, 1894), v. 2,

pp. 177-187 (Macdonald to Lord Dufferin, October 9, 1873).

(c) Pope, (Sir) Joseph, ed., *Correspondence of Sir John Macdonald* (Toronto, 1921), p. 229 (Dufferin to Macdonald, October 19, 1873).

2 Canada, *Debates of the House of Commons*, December 10, 1880, pp. 28-31.

3 *Ibid.*, March 7, 1878, pp. 854, 858-859.

XIV 1 *Canada Sessional Papers*, 1870, v. 5, No. 12, pp. 99-100.

2 Morton, W. L., ed., *Alexander Begg's Red River Journal* (Champlain Society, Toronto, 1956), pp. 515-519.

3 Toronto *Globe*, April 6, 1870.

4 Petition to the Hon. A. Chapleau, dated December 16, 1884, signed by Andrew Spence and W. H. Jackson. Public Archives of Canada, Department of Interior, Dominion Lands Branch, Correspondence File 83808.

5 *The Queen* v. *Louis Riel* (Ottawa, 1886), pp. 147-154.

6 Public Archives of Manitoba, Louis Riel Collection, Louis Riel to Monseigneur Taché, July 24, 1885.

XV 1 (a) Pope, *Correspondence*, pp. 74-75 (Macdonald to Brown Chamberlin, October 26, 1868).

(b) Toronto *Globe*, March 9, 1888.

2 (a) Senate of Canada, Session of 1939, *Report Pursuant to the Resolution of the Senate . . . relating to the Enactment of the British North America Act, 1867, . . .* (King's Printer, Ottawa, 1939), Annex 3, p. 17.

(b) *Ibid.*, p. 22.

(c) *Ibid.*, p. 38.

3 *Dominion-Provincial and Interprovincial Conferences from 1887 to 1926* (King's Printer, Ottawa, 1951), pp. 20-21.

XVI 1 Locke, G. H., ed., *Builders of the Canadian Commonwealth* (Ryerson, Toronto, 1923), pp. 170-172.

2 Smith, Goldwin, *Canada and the Canadian Question* (Toronto, 1891), pp. 268-269, 275, 278-79, 280.

3 Pope, *Memoirs*, v. 2, pp. 335-336.

XVII 1 Rumilly, R., *Histoire de la province de Québec*, vol. 1 (Editions Bernard Valiquette, Montreal, 1940), pp. 155-156.

2 Barthe, U., ed., *Wilfrid Laurier on the Platform* (Quebec, 1890), pp. 52-76.

3 Pelland, J. O., ed., *Biographie, Discours, Conférences, etc., de L'Hon. Honoré Mercier* (Montreal, 1890), pp. 328-333.

4 Toronto *Evening News*, April 20, 1885.

5 (a) *Debates of the House of Commons*, March 3, 1896, pp. 2734-2736.

(b) Skelton, O. D., *The Life and Letters of Sir Wilfrid Laurier* (2 vols., Oxford University Press, Toronto, 1921), v. 1, pp. 464-465.

(c) *Debates of the House of Commons*, March 3, 1896, pp. 2740, 2756, 2758-2759.

XVIII 1 Dafoe, J. W., *Clifford Sifton in Relation to His Times*, (Macmillan, Toronto, 1931), pp. 273-274.

2 *Maclean's Magazine*, April 1, 1922 ("The Immigrants Canada Wants").

3 *Canadian Courier*, February, 1914. Also in Toronto Public Library, *Scrapbooks*, No. 229.

4 *Debates of the House of Commons*, July 30, 1903, p. 7659.

5 *Report of the Royal Commission to Inquire into Railways and Transportation in Canada* (King's Printer, Ottawa, 1917), pp. xci-xcii.

XIX 1 Ollivier, Maurice, ed., *The Colonial and Imperial Conferences from 1887 to 1937* (Queen's Printer, Ottawa, 1954), pp. 153-156.

2 Leacock, Stephen, *Greater Canada: An Appeal* (Montreal, 1907).

3 Bourassa, Henri, *Great Britain and Canada* (Montreal, 1902), pp. 4, 45.

4 (a) Buchan, John, *Lord Minto, A Memoir* (Nelson, London, 1924), pp. 159-160.
    (b) Skelton, *Laurier*, v. 2, p. 380.

XX 1 Siegfried, André, *The Race Question in Canada* (Carleton Library, McClelland and Stewart, Toronto, 1966), pp. 52-58.

2 *Ibid.*, pp. 165-169.

3 *Ibid.*, pp. 119-122.

4 (a) Brooke, Rupert, *Letters From America* (New York, 1916), pp. 64-65.
    (b) *Ibid.*, pp. 51-54.
    (c) *Ibid.*, pp. 54-57.
    (d) *Ibid.*, pp. 79-84.
    (e) *Ibid.*, pp. 102-105.
    (f) *Ibid.*, pp. 126-129.
    (g) Hobson, J. A., *Canada Today* (London, 1906), pp. 28-29, 31-32.

5 Brooke, *Letters From America*, pp. 117-120.

XXI 1 *Debates of the House of Commons*, June 11, 1917, pp. 2187-2188.

2 Bourassa, Henri, *Conscription* (Montreal, 1917).

3 Chown, S. D., "An Open Letter on the Duty of the Hour", *Christian Guardian*, December 12, 1917.

4 Savard, A. and Playfair, W. E., *Quebec and Confederation* (n.p., 1918), pp. 20-22.

XXII 1 *Canadian Annual Review*, 1919, pp. 365-368.

2 "Report of the Committee on the Church, the War, and Patriotism", *Journal of Proceedings of the Tenth General Conference of the Methodist Church* (Toronto, 1919), pp. 290-292.

3 *Royal Commission on Industrial Relations, Report*, published as a supplement to the *Labour Gazette*, v. 19 (Ottawa, 1919), pp. 5-6, 18-19.

XXIII 1 (a) Riddell, W. A., ed., *Documents on Canadian Foreign Policy, 1917-1939* (Oxford University Press, Toronto, 1962), p. 1.
(b) *Ibid.*, pp. 2-3.

2 Kennedy, *Statutes, Treaties and Documents*, pp. 701-702.

3 *Ibid.*, p. 703.

4 Ollivier, *The British North America Acts and Selected Statutes*, pp. 147-153.

XXIV 1 *Debates of the House of Commons*, April 3, 1930, pp. 1225-1228.

2 *Ibid.*, Sept. 9, 1930, pp. 17-27.

3 (a) *Report of the Royal Commission on Price Spreads* (King's Printer, Ottawa, 1937), pp. 12-13.
(b) *Ibid.*, p. 56.
(c) *Ibid.*, pp. 110-111.

4 (a) Bennett, R. B., *The Prime Minister Speaks to the People*, (Ottawa, 1935), Nos. I, pp. 18-19; III, p. 15; IV, pp. 17-18.
(b) *Ibid.*, V, pp. 20-21.

5 *Report of the Royal Commission on Dominion-Provincial Relations* (King's Printer, Ottawa, 1940), Book II, pp. 269-273.

XXV 1 McNaught, Kenneth, *A Prophet in Politics* (University of Toronto Press, Toronto, 1959), pp. 321-330.

2 Aberhart, William, *Social Credit Manual* (n.p., 1935), pp. 4, 13-18, 27, 29.

3 Quinn, H. F., *The Union Nationale* (University of Toronto Press, Toronto, 1961), pp. 206-210.

XXVI 1 (a) Riddell, *Foreign Policy*, pp. 433-434.
(b) *Ibid.*, p. 462.

2 (a) *Ibid.*, pp. 540-541.
(b) *Ibid.*, p. 555.

3 (a) *Ibid.*, p. 159.
(b) *Ibid.*, p. 159.

XXVII 1 (a) *Debates of the House of Commons*, September 8, 1939, p. 36.
(b) Dawson, R. M., *The Conscription Crisis of 1944* (University of Toronto Press, Toronto, 1961), p. 17, f.n.

2 (a) & (b) *Debates of the House of Commons*, November 22, 1944, pp. 6505-6507.

3 *Ibid.*, November 27, 1944, pp. 6604-6606.

4 (a) *Ibid.*, December 6, 1944, pp. 6859-6860.
(b) *Ibid.*, December 5, 1944, pp. 6530-6531.

XXVIII 1 *Debates of the House of Commons*, April 29, 1948, pp. 3438, 3443, 3449-3450.

2 Pearson, L. B., *The Four Faces of Peace* (McClelland and Stewart, Toronto, 1964), pp. 151-153 (Report to the House of Commons, November 27, 1956).

3 *Ibid.*, pp. 226-227 (Address to meeting of Men's and Women's Canadian Clubs, Halifax, April 5, 1957).

XXIX 1 *Debates of the House of Commons,* June 1, 1956, pp. 4552-4553.

2 Speech delivered at Massey Hall, Toronto, April 25, 1957, courtesy of Mr. Diefenbaker.

3 Speech delivered at Civic Auditorium, Winnipeg, February 12, 1958, courtesy of Mr. Diefenbaker.

XXX 1 *Two Priests Censure Political Morality in the Province of Quebec* (Public Morality Committee of the Civic Action League, Montreal, 1956), pp. 7-17.

2 *The Impertinences of Brother Anonymous* (Harvest House, Montreal, 1962), pp. 23, 28-30, 49, 58, 94-95.

3 *Report of the Royal Commission of Inquiry on Education in the Province of Quebec* (Province of Quebec, 1963), pp. 75-82.

4 Scott, F. R. and Oliver, M. K., eds., *Quebec States Her Case* (Macmillan, Toronto, 1964), pp. 133, 135-137, 145.

XXXI 1 (a) Chaput, Marcel, *Why I Am A Separatist* (Ryerson, Toronto, 1962), pp. 28-29.
(b) *Ibid.,* pp. 63-66.

2 *Report of the Royal Commission of Inquiry on Constitutional Problems* (Province of Quebec, 1956), v. 2, pp. 277-278, 326-328.

3 *Le Canada, expérience ratée ou réussi? (The Canadian Experiment: Success or Failure?),* (Les Presses de l'Université Laval, Quebec, 1962), pp. 63-67.

4 *A Preliminary Report of the Royal Commission on Bilingualism and Biculturalism* (Queen's Printer, Ottawa, 1965), pp. 133, 135-139.

XXXII 1 *Royal Commission on National Development in the Arts, Letters and Sciences, 1949-1951, Report* (King's Printer, Ottawa, 1951), pp. 11-18.

2 (a) *Royal Commission on Canada's Economic Prospects, Final Report* (Queen's Printer, Ottawa, 1957), pp. 390-393, 399.
(b) Gordon, Walter L., *A Choice For Canada* (McClelland and Stewart, Toronto, 1966), pp. xviii-xx.
(c) *The Globe and Mail,* Toronto, Dec. 31, 1966.

3 Minifie, James M., *Peacemaker or Powder-Monkey* (McClelland and Stewart, Toronto, 1960), pp. 2-5.

4 Heeney, A. D. P., and Merchant, Livingston T., *Canada and the United States, Principles for Partnership* (Ottawa, 1965), pp. 16-18, 48-52.